To the members, past and present,
of South London Liberal Synagogue.

CONTENTS

ACKNOWLEDGEMENTS

I could not have written this book without the help of a large number of people. They include many of those mentioned in the text whose names have been withheld or changed; my parents, whose stories appear here, as do those of other family members; my husband Anthony, and son and daughter Matthew and Harriet, who waited patiently for me to write 'just another bit' and came up with great ideas; and other cousins, relatives and friends who supplied stories or memories which helped to make sense of the whole.

It would have been impossible to write this book without the help of my friend and researcher Ros Levenson, who interviewed various people (notably Richard Cannon and Carolyn Clark), and who thought through some of the chapters and found innumerable examples of what I was trying to say. Paola Churchill, my indefatigable assistant and friend, printed and edited, found permissions and sought references, and played an essential role in making the book come to pass at all by carving out writing time for me in my diary.

At Rider Books, Judith Kendra, who believed in the book from the beginning, and Sue Lascelles, who edited it, were wonderful supports and colleagues. And Alan Bookbinder and the trustees of the Gatsby Charitable Trust deserve huge thanks for believing in this project and contributing to the costs of research. Clare Alexander, my agent and friend, believed in this from the beginning too, and has been a huge support in thinking books through and helping me frame them.

Willie Kessler provided me with his grandfather's ethical will, which was given to him on his bar-mitzvah and which is a wonderful example of the genre – and for which I am very grateful. Justin Davis-Smith, Chief Executive of Volunteering England, allowed Ros Levenson and me to plunder the research material from the Commission on the Future of Volunteering.

The library staff at the House of Lords provided masses of material for parliamentary questions and committees, and some of that clued me into material I would never have found for this book otherwise. They are wonderful.

And members of my former congregation, South London Liberal Synagogue, who talked to me over the years, whose stories have been changed and anonymised, but from whom I learned so much: thank you to everyone. You can never be repaid.

The author would like to thank the following for permission to use copyright material:

BMJ Publishing Group for extract from *A Friend in Need: why friendship matters in medicine* by David Loxtercamp (2008); Janet Christie for material quoted from *Scotland on Sunday* (29 September 2009); the Cittaslow UK Board of Directors for material from *Cittaslow* (www.cittaslow.org. uk); Elaine Feinstein and Carcanet Press Ltd for lines from 'Getting Older' by Elaine Feinstein in *Collected Poems and Translations* (2002); Guardian News & Media Ltd for extracts from 'Fresh way of life sweeps suburbia' by Lucy Siegel in *Observer* (7 November 2004), 'Anna Bullus's innovation' by Lucy Siegel in *Observer* (25 April 2010) and 'Once upon a Life' by Jeannette Winterson in *Observer* (13 June 2010); Harvard University Press for extracts from *The Denial of Aging: Perpetual Youth, Eternal Life, and other Dangerous*

WHAT'S IT ALL ABOUT?

A well-known public figure came to see me a couple of years ago. I'd known him a bit in a previous life when we were both very young, and he'd aged rather more gracefully than I had, I thought. But when we spoke he told me that in the preceding twelve months he had lost a teenage child, experienced great difficulties in his marriage, and now less and less work was coming his way, particularly on television.

He sounded desperate. 'What's it all *for*?' was his constant refrain as he recalled what had happened to him. His despair was deepened by his lack of answers to the question of why bad things happen to good people; and he combined this with an even more profound set of questions: 'Why am I here? What's the purpose? What's it all about?' There are no easy answers, of course, and his particular issues meant that life was extremely painful for him at that time.

My job as a rabbi and his friend was to try to offer him some comfort, alongside practical advice to encourage him to think about what else he might want to achieve in life, and how he wished to be remembered when he was gone, given the searing pain of how he now remembered his son. My friend had a very particular pain: that of losing a child, a death that goes against the natural order of the generations, which is a profound physical shock as well as emotionally devastating. However, the questions he put to me were those that many of us ask in circumstances far less extreme than his. We'll all experience pain at some point in our lives – be it from broken relationships, death, loss, the feeling of being betrayed, or whatever other form it may take. It is often at these moments that we start thinking about what life's all about – moments when we are somehow distanced from the everyday rush, from the routines of going to work and getting home, having a drink with friends or watching the TV.

As a congregational rabbi, I have spent a great amount of time talking with people about finding meaning in life. It is not usually about their belief in God, although much debate about religion seems to be about that right now. It is much more about having a reason to get up in the morning, about feeling that it's worth carrying on; or, particularly for teenagers, existential questions about how they fit into the world, into society, alongside a certain amount of rebellion against whatever parents or other authority figures tell them they have to do.

Teaching a class of sixteen-year-olds at religion school on a Sunday morning, when they clearly do not want to be there, is a pretty big challenge for anyone. But getting them to focus on what they think about life and fairness, about friendship and purpose, about facing death (no one ever talks to teenagers about death) and about valuing life, is a way of confronting their existential angst. Accompanied by lots of coffee and cakes, it's also a pretty good way to get them talking more generally about how they see their own lives panning out and what worries them. And they have their worries, just as their parents do – just as all of us do.

Indeed, whatever their age or status, many of the people I meet ask me in a bewildered way: 'Is this it? What am I really supposed to be doing with my life?' One old friend began a conversation with me with those words, and continued: 'Once I've finished work (if I'm still lucky enough to have a job), looked after my children and my elderly parents, am I supposed just to have fun? Is that OK?' But it transpired that the subtext to her question was a nagging doubt: 'When things go wrong,' she confessed, 'I just seem to fall apart. Always, in the background, I have this very real fear that I might keel over suddenly and just disappear. And who would care? What hole would I leave?' She was getting older and worried that her life had no point, no meaning, to anyone other than herself. After a series of failed relationships, she lived alone; her children had moved away, although her parents were still nearby. She had no desire for solitude and feared falling apart on her own.

The truth of the matter is that, at some stage in our lives, most of us will have our own worries and concerns about what life is all about. Once we are past basic survival (when the point of life is simply to keep on going, finding enough food and warmth and healthcare to have a life at all), we human beings start fretting about why we are here in the first place, what we have to offer to other people, what it all means, and which bits of our lives are truly worthwhile – if any. Some people have argued that this mental process is what differentiates us from animals: our desire to find meaning, and our apparent need to be needed and have a sense of purpose in life, rather than simple survival. Personally, I do not know whether this is true, and think it would be difficult to design an experiment that might prove it to be so. But I have no doubt that worrying about why we are here, and about whether life has any meaning beyond ourselves or any particular overarching purpose, is part of the human condition.

I know it to be as true of me as it is of anyone else. During my life, I have spent so much time studying and then teaching – first as a student at Cambridge, then as a student rabbi, and later as a congregational rabbi – that sometimes, when I look back, I wonder to what extent all that academic training really helped give me a clear perspective on how I wanted to spend my life. I rather suspect I fell into much of what I did by accident, without working it out beforehand. I sometimes find myself comparing my life to that of my father, who was in many ways a rather shy man, and whose training was quite different from mine in that it was largely shaped by life rather than academia. He not only respected learning but had great empathy for other people and their problems, and would have loved to be an academic, had his opportunities been different. All the same, his life experience taught him to sit quietly and listen, and he taught me to listen – especially when there is little else one can do. The very fact that they are being listened to can bring comfort to others and, indeed, help them find a way through whatever is troubling them, even if the listener has said nothing at all in response. And it may be that listening, and then thinking, working things out, is one way to establish what we really want in life.

Certainly, I can recall the way in which my father would listen as his older brother bemoaned his lot in life. Despite my father having some strong critical feelings about this particular brother, he would patiently ask the crucial question: 'Sig, what is it that you *really* do want to do with your life?' Then he would sit for hours teasing out what my uncle had said. It was quite funny to come across the pair of brothers talking like this when I was a child. As they sat there, they'd look remarkably alike, although my father had more hair. When his brother failed to see what he was getting at, my father would run his fingers through his hair in agitation, till it stood up on end; whilst my uncle would pause their conversation at odd moments to ask how it was that my father had more hair than him!

Much later in life, when I became a rabbi and tried to help others see the broader context to their practical problems of day-to-day living, I began to realise that listening, as my father had taught me, is the first stage in offering support on almost all occasions other than an emergency. Whatever the situation, I have found that being listened to helps people to find something, anything, which fires them up, even when they are depressed or gloomy, which might often be for good reason. Most people mind passionately about something – and it was the process of finding that 'something' and getting them to describe what it was and why they cared so much about it, which made me realise almost everyone draws their motivation and inspiration from a particular source. That 'something' may well be the key to their finding out what the purpose of life is for them personally. But working all this stuff out can be a challenging business, and it's not a task for wimps!

My time as a rabbi has taught me just how hard thinking through a sense of purpose can be. People tend to believe that religions have the answers to everything. And some religious people are probably of the opinion that they do. But I don't think they are right. Religion has, histori- cally, claimed to have some, if not all, of the answers to the question of whether there is any point or meaning to life. But it has often been so preoccupied with general issues of right and wrong, with living a 'good life' or experiencing a 'good death' according to its own rules, that it has not been overly concerned with exploring our sense of purpose as individuals. Religions tend to focus on people as members of families and communities, rather than as autonomous individuals with unique desires, hopes and fears.

Suffice it to say that religion has not, on the whole, been overly preoccupied with whether we are happy. It does, on the other hand, concern itself with our duty to others, and with our obligation to the Church, mosque or wider religious community. It is concerned with what we should give in terms of charity, and it imposes upon its adherents a form of discipline as to how to live their lives. It cares about our spiritual awareness and various forms of piety. And it is usually predicated either on a belief in a single deity or several deities, or on a philosophy, such as is the case with Buddhism, which emphasises trying to reach the highest order of spiritual awareness. In offering followers their guidelines, religions, and their leaders and teachers, may have assumed that simply living a religious life, sticking to the rules, and being 'good' will inevitably make us happy and give us a sense of purpose – but happiness has sadly never been religion's primary goal.

This fact was brought home to me many years ago when I was newly out of rabbinic training college. I found that older members of my congregation were often depressed – and this was at a time before it became widely recognised that older people, particularly those in care homes and other kinds of residential care, suffer frequently from undiagnosed depression. One lady with a formidable brain and a failing body used to ask me in no uncertain terms what the point of life was; she wanted to know why she had worked so hard all her life, brought up three children and gone out to work until she was seventy, earning most of the family income, if all that happened at the end of her life was this. What was the point, for her? We talked a great deal about it, and I hope I gave her some comfort by helping her to realise what she had achieved over the years, and also the significance of the contribution her children and grandchildren were now making to the world, and how that was a legacy she could be proud of, even if her own life seemed to be increasingly limited by her physical frailty.

Once I ceased being a congregational rabbi in 1989, I spent more and more time working on developing policy around the care of the frail and elderly. In my time at the King's Fund (a charity that looks at how the British health and social services can be improved), we took a long, hard look at what was happening to frail older people in London and questioned the level and quality, as well as location, of their care. Once again, it became apparent that there were significant levels of depression among them. When talking to senior citizens who attended a discussion session at the King's Fund, I realised that many of those who were being sent away to care homes outside London (so that their local authorities could save money) were also wondering to themselves what the point of it all had been. What's the point, if I am sent to live seventy miles from my nearest and dearest? Is there any purpose to my next few months and years on earth, or am I just sitting around waiting to die?

These and others like them are existential questions which we ask at virtually every stage of life, young and old – young when we cannot see the purpose of our future, old when we cannot see the point of our lives. Whatever our age, it can be difficult to comprehend what leaving a personal legacy might mean. Listening to more and more people for whom those sorts of question seemed to be central to their lives, I looked at why we might want to think differently about the importance of having a sense of purpose, regardless of age, and how to think it through outside the main religious frameworks.

Indirectly, that experience is what got me involved in volunteering – where people of all kinds, all ages and backgrounds put into practice the 'something' they care about, once they have worked out (often with the help of a willing listener) what that is. When I saw seemingly quiet and shy people, who were often quite subdued and withdrawn, light up when they got involved in land conservation, historic houses or whatever it was that interested them, I realised there was something important for us all to learn here. When I saw young people devote hours and weeks to an older people's project, or to a summer scheme for disadvantaged children, I could see how that voluntary impulse, that desire to do something for others – however depressed and sad we are ourselves – can change how we approach the world and, in due course, our own lives.

❦

This book is mostly about the individual. It's about you and me. It is about what we can see in our lives and about what is lacking, and more particularly about what we can do to improve those lives and fill those gaps, if gaps there are. Throughout this book, I use illustrations from my own and other people's lives (with names and places changed to protect identity and confidentiality where necessary), which I hope will give you pause for thought and bring alive the important questions of meaning, loss and legacy that I'm going to consider in these pages. If I did not use examples from life, these subjects, these ideas, might seem very abstract.

And if we do not take these ideas to heart early enough, we may all too often end our lives filled with deep regret, for, by the time we finally get around to thinking about what really matters to us, it may be too late to do much about it. Then the important emotional and intellectual process of working out what matters to us becomes rushed and unsatisfactory, instead of being a source of inspiration for how we might go on to live our lives – however much life, however many years, we may have left.

I sincerely hope this book will provide food for thought, and perhaps even some answers to the question of whether this *is* all there is. I very nearly did not write it at all, even though I'd agreed to do so and had been given a grant to help pay for the research. And that's because I started by looking at what else was around covering the same ground. Some books were overtly religious or tackled the subject from a specific religious standpoint – which is quite different from the approach in this book. And there were already plenty of self-help guides, many authored by life coaches who probably help their clients but whose writing sometimes struck me as banal or superficial in the extreme.

While I do not want to write a new Samuel Smiles, whose famous book *Self-Help* (1859) helped to kick-start the entire personal development movement, I do not want to dumb down such an important subject as the meaning of life in these pages! Nor do I want to emulate the French psychiatrist François Lelord, the author of *Hector and the Search for Happiness*.[1] The idea of a shrink setting out to determine what really makes people happy is appealing, but to my mind his approach does not draw out lessons of self-discipline or self-awareness sufficiently to be much practical use. Nor do I want to write as Mitch Albom does, much as I admire him.[2] *Tuesdays with Morrie* is a great book, and his others also make you think. But I want to cover wider ground here and not be as faith based as he is, although he has much to teach us.

This is not easy stuff to think about, yet ironically it is all too easy to write about it in ways that strike me as being trite, obvious or 'goody-goody'. In fact, in looking at how we find meaning in our lives, I have found the core themes to revolve around questions of self-discipline, self-examination and compassion, around listening and really hearing others, around empathising and gaining a sense of purpose.

Above all, the process of finding meaning and uncovering a sense of purpose in life is about not allowing ourselves to become isolated, hermetic or sealed into the surreal world of internet connections such as Facebook and Tweeting. They are forms of communication. But they are not about living and breathing friendships or obligations, or about real-life recognition and empathy. And as such they are no substitute for human contact and human effort. And so this book is my attempt to give guidance on how to acquire sufficient self-discipline and make the efforts needed to realise that there is more to 'it' – this precious life – than just the existential-ist experience.

When I was a teenager at religion school, arguing, fighting with my teachers and parents, thinking I would break away from anything Jewish, I was brought up short by a famous saying (which I now use all the time) from *Ethics of the Fathers*, dating back to the first century AD:

> If I am not for myself, who will be for me?
>
> But if I am only for myself, what am I?
>
> And if not now, when?
>
> **Mishnah: Ethics of the Fathers, 1.14**

To my mind, this quote sums up the perennial questions we all ask of ourselves: if I do not live life in my own interests, then who will act in my interest? But if I only live life for my own benefit, what kind of person am I? And, if I don't take action now, then when will I? What kind of person am I? How do I relate to others? And is there any kind of urgency in all of this?

Those rabbis of the first century knew a thing or two. These are some of the basic questions that most of us ask ourselves. And they are the ones we need to answer if we are to live comfortably with ourselves and, more importantly for many of us, with family, friends, colleagues and the wider community. So this book is an attempt to work through some of those questions, giving you, the reader, a chance to engage with some of the people I've met and talked to over my life.

At the very least I hope that this book will offer you some searching questions to think about. I wish I'd had something similar to read when I was younger. And I hope that the experience of considering some of life's most profound questions, chapter by chapter, will help you to think through some of your own questions about human existence, and perhaps even find some answers for yourself.

CHAPTER 1

IS THAT ALL THERE IS?

For I know just as well as I'm standing here talking to you,
When that final moment comes and I'm breathing my last
  breath,
I'll be saying to myself:

[Chorus]
  Is that all there is, is that all there is?
  If that's all there is, my friends, then let's keep dancing,
  Let's break out the booze and have a ball
  If that's all there is.

Jerry Leiber and Mike Stoller, 'Is That All There Is?'

Peggy Lee's rendition of the song 'Is That All There Is?', written by Jerry Leiber and Mike Stoller, hit number 11 in the charts in the USA in 1969 and later entered the Grammy Hall of Fame. The song itself is the perfect existentialist's lament – and certainly a good introduction to the themes of this book. It begs the question of whether there is any meaning to life or, indeed, whether life *has* to have any meaning.

I have found that most of us need a sense of purpose of some kind to give us a reason for being alive, but that sense of purpose can take any number of forms – from a long-term set of goals or tasks that we want to complete in our lives, to a specific set of achievements we would like to list beside our names, however minor these may appear to others. And that is because human beings, by and large, need to be needed, to feel driven, to have a sense of being able to grow and learn and expand their horizons to the very end of their lives.

So, just what *is* it all about? What are life's key questions? In *Alice Through the Looking-Glass*, the famous nineteenth-century children's book by Lewis Carroll (which might not have been written for children at all), some of the characters are chess pieces such as the Red Queen, the White Queen and the Knave. It is as if the meaning of life is only a game in the Looking-Glass world, to be understood purely in terms of set rules. In the final chapter, Alice wakes to find herself back in her room and asks, '… let's consider who dreamed it all'. The book ends with a poem and the final line: 'Life, what is it but a dream?' There are parallels with a well-known passage in Shakespeare's play *The Tempest*: 'We are such stuff /As dreams are made on, and our little life / Is rounded with a sleep…' But is the meaning of life really just the stuff of dreams and games?

Although Lewis Carroll (whose real name was Charles Dodgson), a mathematics lecturer at Oxford, was adamant that he 'meant nothing but nonsense' in his writings for children, there is something odd about the way he leads us into strange, eternal places. Within the crazy chess game in *Alice Through the Looking-Glass*, there is a form of twisted logic at play. Some interpreters have suggested that this shows

Carroll believed life has a logical development and pattern to it, which, although inexplicable at times, ends up in some kind of resolution. Interestingly, some physicists have argued that they too can see a pattern in the universe – that there is, in some way, a design that permeates the whole of creation, which leads to an argument for the existence of God.

In the process of reading *Through The Looking-Glass*, we find that the novel gets 'curiouser and curiouser' as it continues, with Alice and the other characters changing size and appearance at random. Similarly, life itself is partly inexplicable – physicists notwithstanding – and as yet there does not appear to be an absolute meaning to it which everyone can share. Rather, we tend to search for something that makes sense of it to us as individuals, something that we can wonder at. This is not dissimilar to the very different ways in which the world's religions approach the mysteries of life and death, or of creation. What may lead to meditation in some Eastern faiths, for example, may lead to prayers of awe and wonder in Western religious traditions. If nothing else, Alice's adventures may help us realise that there are all sorts of different kinds of meaning and patterns in life.

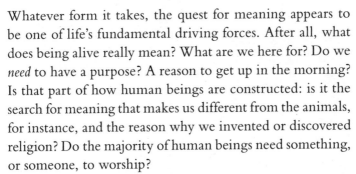

Whatever form it takes, the quest for meaning appears to be one of life's fundamental driving forces. After all, what does being alive really mean? What are we here for? Do we *need* to have a purpose? A reason to get up in the morning? Is that part of how human beings are constructed: is it the search for meaning that makes us different from the animals, for instance, and the reason why we invented or discovered religion? Do the majority of human beings need something, or someone, to worship?

Evidence from ancient civilisations suggests that our

ancestors felt compelled to worship the sun, the moon and other heavenly bodies, and so they created divine figures linked with these, to whom they offered sacrifices or prayer. It was as if they saw themselves as insignificant and needed something bigger – the planets, the city gods, even the universal mother goddess – to give them something to appeal to. The great Greek poet Homer said just as much in the ninth century BC: 'Insignificant mortals, who are as leaves are, and now flourish and grow warm with life, and feed on what the ground gives, but then again fade away and are dead.'

Homer's writings and other classical literature tell us a lot about the gods of the Ancient Greeks and Romans, who seem to have been a rather fractious and imperfect lot. Yet gods they were, and anthropologists and sociologists of religion are divided as to whether it is a fundamental human need to worship god-like figures and look to them with awe and fear for help and mercy, however flawed they may be. Human beings seem to need to search for – even if they cannot find – significance in a universe of billions of stars that apparently ignore us. And that compulsion to search for significance may even increase as new stars and worlds are discovered, as the likelihood of some other form of life on one of them becomes a credible theory once more.

Although the dimensions and nature of the cosmos are such that they are beyond our present understanding, we look to the universe for a sense of what is inexplicable yet magnificent, for ideas of pattern and purpose, and often seem to find within it something to inspire awe and wonder within us. So whether it is a fundamental human need or not, whether there is some kind of biological explanation or not, the fact is for most of us there is a need to find something – even if not a divine being – in which to believe, to give us a sense of meaning.

Richard Dawkins, scourge of religious believers, would probably disagree. He would in all likelihood argue that we – and all living beings – are just 'survival machines, blindly programmed to preserve the selfish molecules known as genes', and that the search for meaning simply fails to recognise that fact.[1] Others might argue that the reality we seem to know is in fact imposed on us by nature. Our inclination to think about concepts such as the meaning of life may be a purely human phenomenon foisted on us by our humanity, just as music, or love or colours are apparently human constructs. Science tells us that there are no such things as music, harmony or colours in the physical world, but only travelling molecules; in the words of H. Von Foerster: 'There is not, external to us, hot or cold, but only different velocities of molecules; there aren't sounds, callings, harmonies, but just variations in the pressure of the air; there aren't colours, or light, just electro-magnetic waves.'[2]

If concepts such as colour or music have no existence outside us, what are we to make of qualities such as suffering and wickedness? Cruelty is to be found all around us in everyday life: pain, evil, not to mention death. Again, perhaps these are simply manifestations of our genetic make-up. But I prefer to think of them as the hidden tigers, lying in ambush and ready to attack the imprudent – to use an image present in the Buddhist Scriptures. And Dawkins' selfish gene does not help us deal with that danger.

With the possible exception of those who're convinced we are only the products of our genetic make-up, many of us will find ourselves reflecting on what life is for – what it's all about – at least some of the time. The majority of us will wonder at some point whether there cannot be more to life's everyday (and not so everyday) experiences than we usually find within them. Most of us want to determine a purpose in our being alive, an overarching sense of meaning in our lives; but at the same time we look at our daily activities and find it hard to see much that's important there, much that nourishes the spirit in the experiences of going to work, going home, doing the chores, dealing with the everyday tasks of domestic administration, paying the bills, going out for a drink or meal with friends, cooking a meal, going on holiday.

Of course, many of us live with a partner, parent or child. We are not alone. Or, if we live by ourselves, we have family, friends or neighbours whom we care about and to whom we feel we have obligations. And sometimes the 'purpose' of life seems to be largely taken up with looking after that person, or cherishing that relationship, striving to keep it alive, or simply worrying about one's children ... But if we look beyond those obligations to others, and strip away the daily concerns of cooking, cleaning, going to work, and start thinking what happens when some of that activity stops when we retire and grow old – then what's left? Is there enough to make us happy? Is it enough to look back on with a sense of pleasure and satisfaction, 'all passion spent' as the seventeenth-century writer John Milton put it so famously in his epic poem *Samson Agonistes*?[3] Did those activities really make us happy once upon a time, even if it may not seem like it now? Was there any point to it all?

Perhaps if we find ourselves looking back with a sense of regret, it is because we simply didn't try hard enough to enjoy things. There is a form of hedonistic philosophy that rests in the saying *carpe diem* – 'rejoice in the day' – a Latin phrase popularised by the schoolteacher character played by Robin Williams in the film *Dead Poets Society* (1989). It is often translated as 'seize the day'; it might be argued that it suggests we should exercise the muscle of enjoyment more and agonise less. And maybe that's not such a bad way to live our lives after all.

The expression *carpe diem* actually comes from an ode by the Roman poet Horace, where it is placed at the end of a verse which tells us it is not for us to know what the gods have in store for us. There are parallels in the phrase with the refrain 'If not now, when?' in the quotation from Mishnah in the introduction to this book, and also with the classic line 'Gather ye rosebuds while ye may' from poet Robert Herrick, which suggests we may not get another chance so we should seize the day.

In his ode, Horace argues not only that we should seize the day, but that we should also forget about tomorrow, because we cannot know what it will bring. To my mind, that way of thinking represents true existentialism, much like Peggy Lee's approach in the song 'Is That All There Is?' For, without looking to tomorrow, it is hard to see the point of having any hope today.

Without hope, human beings find it difficult to continue to live. And that is why most of us do look to tomorrow and plot and plan for the future, often agonising so much in the process that we fail to capture today's joy, today's experiences. So perhaps a measure of a carpe-diem attitude alongside a bit of hopeful planning, saving and being ready for whatever tomorrow might bring (if one ever can be), might be a healthier combination than simply burying our heads in the sand and pretending tomorrow does not exist!

In Primo Levi's famous memoir *If This Is a Man*, he records the few who retained humanity and hope within the horror of the Nazi concentration camps.[4] One of them was Jacques Samuel, nicknamed Pikolo, the youngest and smallest man in the group, who was less of an intellectual than Levi but who spent his time in the camp thinking about maths as much as he could, and thereby continuing to be human, continuing to have hope. He managed to survive and died, finally, in 2010 aged eighty-eight, having spent most of his life living with purpose, yet telling few people, including his own family, about the horrors of his life.

In modern society we need hope too. As public life becomes less and less religious (in the UK at least), there is no longer such an overt publicly shared sense of needing to believe that things will get better, beyond a purely materialistic view of the world. It was, uncharacteristically, President Nicolas Sarkozy of secularist France who argued for a 'blossoming' of religions in 2008, on the basis that: 'A man who believes is a man who hopes.'[5] And, despite the secular world around him, and his own growing scandals of excess, he was right: we need to hope in order to survive, and to feel we have something to survive *for*. This means that working out what it is we wish to hope for – in this life, the afterlife or in the way in which we wish to be remembered – is critical to our happiness.

Yet the philosophy of *carpe diem*, of forgetting about tomorrow and not worrying about whether we have anything to hope for, has had a powerful effect on our modern lives. In some ways, it influenced the let-it-all-hang out hippy culture of the 1960s, when society had had enough of rationing after the war and of worrying about nuclear deterrents. There is no doubt that being able to exercise the muscle of enjoyment is important. So I was delighted to read a piece by Mark Vernon entitled 'Carpe Diem' in the *Observer* Magazine, which suggested we should translate the phrase differently.[6] Instead of 'seize the day', he proposed 'harvest the day'. Now, that means something quite different. It no longer encourages us simply to grab and grasp. Instead, it implies that we have some responsibility for what the day brings. We put into it some of what it gives us.

And, as Vernon makes clear, that attitude suggests another maxim which is to be found in the same poem by Horace and indeed in Jewish teaching of the period. And that is: live each day as if it were your last. This advice is not as blunt and selfish as 'seize the day'. Instead, it suggests that we have to be willing to put a lot into our day and indeed be ready to take a lot out of it, to experience from it as much as we can.

∞

There are equivalent sayings to Horace's maxim in all the world's great faiths. But perhaps one of the most profound comes from the Tibetan spiritual and political leader, the Dalai Lama, who argues: 'What is the purpose of life? I believe that the purpose of life is to be happy.'[7] Later in this book, we'll be looking at happiness – what makes us happy and how we can learn to be happy, without losing sight of the other things that give our existence meaning too. But it might be argued that any discussion of happiness should come with a health warning, as it might promote a hedonistic attitude to life. Few people would argue that individual happiness is the only thing that matters in life, and I'm certainly not claiming that it is. But what I would say is that the pursuit of happiness, and giving ourselves permission to be happy and have fun, is a good thing which can add to other people's happiness – because joy can be infectious.

Of course, we can't be happy all the time. Grief, loss and sadness are all part of normal life as well. But unless we aim for a life that includes a good measure of happiness, we quite possibly won't have the inner resources to be much use to others when they experience hard times, and we may not be able to cope with the periods in our own lives when happiness seems elusive.

As we'll see, happiness is something that governments have begun to talk about too. A recent Swedish paper is particularly interesting as it looks at happiness in relation to government rather than just individuals. It states:

> Our hypothesis is that quality of government – defined as effectiveness, impartiality, rule of law and no corruption – is a factor, a prerequisite, behind aggregate levels of feelings of happiness and satisfaction with life among populations across the Earth. Quality of government makes people happy. And it makes people happy in rich countries as well as in poor countries. Maybe not Big Government, but certainly Good Government, is an essential recipe for making citizens more content with their lives. That is our strange hypothesis.[8]

The UK's coalition government has also made a decision to weigh up its citizens' happiness, as well as their material wellbeing, as part of their assessment of how well we are doing as a nation.

Much of the real work in finding happiness lies in thinking about it for ourselves. However, we cannot ignore the arguments of the great philosophers and religious teachers here: they have made an enormous contribution to how we think. John Rawls, an American philosopher, argues that wellbeing lies in making (and presumably sticking to) a rational life plan.[9] He argues that there is more to life than economic wellbeing, yet he does not explain precisely which activities are valuable or what a rational life plan might look like. His book is designed to be personal, more concerned with how we function as individuals and small groups, family and friends, than with the politics of wellbeing for the wider society.

Although in this book I will be focusing more on the personal than on the political, it is certainly the case that, for many people, taking up a cause and becoming an activist fired up with a sense of purpose is what gives life meaning. In some political philosophies, a 'cause' can become an entire way of life. Certainly, thinking back to the Communists of the 1930s, Communism often became a way of life for its followers and justified actions in their eyes that might otherwise have seemed unacceptable, such as, much later in East Germany, spying on neighbours and even family. Today, it has become apparent that, for some young adherents, terrorist organisations may become an all-consuming passion that is so important, so central to the 'purpose of life' for them, that they are prepared to give up their own (usually pitifully young) lives for it.

To consider the wholly positive aspects of devoting ourselves to a cause, it is clear that people are ready to take considerable risks if they believe it is for something worthwhile, be it a case of firefighters pulling people from an inferno, or passersby diving into the sea to rescue a drowning child, or people who regularly go out in lifeboats or do other risky forms of charitable work. Some of this is about fulfilling a sense of service, but for others it is the motivating force, or one of the motivating forces, that gives them a sense of purpose in being alive.

Whoever we are, everyday life throws up a number of important questions that we need to think about in order to get the most out of our lives. I believe that these can be grouped into three main subject areas:

MEANING

As we have seen, it's important for most of us to find a sense of meaning in our lives. We need to be able to identify a purpose so we can work towards it. Without an underpinning sense of meaning, life can feel a bit pointless; our only goal lies in reaching out towards the next set of sensations, the next rush of activity that heightens our awareness of ourselves or others, the next object of desire to be acquired. Everything refers back to ourselves, or those nearest to ourselves, and selfishness becomes not only the norm, but is the only personal quality that makes any sense to us.

Yet, as later chapters of this book make clear, selfishness and being self-obsessed are hugely damaging qualities. The desire to acquire more and more, to fill our homes with more 'stuff' and wear ever more expensive clothes on our backs, has been a major part of the late twentieth- and early twenty-first-century Western way of life. Acquisition is good. More means feeding the markets. More keeps the economy turning. But there is now – finally – a reaction, a fashion for make-do-and-mend, for living with less, and on less.

Is the current fashion for thriftiness a denial of selfishness – or simple self-denial? Or is it about a desire to protect the environment and rule out waste? Is it even a manifestation of sentimentality, harking back to a time when people seemed to be happier, more content, when there was rationing and people darned socks, and the lack of availability of desirable objects (in wartime it was sweets, nylon stockings, curtain fabric) somehow made us nicer, finer people? Others have tackled this issue head on, most notably Oliver James, in his ground-breaking work *Affluenza*.[10] Far from arguing that we should revert nostalgically to the rationing of wartime, he points to the current rise in mental illness, more profound in the UK and America than in mainland Europe, and suggests that it is important for people to define themselves independently of their possessions and to find value elsewhere. He notes that people living in poverty in much of the developing world do not appear to suffer from many of the disorders that are so common in the West, where our desire to acquire and the tendency to define ourselves by what we have, rather than by who we are, is so deeply rooted.

LOSS

It's important to learn to live with loss – which might come about through the death of another, or simply through the death of our own hopes, dreams and even the fading of physical beauty with increasing age. Unless we are simply to fall apart under what seems to be a crushing and pointless blow, we need to find ways to address loss, cope with it and extract something good from it, something that strengthens us – and that is more enduring in the long term than the immediate searing experience of loss.

The ways in which we grieve may help us to extract meaning from loss. But there is a more fundamental issue. We all know the saying: 'Better to have loved and lost than never to have loved at all.' That is, literally, a truism. But the point of it is that the very experience of loving and being loved will eventually be something to rejoice in (once the acute pain of loss has lessened). Loss means that there was once a gain. Loss implies that something good went before. So loss, however painful, ought to imply that there is something to be remembered with delight, with affection, with love.

Bereavement counsellors often point out to those who are widowed that a sense of loss implies something good went before – and a very good job they usually make of this too. But I nevertheless believe it is something of an indictment of society that people who are grieving should need bereavement counsellors as the norm, rather than if they have exceptional problems in coming to terms with their grief. Where are we as friends? Where are we as willing listeners, hearing the bereaved talk of those they have lost, and why aren't we there asking questions, encouraging the outpouring of grief? We could and should be so much better as people, as friends, in helping others come to terms with loss, yet all too often we seem to have lost the art of listening, the art of bringing quiet comfort.

Learning to live with loss is far from easy. When it comes to death, we are short of rituals in the West to enable us to grieve in the first instance (with the exception of a few faiths and cultural minorities). We have brought in bereavement counselling, but that sort of work involves the private processing of grief, not a communal way of acknowledging and working with loss. And life brings with it so many losses. The older we get the more beloved people – and indeed animals and even inanimate objects such as houses – we will 'lose'. Some of these losses will bring us great pain and sorrow. Yet dealing with these experiences, growing from them and learning from them – and perhaps even doing something good because of them – is part of beginning to live with loss.

There is a wonderful Buddhist story about loss that has universal application. It comes from the tales of Kisagotami, taken from the parables of Buddhaghosha (a name used by several Buddhist writers).[11]

> Kisagotami became in the family way, and when the ten months were completed, gave birth to a son. When the boy was able to walk by himself, he died. The young girl, in her love for him, carried the dead child clasped to her bosom, and went about from house to house asking if anyone would give her some medicine for it. When the neighbours saw this, they said, 'Is the young girl mad that she carries about on her breast the dead body of her son!' But a wise man thinking to himself, 'Alas! This Kisagotami does not understand the law of death, I must comfort her,' said to her, 'My good girl, I cannot myself give medicine for it, but I know of a doctor who can attend to it.' The young girl said, 'If so, tell me who he is.' The wise man continued, 'Gautama can give medicine, you must go to him.'
>
> Kisagotami went to Gautama, and doing homage to him, said, 'Lord and master, do you know any medicine that will be good for my boy?' Gautama replied, 'I know of some.' She asked, 'What medicine do you require?' He said, 'I want a handful of mustard seed.' The girl promised to procure it for him, but Gautama continued, 'I require some mustard seed taken from a house where no son, husband, parent, or slave has died,' The girl said, 'Very good,' and went to ask for some at the different houses, carrying the dead body of her son astride her hip. The people said, 'Here is some mustard

seed, take it.' Then she asked, 'In my friend's house has there died a son, a husband, a parent, or a slave?' They replied, 'Lady, what is this that you say! The living are few, but the dead are many.' Then she went to other houses, but one said, 'I have lost a son'; another 'I have lost my parents'; another 'I have lost my slave.' At last, not being able to find a single house where no one had died, from which to procure the mustard seed, she began to think, 'This is a heavy task that I am engaged in. I am not the only one whose son is dead. In the whole of the Savatthi country, everywhere children are dying, parents are dying.' Thinking thus, she acquired the law of fear, and putting away her affection for her child, she summoned up resolution, and left the dead body in a forest; then she went to Gautama and paid him homage. He said to her, 'Have you procured the handful of mustard seed?' 'I have not,' she replied; 'The people of the village told me, "The living are few, but the dead are many."' Gautama said to her, 'You thought that you alone had lost a son; the law of death is that among all living creatures there is no permanence ...'

Later in this book I will be writing about individuals' experiences of coping with loss, as well as about different cultural approaches to dealing with bereavement. But I will also be discussing how we in British society should open our eyes to the inevitability of loss and do something, however haltingly, to develop a language, a series of rituals and customs, to help us talk to each other and share that sadness together.

LEGACY

Thinking of loss, I believe that it's important to think *now* about what we intend to leave behind us when we ourselves die – our legacy – rather than wait until we're on the point of death to do so. How do we want to look back on our lives when we're seventy, eighty or ninety? And why are relationships more important than anything else for most of us? Is there more to how we might be celebrated after we are gone than whether we remembered to send our niece a birthday card or kept a note of our cousin's wedding anniversary?

There is a fashion of sorts – particularly in the United States – for academics and others to deliver a sort of 'last lecture', the lecture they would give about what really matters to them if this were the last lecture they physically were *able* to give. Randy Pausch, a distinguished professor of computer science and human-computer interaction and design at Carnegie Mellon University in Pittsburgh, Pennsylvania, learned that he had terminal pancreatic cancer in September 2006. He gave a talk entitled 'The Last Lecture: Really Achieving Your Childhood Dreams' the following September at Carnegie Mellon, which became a popular YouTube video.[12] As a result, he co-authored a book called *The Last Lecture* on the same theme, which became a *New York Times* bestseller.

His was not some 'pretend' last lecture following the prevailing fashion, however, but the real thing. Given that he wrote it when he had only months to live, having moved his family hundreds of miles to be nearer his wife's family (so that they could provide support after his death), it is clear that the lecture was of great importance to him. In order to write it, he ignored the boxes piled up everywhere around him – to his wife's considerable irritation. Not only that, but when he delivered the lecture, he did so in a decidedly upbeat manner, even doing press-ups on the floor of the lecture theatre to prove that, despite having only months to live, he was 'in good shape'. His determination to give this lecture, to produce his thoughts, to make one last statement, suggests it was important to him to leave a public legacy of his ideas and his philosophy, in addition to his intellectual legacy in his academic work and his emotional legacy through his wife, children and friends.

I suspect that, if we were to give the matter the same degree of thought as Pausch did, we would agree with many of the wise thoughts he included in the lecture (and in the book). For instance, besides the humour of the press-ups, he included the much more challenging assertion that if someone cares enough about you to criticise what you are doing, you should not take offence but be grateful. That is a far cry from our usual reactions to criticism, and it's also far from stupid once we pause to think about it.

There's another theme which we'll be returning to time and again in the course of this book, and that is about taking advantage of the opportunities that come our way – be they sabbaticals, the chance of a holiday, invitations to do something we've never done before, or whatever other form they may appear in.

Opportunities aside, I will also explore the benefits of planning our lives and making lists (pure joy to this inveterate list-making author)! Again, this is a theme to which we will return, and it will encompass making lists of what you'd *like* to achieve in the course of your life … Some people may think at first that this seems like a crazy, uptight thing to do: imagine planning one's life like that, with that degree of formality, that degree of planning! But I hope to show that there is something very appealing in the idea of thinking hard about what we wish to have achieved by the end of our lives, and trying to organise ourselves so that we get at least some of it done and don't end up feeling that we've wasted our time on this earth. Again, when considering how to find meaning in life, this deceptively simple technique might provide inroads into establishing meaning, or at least a sense of purpose, for ourselves.

In his book, Pausch argues hard against spending our time complaining, suggesting instead that we should simply concentrate on working harder. He comes over as a bit of a workaholic, but also as someone who believes that hard work brings real benefits, not only in terms of achievements measured by others, but also in the sort of satisfaction that work can offer us individually.

Pausch's last lecture explores three other themes that we will return to in these pages. First, he makes a point about the importance of apologising properly. His view is that if you are going to apologise – and he argues that it should not be that hard to do so – then we should do so with no caveats, no ifs or buts. 'I am truly sorry if you feel upset' will not do; 'I am really sorry for hurting you' sounds much better. Were the apology to be accompanied by a bunch of flowers and a personal visit, it may even seem – and be – genuine. If we know that we have hurt someone, we should not feel in the least embarrassed about apologising to them.

Second, he argues that we should never give up: if we have things we want to do, things we want to achieve, then, however difficult they may seem, we should keep trying to achieve them; we should always be ready to have another go, and another, and another. If we have made a plan of what we want to achieve in our lives, then not giving up on it is no bad thing – and is likely to give us a sense of purpose for years to come.

Lastly, Pausch argues in favour of taking out an emotional insurance policy … that is to say, he advises that every once in a while we should look at ourselves and try to put ourselves in order. This means looking honestly at our relationships, at how we feel inside ourselves, at life's satisfactions and dissatisfactions. It involves undertaking a form of personal audit – to which we will return. Through it, we can learn a lot about ourselves, grow and, even more importantly, come nearer to achieving some of our life's goals. Whilst that may sound rather psychotherapeutic to some readers (and to others just reinforce how valuable psychotherapy can be), Pausch's emotional insurance is not, principally, about psychotherapy, but about personal work, about self-aware-ness, about thinking and reflection time, about the need to examine ourselves coolly, in the harsh light of day.

But it is also more than that; Pausch believes strongly in the benefits of looking closely at ourselves and at our relationships. That means looking at how we treat others – family, children, friends and acquaintances. With the possible exception of those few human beings who have a natural hermit-like tendency, most of us are social creatures and gain much of our meaning and pleasure in life from our engagement with other human beings. The way in which we think about friendship and nurture our relationships is a key part of learning to live the good life, and an important element of learning to value what matters – our friends and our families, for example, rather than material goods. In the next chapter I am going to consider how and why friendship matters.

CHAPTER 2

BEING A GOOD FRIEND

If a man does not make new acquaintance as he advances through life, he will soon find himself left alone. A man, Sir, should keep his friendship in constant repair.

Samuel Johnson (1709–1784)

There were two friends in particular with whom I kept closely in touch from childhood to adulthood. We were at secondary school together from 1955 to 1968 – all bright, all less than athletic. One of the two is now widowed but, having brought up three wonderful children, she has recreated herself, works full time, is full of ideas and enthusiasm and, despite no doubt still wanting more out of life, she's a real star. We do not see each other all that often, but we are absolutely there for each other – it's the kind of friendship that you know will last for ever; in fact, it feels as if it already has! I officiated at her son's wedding recently, and it's as though the family links between us are written in stone.

Sadly, the other close friend from my schooldays died a few years ago from breast cancer. We saw each other only occasionally during her final illness, as if somehow she didn't want me to see her like that. In the last few weeks, I visited her a few times, but it was oddly hard to talk about what was really happening to her – and I regret that very deeply. I officiated at her funeral and, indeed, more recently at her mother's; but I have been left with the sense of a friendship that I should have nurtured more, of a greater love that I could have given if she had been less reticent and I less busy.

And that has left me with permanent regrets: we can't go back to unpick what we did not do for a friend who is no longer alive. It's an object lesson, because friendship is not something we can take for granted. Nurturing a friendship requires hard work and energy. It means noticing what is going on and keeping our eyes and ears open. It involves making the effort to stay in touch even if we are frantically busy.

Having heard older people say time and again that they can count their close friends on the fingers of one hand, I can see how easy it is to lose those who truly matter to us. If we neglect our friendships, it is often too late to step back into the role of being a true friend when things get tough, because the groundwork for being able to talk about what is really important is simply no longer there.

Friendship takes many forms, of course. From professional friendships to those offering personal support in times of crisis, from organised networking to our oldest friends, whom we may have known from the age of three or four – and to whom we can still say anything … These are all kinds of friendship that we ought to cherish. And occasionally friendships can grow and transform themselves when the need arises, as terminally ill Bruce Feiler discovered when he set up his Council of Dads, a circle of close friends whom he asked to act like fathers to his daughters when he died (see Chapter 2).

Most of the world's great sayings about friendship are clear that we had better treasure it – and they are equally clear that, without it, life is a desert. We should cherish our friends, who can give our lives a fundamental sense of purpose if only because of what they may need from us; and, at the other extreme, because we can do things together, learn together, achieve together, enrich each other in all sorts of ways – with the whole adding up to more than the sum of its parts.

There is something particularly significant at play in our friendships today. Increasingly, social scientists and commentators argue that, as the institution of marriage continues to decline and social activities such as church-going, clubs and other communal pursuits are on the wane in the West, people are putting more and more emphasis on their friendships. To add to that, given our increasing social mobility, whether through moving home or simply getting in a car and driving thirty miles, the local community is less likely to offer the support it once did. The ease of travel, of relocation (which splits up traditional family units), therefore makes it all the more likely we will look for support from our friends, who may in due course become more important to us than our communities and even our families, despite our deep ties with those.

Of course, these factors vary from country to country, and the ease with which people leave one place and go to another for work varies immensely as well. In the UK, it is said that most people still live within five miles of where they were born – although that does not necessarily mean that they engage with their local communities. Other countries are very different, with people living much further from where they started out. In the United States, for example, moving from state to state for work is commonplace – which is why all the planes, trains and even freeways are full to bursting at Thanksgiving, when almost all Americans go back home to family rather than to friends. (Interestingly, it seems that although people in the States make close friendships in situations where moving is the norm, the family unit remains more important than those bonds. People often comment anecdotally that Americans are wonderful friends while you are there, but will forget all about you when you are not! However, my experience has been quite different, with my friends in the United States being amongst my very closest: they make immense efforts to stay in touch by email, phone and occasional long trips, which I value more than I can say.)

Besides friends replacing family in certain circumstances, there is an increasing tendency for people to take part in what were once considered purely social activities by themselves, without embarrassment, as Robert Putnam argues so conclusively in his book *Bowling Alone: The Collapse and Revival of American Community*. Using bowling as a metaphor, he claims that civil society is breaking down as Americans become more disconnected from their families, neighbours, communities and the state itself. Whereas in the recent past thousands of people used to belong to bowling leagues, today they're more likely to bowl alone. This increasing social isolation and the fragile nature of friendship combine to create a recipe which requires those friends we have to work far harder for us when it really matters.

So what does friendship really mean in today's world? In his book *The Meaning of Friendship*, Mark Vernon discusses this problem very succinctly: '... whilst many people, at both a personal and social level, are turning to friendship, few are asking just what it is they are turning to. We need to ask a question and we need philosophy to pursue it: what is friendship?'[1] He suggests that not since the ancient Greeks has friendship really been thought about philosophically. In his *Nicomachean Ethics* (1155a5–6), Aristotle makes it clear that friendship is central to his philosophical thought: 'Nobody would choose to live without friends even if he had all the other good things of life.' Today, we need to work out what we really mean by friendship and what we feel about it, precisely because we are asking far more than we once used to of our friends.

Throughout our lives, our friendships will change. As children, we have 'friends' whom we ask to birthday parties, for example, but even at this early stage little girls and little boys often behave quite differently: the friendships of girls tend to be focused on other girls, with conversation and self-revelation playing a central role, whereas the friendships of boys are often focused on a shared activity and conversation is unnecessary.[2] Yet both sexes can be cruel to the child who does not quite fit in, with the problem of bullying being taken very seriously in schools these days.

That said, I remember a child in my primary school who had a hole in her heart: although she could not join in everything because she was too weak, she was completely included by the children in our class. We could sometimes be nasty to others, but Gillian was one of us even if she could not take part in whatever the activity was. I think I was probably especially welcome as far as she was concerned. She wasn't allowed to do a lot of running around, skipping or jumping, and, as I was so hopeless at physical activities (as I still am, with no hand–eye co-ordination at all), I was all too often keen to sit out of the frame with her! Tragically, Gillian died aged nine during surgery, but I am glad I have such happy childhood memories of our times together.

Older children such as teenagers can forge incredibly important friendships too, but these often operate within gangs. At this stage friendship becomes quite intense; for instance, girls who see each other all day at school will then spend half the night on the phone with one another. In most of the Western world, the streets of towns and cities are alive on a Saturday night with groups of young men and women – usually separately from each other. The girls always seem to be wearing too little in cold weather, whereas the boys seem not to have dressed up at all; but perhaps that is only because I am observing them with the jaded eyes of someone who no longer belongs to that world and, as an outsider, I simply don't understand the language of their fashion code!

I pity the teenager who develops less quickly than his or her peers, or who has Asperger's and cannot interpret the subtle behaviours at play: it must be very difficult, not to say lonely and terrifying, if your potential social life is moving around in a gang from which you feel excluded. Adolescence can be a particularly trying time in which we're either in or out of favour, and especially hard on those who don't quite belong to the main clique.

I witnessed this as a congregational rabbi, when one or other of the teenagers in the top class at religion school just did not fit in, and consequently could not go out with the others on Saturday nights. Even worse, for teenagers can be very cruel, they would find themselves isolated around the classroom table too.

Most of us will know teenagers who stay in their rooms, playing computer games, and I wonder just what kind of friendships they are forming online, when they cannot function with their own peer groups on the streets of their local town. Not being part of 'the gang' can, of course, lead to problems socialising in later life.

We have already seen how boys and girls, men and women, have different kinds of friendships. If we glance around us this may seem obvious. For example, I belong to a mixed book group, but most of my friends belong to single-sex groups. Book groups themselves seem to be more of a female activity than male, for which there are various possible explanations. Some say that book groups act as surrogates for gatherings of friends, and it's true that the book in question might not be discussed for very long before the conversation turns to other matters. The women in my book group often chat about other subjects, and more emotionally, than the men do.

Here's another quick example: a friend who runs a gastropub told me that he is amused by the extent to which the men will prop up the bar watching the odd bit of sport, occasionally shouting support or criticism, but otherwise somehow quietly communing with each other, although they say little of a personal nature at all. On the odd evening that he gets a group of women in, he says the pub becomes like a different place entirely – shrill, full of laughter, with the most intimate details of the women's sex lives and their problems with partners and children being openly discussed, often between those in the group who do not seem to be particularly close. Now and again, he gets the impression that they will readily disclose the most personal information about their private lives to other women they have never even met before!

It is clear that men and women do by and large bond with their friends differently. It is also clear that women rely on their friends more than men do for things such as emotional support, as well as practical help with children and parents. But there is probably something deeper in all this than mere learned behaviour. It is as if the very nature of friendship differs depending on whether it is defined by men or women: in my book group, for instance, there is joshing and physical contact amongst the men, but not much talk, whilst the women talk and talk, but do not necessarily touch much except to greet and later say goodbye to each other.

Moving on to friendships across the sexes, between men and women – and I have always had many male friends – here the texture changes yet again, to lots of talk, of course, but a different kind of talk from that between women. Although I do not adhere to the extreme stereotypes some take from John Gray's *Men Are from Mars, Women Are from Venus*, in which the ways in which the sexes think, speak and behave are seen as being radically different from each other, I do agree with much of what psychologist Carol Gilligan says in her book *In a Different Voice*.[3] She argues that men and women phrase things differently although they actually mean the same thing, and that they exhibit different body language when they mean something the same. And it is interpreting that body language and those words correctly that is essential if friendship is to exist between a man and a woman.

As we have already seen, friendships are not static and will change depending on where we are in our lives. At university, for example, or early on in our careers, we may make large numbers of friends of both sexes, but few of those friendships will last for many years. The ones that do are with our real friends, and they matter – but they may not be the people who we thought would end up being the closest to us when we first got to know them. The individuals whom we marry, live with, divorce or separate from, socialise with and argue with, also affect our friendships. Splitting up with a partner often means losing those friends

28

who 'side' with one party or the other, even though they initially plan to stay in touch with both partners.

Divorce can create an appalling loss of friendships as the split takes effect. If, for instance, the divorced or separated person has familial caring responsibilities, such as needing to see children who live for half of the time with the divorced partner, he or she will have even less time – and probably energy – with which to maintain friendships. The damage to friendships can be particularly acute when there are long fights over custody and money, and where all the energy is taken up by those fights. By the time it is over, friends may have disappeared, been sickened by the fight or simply be too busy and preoccupied with their own concerns.

There is also the situation of many middle-aged people, single or with partners, married or in informal relationships, who may have made many friends earlier in life but who suddenly find themselves caring for their parents or elderly relatives. In these instances, friendships may also dissolve because there is simply no time to nurture them.

So friendships change and our attitudes to them change as well. Yet our need for friends, and the absolute necessity of nurturing our friendships, has never been greater, as we find ourselves with an ageing population, as separated by innovations such as the internet and modern travel as we are brought together by them, and as the traditional locations for communal bonding continue to disappear.

The nature of friendship today is complicated by the fact that we often call people our friends who would never have been described that way in a previous age. For instance, nowadays we increasingly call our work colleagues and acquaintances friends; and in some cases we may even be willing to pay for friendship. Mark Vernon makes that point very strongly in *The Meaning of Friendship*. When he suggests making a list of our friends, or of the people we might describe as friends, he notes that the list might include: 'Your partner. Oldest friend. Mates or girlfriends. One or two family members. Work colleagues. Neighbours. Family friends. A boss perhaps. Therapist, music teacher, personal trainer?' He continues: 'It soon becomes obvious that friendship is nothing if not an amorphous thing. Your friends share something in common, perhaps your goodwill for them. But qualities of friendship, like the degree to which you trust them or rely on them, are pretty diverse. They are far less coherent, and for the most part far less strong, than, say, the qualities that tie you to your family.' Precisely so, and when he includes the therapist, the music teacher and the personal trainer in his list, we have to ask ourselves whether those sorts of friendship are ever really reciprocal, or whether we have now got to the stage where we 'buy' our friends, or at least regard it as normal to pay, without any reciprocity, for some of the things we might once have expected our friends to do for us (and us for them) in a previous generation as simple acts of kindness, for free.

After all, I expected friends in my Jewish community to come to both the funerals and the prayers for my parents after their deaths, which they duly did, whether or not they knew them. Similarly, I expected to receive phone calls to check I was OK after they died, and I expected, and did in fact receive, huge support when I had a seriously sick child – our daughter Harriet was ill, and our neighbours in Clapham were wonderful, cooking and taking care of us; and the members of our local Jewish community, for whom I was rabbi, also offered their support by visiting, cooking and cleaning for us too. That is what friends do.

Although some friends will naturally withdraw that level of support when it becomes less needed, the best of friends will stay in touch for a little longer to get the daily bulletin and ask what else they can do to help – and, as they are real friends, we are prepared to tell them. That sort of unconditional friendship is wonderful, enriching, fun and rewarding: it is, literally, priceless. Tragically, we can become friendless if we let such friendships slide and do not reciprocate when we are offered kindnesses. Besides the possibility that we may need to draw upon the goodwill of others some day in the future, there is something wonderfully fulfilling in mutual acts of kindness offered without restraint.

Nevertheless, it appears that we are increasingly willing to pay for our friendships these days! The American web-based company Rentafriend is the brainchild of Scott Rosenbaum, who got the idea after reading about similar websites in Asia, where people are willing to hire someone to take to a work or family event. When he transplanted the idea to the United States, he decided to make it more of a friendship-come-social-networking site, designed to take advantage of the fact that nowadays people often work long hours, leaving limited time to meet new friends, and live far away from the place where they grew up, so are no longer in touch with their childhood companions.[4] Journalist Claire Prentice tried it out, and met a woman called Jenny Tam in a bar in New York through the website. She writes: 'It could be the beginning of a beautiful friendship, but it was all arranged online via Rentafriend.com. And if I want to see her again it'll be in the knowledge that I have to pick up the tab.' Her 'Rentafriend' date, Jenny Tam, confessed that she would 'definitely be open to transitioning from being a rented friend to a regular friend, but I haven't met anyone I like enough to do that yet'.

Having originated in America and Canada, Rentafriend has spread its wings, launching a UK site in 2010. When asked whether he is exploiting people's insecurities, Rosenbaum replies that he believes he is helping people: 'As the internet has replaced face-to-face time, there are a lot of people out there who want to get out and socialise with new people but it has got harder to meet people.' But others, such as Jonathan Alpert, argue that 'a rent-a-friend is an oxymoron, friendship is something which by its very nature is nurtured and deepens over time ... I can't imagine it feels good to know that you are paying by the hour'.

The concept behind Rentafriend is not in any sense about friendship as most of us would recognise it. This was confirmed for me when I met up with someone who told me that, feeling lonely, she had used another service similar to Rentafriend. Her view was that it felt as if she was simply paying for company, and that it was not like friendship at all.

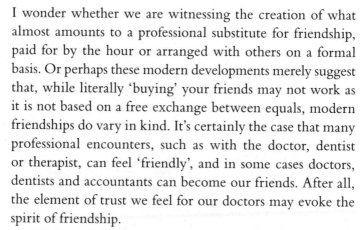

I wonder whether we are witnessing the creation of what almost amounts to a professional substitute for friendship, paid for by the hour or arranged with others on a formal basis. Or perhaps these modern developments merely suggest that, while literally 'buying' your friends may not work as it is not based on a free exchange between equals, modern friendships do vary in kind. It's certainly the case that many professional encounters, such as with the doctor, dentist or therapist, can feel 'friendly', and in some cases doctors, dentists and accountants can become our friends. After all, the element of trust we feel for our doctors may evoke the spirit of friendship.

Whilst I was working on this book, an article in the *British Medical Journal* by David Loxtercamp, from Maine in the United States, was pointed out to me.[5] He had been prompted to write it by the death of a doctor called David Demuth, who had been awarded the title 'Physician of the Year' in the United States and who was aged only fifty-eight when he died. This man had done everything for his patients, from night calls and delivering babies to accompanying patients to see specialists and visiting them in hospital. Arguably, he was burnt out. But in his article, Loxtercamp goes on to advocate that physicians should normally and properly act as friends to their patients. While this may seem unprofessional to modern thinking, I think he has a point:

> … the busy doctor left us with more than the example of his self-sacrifice. He coached us to 'listen to your patients. Most of the time, they'll tell you what's wrong with them.'

He adds: 'We become friends and family with our patients', which may seem surprising to some. Friends with our doctors? Surely not, although we may trust and respect them. Yet the doctor who looked after my family from 1978, when we moved to south London, until his eventual retirement, became a close friend of us all. He even came to Jewish festivals with us until his death in 2006.

Loxtercamp argues that it was his father's example as a small-town physician that prepared him to 'become friend and family' to his patients:

> If a friend in need is a friend indeed, the family doctor never wants for candidates. The patient may claim the need, but such a distinction hides a deep and reciprocal dimension to the doctor–patient relationship. We become friends. Yes, the doctor is paid, licensed, and ethically

bound, but these qualifiers cannot rinse the
essential humanity from each visit ... A patient's
longing for understanding and advocacy, coupled
with the doctor's desire to satisfy it, forges the
therapeutic alliance. Belief in their shared plan
of treatment powers the placebo effect. Why,
then, are we surprised when patients call us both
doctor and friend? More telling, why does the
juxtaposition make us nervous?

If you trust someone to be there for you until the very end,
if you trust them to listen to you and not spill the beans or
release confidences when you are sick and scared, what is the
recipient of those confidences to you, the person providing
them, but a friend – even if your friendship has a professional
basis? Loxtercamp ends his article with a reflection on what
that friendship means:

> What I am talking about is genuine friendship –
> it is a bond that hinges on listening and waiting
> and letting another take the lead. It knows the
> luxury of time and right timing. It matures
> with affection and mutual regard; it accepts the
> risk of self-disclosure and unveiled emotion. Its
> purpose is more than the pretext; we enjoy one
> another, even when in pain ... We lose nothing
> by loving our patients, but what could we gain?
> We might learn something about friendship,
> something that has evaded us outside our careers.
> We could see a future where we, like our
> patients, inevitably change, suffer, and decline.
> We will discover chinks in our armour, flaws in
> its design that keep us socially stuck and isolated.
> We can expect kindness and warmth from the

less injured, more emotionally evolved of our
patients who once seemed to need our care. We
will open ourselves to the full scope of human
drama and the many choices at our disposal for
responding to life's tribulations.

It is a surprisingly moving reflection. And it begs many
questions. Is friendship by its very nature reciprocal, or is
it legitimate to describe the therapist as 'my friend' or the
personal trainer as such for that matter? For, on the whole,
we tend not to think of our professional advisers – our
lawyers, accountants, doctors – as friends, and yet that is
very often what they end up being.

However, if we do include as our friends the therapist, the
music teacher and the personal trainer (who is often more
physically intimate with us than most other people), then
surely this must also beg the question as to whether we have
forgotten how close it is possible for our 'nonprofessional'
friends to be to us physically as well as socially. A warm
hug from a close friend can bring immense comfort in its
wake, yet it is remarkably common for people to pay to have
someone touch them, such as a physiotherapist, an osteopath
or an acupuncturist. These are people who are 'licensed' to
touch us, in a society where touching people in other circumstances can be judged to be assault.

So many people, especially older people living alone,
relish the weekly physiotherapy session in which they enjoy
the connection of touch; I have found that they will gladly
pay for aromatherapy or massage, treatments that provide
many benefits of which touch is not the least. Indeed, there
are those who argue that the popularity of physiotherapy
amongst older people with arthritis lies in the fact that they
are being touched by someone – not abusively, but warmly,
with care, to bring relief from pain.

We human beings respond well to touch and to efforts to care for us, yet all too often people are frightened of touching someone unless they know them very well, fearing they will be accused of assault, as hospital staff have been warned, or abuse. Sadly, this means that the American-style hug is relatively uncommon in the UK, where most of us remain chary of kissing or hugging relative strangers.

There are some formal friendship arrangements that seem to work especially well. In Australia there are now agencies that provide paid friends for older people who live isolated lives. These friends take them out, play Scrabble with them, visit them and generally take part in the sorts of activities that family members would do with the older person if they lived nearer. And the system seems to succeed very well, with many of the older people saying that many of those who initially befriend them in return for payment do genuinely become their friends!

So paying for friendship might not always be a bad thing: it may simply depend on the circumstances. Homeshare International, for example, is a charity that enables an older householder to offer accommodation to a younger Homesharer in exchange for an agreed level of support, such as light household duties. It's an arrangement that often leads to long-term friendships across the generations. In my mother's case, it even led to one of her Homesharers getting married from my mother's flat – and insisting that my very frail mother went to the wedding, something she agreed to do even though we, her family, couldn't persuade her to go out at all!

Older people often rejoice in inter-generational friend-ships. A number of voluntary organisations have created different kinds of 'rent a granny' schemes or programmes that enable older people to become mentors and surrogate grandparents to young people who are in trouble or at risk of offending. Early evaluations of these schemes and others like them reveal some promising results: despite being hard work on both sides, a lot of older people who are at risk of being isolated say that these schemes genuinely transform their lives. Much of this is not difficult to organise and the contact between the generations is greatly appreciated. There can be powerful benefits for everyone concerned. Friendships aside, such schemes allow older people to feel connected to a younger world and enable younger people to ask questions they would never ask their parents, or even their own grand-parents, about how things once were and whether older people had the same sorts of feelings when they were young as teenagers do now.

As a girl I was part of Taskforce, an organisation set up by Anthony Steen (later to become a Member of Parliament), which aimed to get school kids to visit older people. I remember going on my own to visit Charles Larkworthy, an old man living in a single room in Belsize Park. I loved it, and he became a real friend. His life was so different from mine and my family's. He was slightly wicked, with a great sense of humour, and he had a wonderful girlfriend with a delicious gravelly voice who tried to hide his mildly porno-graphic magazines from my delicate eyes; but he was lonely and housebound much of the time. I was devastated when he became ill: I visited him in the hospice, and then went to his sparsely attended funeral, where I knew almost none of those few people who came to pay their last respects.

Later, with my friend Barbara, I visited an old lady in a care home near Finchley Road tube station. Although we all enjoyed it, it was not a real friendship – we were simply visitors, providing a break from her daily routine. While her English was poor, our Yiddish was non-existent, and the communication between us was not good enough to enable us to learn much about her. Even so, I think that sort of inter-generational visiting arrangement to be worthwhile for both sides, even if it does not deepen sufficiently to become a real friendship.

As a general rule in Britain (unlike, say, in France and Italy) we don't have large family meals at which four generations sit down at the table together. This being the case, older people can find themselves fairly isolated, particularly when they are widowed or many of their friends have died or gone into residential care. That makes it all the more important that we do all we can to look after our surviving friendships when we are old.

It is very hard to make real friends. Indeed, there are real issues about whether, as one gets older, it is possible to make many new friends at all. And yet our friends are such an important part of our wellbeing throughout our lives. They help to encourage a sense of self-worth within us. They make us feel we are worth knowing, fun to be with, interesting, funny, sensible and supportive. They reflect us back to ourselves in a positive way. That is one reason, amongst many, why we need friends. One of the most reaffirming things about ourselves is the knowledge that we have friends who want to spend time with us, but, more importantly, who will be there for us when the chips are down.

Everyone knows how hard it is for the child or the teenager to be 'unpopular'. The same is true with adults, although we do not verbalise it in the same way. Other adults around us can affirm what we are doing, ask us questions, care about our welfare, make us feel better about ourselves, or make us feel part of a group that has a purpose, even if it is not explicit. No coincidence, then, the men often go to the pub with their 'mates'– and that often there is quite a deep bond between them, even if little seems to be shared emotionally. No coincidence, then, that men – and women – go to sporting events together, to rejoice in each other's pleasure when their team does well, and to commiserate when it does not. And it's no coincidence that women in particular join book groups and societies where the very act of engaging in discussion can make us feel interesting, valued and fun to be with, and the group itself becomes a bond of friendship, even if we did not feel particularly close to the other members before.

Former Professor of Geriatric Medicine Raymond Tallis argues with fierce conviction that one way of using the festive season – the season of goodwill – is by 'remembering auld acquaintance' and also thinking about making new friends in the months to come. Tallis reasons that it's the perfect time of year in which to examine the nature of our friendships; and also to look at how we might resurrect the spirit of friendship in the challenging relationships we sometimes have with our relatives. He believes that the season of goodwill raises questions about 'our connectedness with and our separation from others': it can remind us of the fact that much of life's meaning is to be found in being with others for the simple pleasure that we derive from their company. Tallis also notes that we benefit from the 'ethical satisfaction' of providing mutual care and support for each other; and he makes it clear that 'much of the meaning and purpose of life' lies with friendship: companionship and caring support.[6] And yet everyone I know who's been widowed, man or woman, young or old, has said the same thing to me: 'You never know who's going to be really supportive, and it's not the ones you expect to be ...'

In a way, the idea of friends who fail us, who do not come through for us when we need them, is truly horrifying. If friendship is important, then it must matter most that we give support to our friends during the hard times; that we lend a hand, give them meals and take them out, and make sure they have things to do that will help them through.

Recently, when I had surgery on my foot and was house-bound for weeks in Leamington Spa, I found people whom I did not know at all were enormously helpful, and people whom I knew only slightly showed me such support, love and genuine friendship (which I firmly believe should be recip-rocated if they ever find themselves in similar circumstances) that I was really surprised. It was as if my somewhat pathetic and cabin-fever-suffering state inspired people to make a huge effort on my behalf, and it also warmed what were not particularly close friendships into something quite different.

It is clear that particular circumstances such as illness, bereavement and common causes in politics or volunteer-ing can bond people together however old they are. But it also seems self-evident that, for friendships to thrive and survive, we need to be observant, make phone calls, check on our friends, and, as we get older, make sure they are all doing reasonably well in, say, bad weather, or if they have a cold or flu.

Some of us believe that old friends are the ones with whom you can pick up where you left off even if you haven't seen them for ages. Others say that you have to nurture your friendships as an on-going process. As someone who has been incredibly busy these last fifteen years, with a mixture of very demanding jobs (e.g. at the King's Fund and in the House of Lords), as well as caring for elderly parents and living between Leamington Spa and London because my husband is at Warwick University, I feel as if I have not always nurtured my friendships anything like enough and that I see my friends all too rarely. I really wish that I saw them more frequently, but, more importantly, that I had the time to relax with them, to spend quietly with them. That enforced six-week break when I had surgery on my foot gave me the chance to spend a bit of time with old friends catching up, as well as making new friends, and although the rest of the experience was ghastly, that one element gave me huge pleasure.

Personally, I do not believe it is easy to pick up exactly where you left off with friends, however old and loyal and wonderful they are: there is just too much missed information, too many emotional trials played out, which is why I believe that we do need to nourish and nurture our friends continuously, and why I also think that we need to think harder about what being a good friend means.

We need to think harder, too, about what we stand to gain from friendships. The Platonic concept of friendship suggests that there is always more to find out, more to discover, more to enjoy in good friendships. And that must be true. When I hear people talking of their friends being 'a trifle dull', or how they are going to do an 'edit' of their friends, I wonder two things: first, whether the person doing the describing is perhaps not a bit dull themselves, missing the point of where the boredom in the relationship emanates from. Second, and importantly, I wonder whether they have made enough effort to find out what might be exciting, interesting, valuable or admirable in the 'friend' of whom they are being so dismissive.

It seems to me that real friendship requires considerable effort, although in some respects this is less true of family relationships. With family, there is a more obvious obligation, but with our non-related friends it is different – friendship needs looking after, cherishing, nourishing, and a deliberate effort has to be made to gain mutual pleasure from each other's company. After all, we don't really need to stay friends with someone who isn't related to us; whereas, however irritatingly, we cannot easily cut our blood ties with fractious members of the family even if we choose not to see them.

Inevitably, when family ties are broken through divorce or death, sometimes friendships also fall into disarray. Whereas it seems that widowers get asked out all the time, I am frequently told by widows that they don't get invited to dinner because of the sheer numbers of them at a certain point in life. Besides, people in couples don't always seem to like having singletons at parties; perhaps they feel threatened by the widow who is pretty, easy company and, quite simply, available ... All of which I find deeply shocking. And yet I hear it time and again. According to the philosopher and essayist Francis Bacon, friendship cuts grief in half, yet where are we when people are grieving? If those who have been bereaved say that people are not necessarily terribly supportive, what does that say about us as their friends?

There are complicated reasons as to why we are sometimes not as supportive to widowed people as we should be. However good friends they were with the couple as a pair, there are those who feel it was the person who has died who was their 'real friend'. For others, there is a simple inability to know what to do or what to say to someone who has been bereaved, which leads to their doing nothing. All the same, not asking a recently widowed friend over for supper, not taking them to a play or film, not spending time with them or going for a walk, seems to me to be a display of worryingly poor friendship.

But poor though it is, at least there is usually some connection there. Most shocking is the growing evidence that there are plenty of people in our society who have no one and who face death alone. Then, once dead, they are not discovered until the smell gets so bad the police or the gas people are called. Apparently, around two hundred funerals a month in the UK are unattended by any mourners.[7] In 2008, Lucy Cohen made a film about these people, 'Watch Me Disappear', in which she argued that with our increasing reliance on online social networks, it is, ironically, easier to disappear. If we cut ourselves off from all social transactions with the real world; if, for instance, we do not have our milk or newspapers delivered to the doorstep every day, or collect our bread daily as is the case in France or Italy, then who's to know if we are no longer around?

Because of strict data protection rules, if an adult member of our family were to try to get in touch with us, they can only succeed if we let them – and a surprising number of us do not let them. It is far more common for older people than the young to become socially isolated and die alone with no one to mourn them, because we shed relationships as we get older, and form fewer new ones.

In September 2010 the news was full of the remarkable story of eighty-nine-year-old Eileen Nearne. She was so quiet and unassuming no one knew she had been a British spy behind enemy lines during much of the Second World War. She died alone in her seaside flat with, it seemed, no one there to mourn her passing. But after considerable publicity in the British media, the various heads of the intelligence services and a couple of nieces did in fact come to mourn her at her funeral. Yet they had not been there for her in life. Was this a case of self-imposed loneliness and isolation? Probably. But what is the nature of caring for others if we do not keep a watch out for people on their own in circumstances such as those, however much they appear to decline our offers of friendship or help?

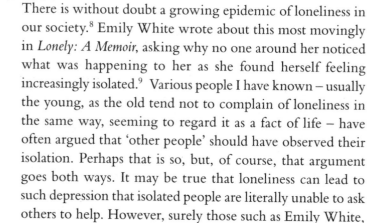

There is without doubt a growing epidemic of loneliness in our society.[8] Emily White wrote about this most movingly in *Lonely: A Memoir*, asking why no one around her noticed what was happening to her as she found herself feeling increasingly isolated.[9] Various people I have known – usually the young, as the old tend not to complain of loneliness in the same way, seeming to regard it as a fact of life – have often argued that 'other people' should have observed their isolation. Perhaps that is so, but, of course, that argument goes both ways. It may be true that loneliness can lead to such depression that isolated people are literally unable to ask others to help. However, surely those such as Emily White, who find themselves alone, also have an obligation to look actively to others for support and to make a concerted effort to ask for help?

In my view, loneliness is not an illness, although there are some who would suggest it is. It is about a state of mind and a lifestyle – and it is also about how we, collectively, have organised society so that meeting people becomes ever more difficult, so that we move around more yet socialise less. It is not the case that simply getting a grip on ourselves, going out more and meeting people will provide an easy solution to loneliness, which is what some charities and psychotherapists suggest – although perhaps it may help. Attachment is not always a matter of choice and loneliness can result from someone beloved dying or simply leaving us; the resulting sense of bereavement all too often needs to be dealt with before the person is ready to go out and start creating relationships again.

During the course of my work with older people, I have come across many who live isolated lives without experiencing great loneliness, at least in part because they know their lives have had real meaning – and they are sustained by memories of love in the past. This is something we would do well not to forget, for our lives are made up of our memories of relationships as well as those relationships we enjoy here and now. So, in view of the fact that some of us are content with our own company, simply to argue that our being lonely is something other people ought to notice – and put a stop to – does not seem to me to be correct. But nor is the argument that we should simply get out more.

～

So why exactly do we need friends? Is it to prevent us becoming isolated, nerdish, eccentric and even downright peculiar? When I wrote a piece for the *Guardian* newspaper in early 2010 about the danger of networking sites replacing 'real' friendships, I was taken aback by some of the comments on my piece, including those from self-styled loners who obviously felt I was a bit of a Luddite, unable to derive any proper benefit from social networking sites and too concerned with physical touch and presence.[10] Yet it seems to me that there is something perverse about the person who spends lots of time 'networking' online, but who does not go out to meet any of the people concerned. I have no objection to the internet *per se*; indeed I have found it life-transforming when using it to make arrangements, book tickets, check where venues are and so on. But the corny invitation popping up on the email list on a daily basis, often from someone we hardly know at all, asking us to become their 'friend' online, is what concerns me. What kind of 'friend' is that?

The internet, however much it has transformed our lives for the better, is no substitute for meeting people in person, getting out there and making friends. And that's the point. Once people become hooked on their computer screens, in some cases they go out less and less. I wrote in the article: '... we human beings are social creatures; we need other people to sustain us. More to the point, others need us to sustain them, particularly old, lonely and vulnerable people – or the young, frightened and uncertain. A message on email, however welcome, is not as good as hearing a human voice. Hearing a human voice, however welcome, does not compare with meeting face to face.'

Perhaps my critics are right to say I am being a little old-fashioned about all this. But I am not alone. I was comforted to discover that Raymond Tallis was writing about this subject at much the same time I was, and arguing that there was something concerning in the 'e-friendships that we may cultivate in the illusion that, even if we are unloved close up, we may be appreciated for our true value at a distance'. In his piece, he continues that 'screen-mates, alas, are remote from the real mess of the real world in which real friend-ships are formed and tested and deepened'.

Before I consider giving in and joining up, maybe I should be wary, as I have been, of promoting my Facebook page and 'befriending' anyone who wants to find out all about me. I worry that the information people put up on their pages is simply too readily available to those who may want to use it for nefarious purposes. What happens online is further complicated by the very public nature of Facebook and other networking sites. Whilst Friends Reunited and other such sites have obviously made many people very happy, they mean that we share our news – and our views – in public. It becomes a deliberately public display of matters that were once considered the raw materials of our private lives.

I am also concerned that our increasing reliance on the internet for our friendships has a detrimental effect on the very old and the very young, on those who cannot use the technology and on those who do not want to. And that it may also have a very negative effect on those who enjoy using networking sites if they do not balance that use with networking in real life – going out, meeting people and forming social connections.

Whilst I accept that the internet can be a wonderful means for getting in touch with old friends, I still believe that there is a danger of it numbing us to the need for human contact that most of us have. Older people who live alone often speak of how they force themselves to go out simply so that they see other human beings, whether or not they speak or have any interaction with them beyond a smile of recognition. The gradual replacement of bank clerks with cash machines, of checkout staff with automatic tills, and the lack of a bus conductor or even driver to talk to if we have a bus pass means that we do not need to speak to or negotiate our day with anyone.

All of this leaves me wondering whether Facebook friendships are real, or whether they are perhaps almost a deliberate means of replacing the physical world, which increasing numbers of people today seem to find dangerous or threatening. Some of the respondents to my *Guardian* article pointed out that their virtual friendships were not only real (to them, if not to me), but that they or their siblings had actually met their partners though social networking sites and in some cases even married them! They accused me of not really understanding how these sites work, which is, to some extent, perfectly fair comment. Yet I can't help wondering whether listing – flaunting almost – our numbers of 'friends' and their photos on Facebook is done just to make us feel we have a wide circle of friends when, in fact, most of them are nothing of the sort. It feels as if the meaning of the word 'friend' is drifting into acquaintanceship or to denote loose groups of people with common interests and concerns.

My concerns go wider than social networks on the internet. Carole Stone has written prolifically about networking and is herself the most accomplished networker I know.[11] Her networking is real, in person and predates the rise and rise of social networking online. She has a database of over twenty-one thousand people, can put a face to over ten thousand of them and mixes socially with up to a thousand. Yet how many of these are close friends? She herself would only claim a couple of dozen.

Nevertheless, she achieves amazing things through her networking, using it to link up people who she thinks could benefit each other. That is a very generous sort of friendship in my eyes, but as it covers a large number of people, the support, long-term energy and ability to talk about real problems which go with close friendships simply cannot happen on a scale such as this.

So maybe the answer is to issue a health warning of sorts. Instead of indiscriminately stating that we should not spend all our time on the computer screen indulging in social networking, perhaps I should suggest that we use networking to make the links we want and then do everything we can to meet in person – but if we are unable go out and cannot physically meet other people, then it's to be argued that social networking online is infinitely preferable to making no contacts at all.

In my view, true person-to-person friendship runs deeper than all the words and messages of emails and online interactions, useful as these are. While I was working on this book, Bruce Feiler, an American man in his forties, was diagnosed with an osteosarcoma, which is an extremely rare form of bone cancer with a very poor prognosis.[12] His treatment was painful, sickening and scary, and he thought he would die. He had small twin daughters, and feared he would not be around to see them grow up. He decided to make contact with his closest friends to set up a 'Council of Dads' so that, should he die, they could take on some of the parenting role for his two girls. Knowing him from different stages of his life, and bringing with them different talents, none of the friends turned him down.

He went to see them individually and set out what he had in mind. But the interesting thing was that what had started as a list of separate friends turned into something else – a kind of 'Stonehenge assembly' as he put it. The men came together as a group and collaborated to forge a strong connection with Feiler's daughters.

The whole makes for an extremely moving read: what emerged was a new form of friendship – the Councillors, as Feiler calls them. They created a support network into which his oncologist also fitted in the role of surrogate father whilst Feiler was ill. The group continues to work with his family, so that the support mechanism persists despite his being still alive, with a real strengthening of bonds every which way.

But there really need to be questions asked about this example. What kind of society needs a dying man to make such a formal arrangement to look after his daughters? Why would his friends not step in naturally and automatically? And, as I discovered when I broadcast about Feiler's work in spring of 2010, why does it not seem as easy for a woman who is dying to do the same – to ask her women friends to help provide mothering for her children? Is it because the idea of mothers dying young was once commonplace and is culturally ingrained in us? Women often used to die in childbirth; hence the common theme in fairytales of the 'wicked stepmother', a figure of hate when often she does her very best. On the other hand, young men die in war and in famine. But somehow women are either seen as tougher and more capable of getting on with it; or, perhaps, because women cherish their friendships differently, their women friends show an unsolicited interest and are naturally prepared to take on some of the mothering of their children without being asked.

In describing his group of friends, Feiler talks about the bonds that men make in the army. Having developed the thinking behind his group, and having become more and more interested in male friendships as a result, he joined up with the national Fatherhood Initiative in the United States to develop a five-step plan so that fathers in the military could also develop their own 'Councils of Dads'. If, as he suggests, the military uses 'male intimacy as a plank of modern warfare', then the team spirit should extend to supporting each other's children. Given the risk of dying in active service, setting up Councils of Dads is a sensible precaution, and it also leads to a new – and different – form of male intimacy.

Feiler suggests that Councils of Dads are a natural

evolution from the idea of godparenting. Traditionally, godparents took some responsibility for the spiritual upbringing of their godchildren. In Feiler's fresh approach, it offers more of a secular approach to adults (in this case men) taking a deliberate interest in and, should the need arise, developing a readiness to provide for the welfare and upbringing of a great friend's children.

It is a wonderful development; one that could and perhaps should be replicated worldwide – giving depth to friendship and adding to a sense of purpose in our being alive, particularly when someone dear to us no longer is. I am particularly interested in what the hands-on support provided by Feiler's doctor and his Council of Dads has to tell us about the looseness of our 'friendships' on Facebook, or the so-called friends we barely see and hardly know. Loxtercamp and Feiler, the anonymous people who give real support during bereavement, and the friends who genuinely seek out and befriend an isolated older person – surely these are the real friendships in terms of everyday quality over online quantity? They tend to their friendships and realise their value, and they know that time, energy and thought need to be given to nurturing those friendships and maintaining them.

So what can we do to make ourselves better friends, besides nurturing the friendships we already have? Human beings have felt the need to have friends and have celebrated friendship since time began. In the Bible, the close relationship between the future King David and the present King Saul's son, Jonathan, is depicted as what we might now call a 'passionate friendship'. The two young men play together and fight together, are close to each other and love each other. Some recent commentators have suggested that they might have been gay lovers, but it is more likely that they represent the embodiment of a close friendship between two men who are mutually involved in each other's lives. Theirs is more like Aristotle's description of what friendship can be: 'Friendship is one soul inhabiting two bodies.'[13]

And, of course, there is the quotation from the Gospel of John in the New Testament about the importance of male bonding, which is still used to strengthen young soldiers' resolve in times of war: 'Greater love hath no man than this – that a man lay down his life for his friends.'[14] There are similar teachings in Islam, as well as the very sensible warning to be careful who our friends are. The Holy Prophet says: 'Man is influenced by the faith of his friends. Therefore, be careful of whom you associate with', which is mirrored in the Hebrew Bible by the text: 'The righteous should choose his friends carefully, for the way of the wicked leads them astray.'[15] [16] So scriptures and ancient writings of all denominations think that friends are important, but we need, they say, to choose our friends wisely.

So what is the nature of a good friendship, wisely chosen? Is it to put things down instantly in order to rush round and help a friend in a crisis? If so, there is clearly a sense of purpose at work and a strong sense of connectedness. Or is it to be the calming presence to others in times of stress?

Being a true friend might also mean being critical; it might entail telling what seems to be the unpalatable truth when powerful forces of one kind or another are stacked up against us. When we speak out, we may be temporarily unpopular, but at least we will feel very alive and be seen to be struggling to achieve a good outcome for our friends. To repeat one of Randy Pausch's lessons from his last lecture, criticism is not something we should unquestioningly resent: it may be a sign of true friendship.

Do we need to see our friends often in order to maintain that sense of connectedness; or is what matters something to do with the texture of the relationship, and the extent to which we trust one another? The pattern of having lots of friends in our twenties and thirties will change as we grow older. In the busy years of bringing up children, which often coincide with caring for increasingly frail parents, many of us stop looking after our friendships. We may turn into less than good friends, yet ironically we may need our friends more than ever just as they need us at that stage in our lives. And it is really important to retain some friends from earlier points in our lives as well as to make new ones. In trying times, friendships will certainly make us feel good about ourselves, and influence the ways in which we will look back on our days.

I am nowhere near the end of my own life yet, I hope, but as I look back I find that some of my best memories are surprise outings with friends, or completely unexpected gestures of friendship: a few weeks ago, an old friend sent me a bunch of flowers because he was thinking of me. The gift was not apropos of anything – not my birthday, not a celebration, there was nothing to be congratulated for or thanked for – it was just an extravagant gesture of friendship. It meant a huge amount. Oddly, I had been thinking about him that same day, but we had not seen each other for months.

Occasional gestures to spoil our friends and surprises that show we are thinking of them are immeasurably life-enriching – not just at Christmas, Chanukkah, Eid or whenever, not only on birthdays or to sympathise or to celebrate – but simply as a sign that someone is in our thoughts. These simple acts really do help the world go round, and are a source of unexpected pleasure: people love them.

There are times, naturally, when friendships come to an end. There was a period in my own life when certain individuals whom I had considered to be relatively close friends became so different to me politically – and I have always prided myself on having friends across the political spectrum – that we simply could not remain close. And there are other occasions, such as when children grow up, where those friendships with the parents of our children's friends simply fizzle out. And yet it can go the other way; I know of instances when, although the children themselves are no longer friends, the parents of those children remain close. And this can involve people of diametrically opposed views and very different approaches to life, and becomes a source of huge pleasure and fascination.

I believe that being a good friend, supporting others in the bad times, is a great test of being a good and caring person, however banal that sounds – and also that we can usually do even better. When we have friends who are widowed, divorced, separated, seriously ill or going through a hard time, we need to ask ourselves the questions: did we help? Were we there for them? Are they there for us? Were we also there for them at other, calmer times? As somebody who has worked hard all her life, and who also cherishes the company of others, it seems clear to me that the forging of enduring friendships matters more in terms of life satisfaction than simply ploughing on with a career, or focusing on the day-to-day running of a family. Friends matter, and nurturing friendship, and enjoying it without expecting too much from it, or taking the view that we need a payback from it, is something we should add into the list of things to do as we get on with our lives: true friendship will make us feel immeasurably emotionally richer, and, indeed, happier.

CHAPTER 3

LEARNING
TO BE HAPPY

*What everyone wants from life is continuous
and genuine happiness.*

Baruch Spinoza (1632–1677)

Happiness. I remember that feeling so well as a child. It would be particularly strong whenever I returned home from holiday with my parents. We'd drive up to our block of mansion flats, which always looked enormous when we got back, then park and start unloading the luggage. And I always felt a rush of pure joy at being home. I had been happy on holiday, of course, but it was that feeling of contentment, of being pleased to be back, of enjoying the feeling, the smells, the familiarity of it all, that always made me profoundly glad to come home – and still does.

I recently talked to a couple of friends about feeling happy as children. One said she remembered that sense of endless free time at the start of the summer holidays, and the feeling of pure unadulterated happiness when you knew you could do what you wanted for six weeks: be indolent, play, go on holiday or just hang out. She says she has never been so happy since! And another friend remembers the pure joy of being allowed as much ice cream as she could eat on her birthday! I think it would have made me sick, but she says she never felt nauseous, just full and happy; and brimming with the awareness that she was doing something that she knew, even then, was not very good for her, but which was simply blissful nevertheless.

I might not have shared that particular experience, but I do remember going to buy a new dress with my grand-mother, who was extremely indulgent, when I was about six years old (she bought new clothes for all her grandchildren for the Jewish holidays). She allowed me to buy the most unsuitable blue dress, which had endless net petticoats – the height of fashion and desirability for any self-respecting six-year-old at the time. And I was blissfully happy. My mother was not: the dress needed to be dry-cleaned every time it was worn, which was expensive and in her view ridiculous. But I was pleased, and I still remember the extraordinary joy I felt every time I wore it, till it got too small!

Happiness sounds simple, but it can be so difficult to talk about. Song lyrics about happiness, which are to be found all over the place, tend towards the immensely cheesy, or even to the faintly embarrassing. Yet happiness pure and simple is what we all want, although it may make us cringe to be open about our desire for it and it often seems that we don't quite know what it really is or how to achieve it.

Here's a little experiment: ask people you know if they are happy. They will probably be very surprised by the question unless it's linked to the enjoyment of a major event such as a birthday, the arrival of a new baby, a special night out, winning a prize or getting a new job. You will probably find that at least some of the people you ask can't or won't give you a straight answer. 'It depends what you mean by happy' is quite a common response. And, of course, the pure happiness I remember from childhood is not the way in which I usually feel happy now. These days, there is less of a sense of the exultation that I remember (except occasionally, when I'm lucky enough to listen to a magnificent performance of music) and more of a sense of contentment, of feeling 'happy in my bones' as my mother used to say, and of being generally content with my family, friends and life. We change throughout our lives, and the ways in we experience happiness change too.

Yet, whatever age we are, happiness is something that we need to think about seriously and pursue actively. It is a worthy goal throughout our lives. Happiness, joy, pleasure – call it what you will – is part of what can give us a sense of meaning. The pursuit of happiness is a deserving objective in itself, although we usually tie it to some other goal whose fulfilment we hope will make us happy. Living with a sense of contentment (which, to my mind, suggests a gentler way of being happy than the full-blown exultation of youth) can give our lives meaning through a sense of gratitude, through the wish to maintain that sense of equilibrium, and also through the desire to help other people achieve the inner harmony that we have found.

As we will discover, many of the later chapters in this book touch upon happiness in some way. For example, some of us define happiness in relation to taking risks, others in relation to volunteering or being a good friend and neighbour. But in this chapter I want to examine happiness as a concept in its own right, to ask what makes us happy, and whether and how we can learn to be happy – and, indeed, whether we should.

Of course, thinking about happiness is not new. In 1776, the American Declaration of Independence cited as its goals 'life, liberty and the pursuit of happiness':

> We hold these truths to be self-evident, that all men are created equal, that they are endowed by their Creator with certain unalienable Rights, that among these are Life, Liberty and the pursuit of Happiness.

In Britain, as in many other countries, the influence of the social reformer Jeremy Bentham (1748–1832) and the philosophy of utilitarianism had a huge effect on social policy and political life. The rule of utility is that what is good is whatever brings the greatest happiness to the greatest number of people.

Interestingly, although happiness has been studied by philosophers since ancient times, happiness studies as an explicit subject in its own right is the newest of academic disciplines. These days, it is as much a subject for sociologists, psychologists, economists and political theorists as for philosophers. We now see politicians debating the nation's contentment and examining how to ensure happiness for the population, or at least for the greatest number of us. This is now a standard part of political dialogue, a modern political trend that comes largely from the work of Martin Seligman, Nick Baylis and others who have pioneered what they call 'positive psychology'.[1] They argue that, instead of focussing on what makes people unhappy and what happens when things go wrong, we should be thinking about what it is that makes life go right for some people.

Martin Seligman, the founder of this type of thinking in the United States, argues that 'while psychologists knew virtually all there was to know about depression, they knew almost nothing of the secrets of a happy life'.[2] The issue for Baylis, Seligman and their colleagues around the world is whether we really can find out what makes people happy. Increasingly, they think they know: 'The happiest people surround themselves with family and friends, don't care about keeping up with the Joneses next door, lose themselves in daily activities, and, most important, forgive easily.'[3] If that is correct, as Selgiman and others argue it is, then is this a formula we can 'bottle', as it were, and give to the majority of people in our population? And, if so, should we be doing that?

The British economist Richard Layard has also done a great deal of work on what does and does not make us happy and, indeed, thought a great deal about what bottling the answer might look like.[4] His solution does not include age, gender, looks, IQ or education, except to the extent that these factors affect income – although, as we shall see, some would disagree on most of those exclusions. However, he rates the importance of family relationships above all, alongside other factors such as finance (of which more below), meaningful work, community and friends, personal freedom and personal values such as our attitudes and philosophy of life.

The emphasis on meaningful work is instructive: most of us long for holidays and breaks away, and some relaxation is certainly beneficial. But the main element in what makes people happy, according to Swedish research, is the pursuit of a goal alongside good personal relationships.[5] It is not even about reaching the goal, but more about remaining active and striving towards whatever it is that we wish to achieve, which could involve either paid or voluntary work.

Not only that, but if the evidence from the John Lewis Partnership in Britain is to be believed, hard work combined with a sense of being well looked after and in some respects in charge of our own working destiny – as an active 'partner' in the process – are likely to lead to greater contentment and happiness, greater motivation and a sense of vocation at work. As a result of such a supportive environment, John Lewis staff were found to be much more inclined to cooperate with their directors in order to achieve increased profits for the company as a whole.[6] So convincing is the company's success that politicians across the spectrum are looking at the model to see whether they can use it to bring greater commitment, a sense of shared ownership and improved productivity to many of our public services.

In my time as Chief Executive of the King's Fund, I became very aware of the caring culture that was deeply ingrained into the organisation as a whole. There were, for example, generous funds for Christmas parties, good provision of subsidised meals, a very good pension scheme and sympathetic hearings for people who wanted to undertake additional training or education. Without doubt, the supportive atmosphere made the King's Fund a wonderful place in which to work. It made people smile. And, when we had to take some tough decisions because of financial shortfalls, I became very aware that it was important not to remove the things about the organisation that made the people there smile.

On a slightly cynical note, our own behaviour gets other people to mirror what we do to some degree; therefore our learning to smile more often brings out smiles in other people. Conversely, while working in a supporting and caring environment clearly makes people happy, a toxic environment can cause considerable unhappiness. And unhappiness can result in lack of productivity.

Layard has campaigned – as an economist – for a far greater availability of cognitive behavioural therapy (CBT) for people with depression in the UK, and he has successfully persuaded the UK government to find the money for it (although there is still some doubt as to whether it is being provided by the health services in sufficient quantity and quality). His argument is that depression costs the country a great deal in, for example, wasted energy and days away from work. In his research he touches on the human cost of depression, although he does not plumb the depths of what it means to be seriously depressed – what it feels like to be unable to get out of bed, with no sense of meaning or purpose, and no will to do anything at all.

I talked to a friend recently who has been through terrible bouts of depression, mostly since her forties, although she thinks on reflection that they must have started when she was a child. She certainly has no recollection of those moments of pure joy that I can remember as a little girl. She told me that she has been seeing a therapist for years, yet it is still as though she sees the world through dark glasses. What is a bright blue sky to me appears grey and overcast to her, and when she thinks of the future it looks bleak, whereas I am naturally pretty optimistic. Her life has not been very different to my own, so I don't think that her depression can be the result of outside circumstances, but is perhaps more likely to do with her personal chemistry – with how she is made and how her brain functions. She is really looking forward to old age because her doctors have told her that, if she is lucky, her depression will burn itself out by then, given the recent evidence which suggests that women's mood changes are often linked with hormonal fluctuations during the menstrual cycle.

I really feel for her. The inability to experience those

life-enhancing moments of pure joy damages her life. Although she tries incredibly hard to 'put a brave face on it' and to carry on as normal, she often does so with the most leaden of steps and is sometimes only just able to get out of bed. Hers is a case of diagnosed clinical depression. Judging from her experience, it seems clear to me that as a society we do not take this condition seriously enough, or, indeed, feel sympathetic enough to those who suffer from it.

For this debate should not only be about what serious depression costs the economy and the nation. There are immense human costs involved as well. Layard's premise, that governments should concern themselves with the wellbeing of the people – their citizens – because citizens are more affected by happiness (or lack of it) than by wealth, and mere economic prosperity, is not enough. In his view, this is an issue on which politicians should act.

Of course, there have been many critiques of Layard's theories and many who doubt his conclusions. Indeed, several American critics argue that he does not take into account economic freedom as a cause of, or foundation for, happiness, and that some of those societies which provide a variety of supports and free social services (such as health-care) for their populations do not necessarily find that their populations are any happier than those, say, in the United States.

Somewhat earlier than Layard, the most famous economist of the twentieth century, John Maynard Keynes, was known for his view that:

> ... The economic problem will take a back seat where it belongs and the heart will be occupied ... by the real problems, the problems of life and human relations, of creation and behaviour and religion, ... (then) man will be faced with his

permanent problem – how to use his freedom from
pressing economic cares, how to use the leisure,
which science and compound interest will have
won for him, to live wisely, agreeably and well.[7]

So economists did not always put economic growth before
everything else, nor do political theorists today, although
it is still somewhat unorthodox – *pace* the new science
of happiness – to say so. Modern critics of our market
economy, and the way it puts maximisation of profit and
unlimited material growth above human wellbeing, would
agree. The Archbishop of Canterbury, Dr Rowan Williams,
has stated that the central question for us in light of current
doubts about the global market economy is how we think
about shared wellbeing: 'Theology does not solve specific
economic questions (any more than it solves specific political
or scientific ones); but what it offers is a robust definition of
what human wellbeing looks like and what the rationale is
for human life well-lived in common.'[8]

Money can't buy happiness. (Or love!) True, it's a piece
of conventional wisdom, a cliché perhaps, but one that
most people would agree with. Materialism has even been
described as 'toxic for happiness' by University of Illinois
psychologist Ed Diener. However, that is not to say that
money can't make life easier. Although having enough
in the bank to deal with a roof repair may not obviously
equate with happiness, the feeling of security that comes
with having a bit of money to spare certainly makes it easier
not to be unhappy. And while so many of life's pleasures
don't require vast amounts of money, having some spare cash
opens up choices and possibilities that can, at the very least,
extend the range of ways in we choose to enjoy ourselves.

I don't think that we should underestimate the high cost of simply maintaining a reasonable standard of living. While, as we will see elsewhere in this book, there are those who take pleasure in the simple life and others who have successfully downsized, most of us still need a certain amount of money in order to enjoy life as we would wish. A recent article on a financial website reported on a study which estimated that, on average in the UK, we would need a home worth £500,000 and a salary of £42,000 before considering ourselves financially content: 'Britons would also need at least two foreign holidays every year and have more than £33,000 in savings and investments to regard themselves as well off.'[9] Although financial contentment is not the same as happiness, and we may disagree about the figures, a link between financial security and happiness exists for most of us, even if financial security does not inevitably contribute to communal, societal wellbeing.

I found myself chatting to a friend about this: she confessed that she had lost a lot of financial security when her husband died many years earlier, but that she later gained some back when her mother died and left her the proceeds of a very valuable house. She said that she felt much, much happier when she was financially secure and that it is simply untrue, in her view, that money does not buy happiness. If having enough money means you do not have to worry about how you are going to pay the bills, then, she says, without doubt it does buy a form of happiness. And she certainly now regards herself as content and free from financial strain – a great blessing, in her book.

Economist Richard Layard argues that we can feel wealthy in comparison to those around us, regardless of how much we earn or receive. Whether an individual is happy depends on how his or her income compares with the norm. He thinks that those who earn an average or higher income are likely to be happy with their financial condition, while those who fall well below the average are more likely to rate themselves as not happy. This may sound obvious, but the focus on comparisons with others rather than on a particular amount of money is an interesting and surprisingly controversial one. It is, arguably, also a reason why economic growth does not necessarily improve happiness, because we compare ourselves to others in a climate of changing levels of income.

It's also interesting to consider whether receiving unexpected windfalls can increase happiness. Judging by the enthusiasm with which people play lotteries in spite of the gigantic odds against their winning serious money, it appears that many people think a big win would make them very happy indeed. In fact, Professor Andrew Oswald and others have suggested that winning just £1,000 could be enough to change a person's outlook on life, although a win of less than £1,000,000 is unlikely to have a lasting effect on a person's happiness. Oswald said: 'We found a strong link between financial windfalls and being happy and having much better psychological health.'[10] However, research also suggests that a strong marriage and good health are more likely to make people feel content than money.

Although Oswald's study shows a link between windfalls and wellbeing, and a serious lack of money can clearly cause problems, there is evidence that money really does not buy happiness, in the sense that it can't guarantee contentment or lead automatically to our being happy. A paper from the University of Ulster concludes that there is a distinction between people's satisfaction with their standard of living and their happiness.[11] The standard of living is one source of happiness, but it is not the most important source. The most important source of happiness is good health. Another considerable source of happiness is whether the area in which a person lives has a strong sense of community. A third source of happiness is age, with younger people being generally less happy than older people (we'll be returning to this last point a little later on). The thing to note is that each of these three considerations has a greater influence on the level of happiness than the standard of living.

There is also some suggestion that Britain is less happy today than during the 1950s, despite the fact that we are three times richer. Could this possibly be one reason why there is currently such a renaissance of what would once have been dismissed as old-fashioned pursuits (but which we now call 'retro') – such as the renewed interest in baking cupcakes, flower-arranging and all things domestic, as embraced by a new cohort of Women's Institute members in the most unlikely of urban areas? Whether our understanding of happiness has become increasingly confused with nostalgia, or whether it's simply the case that the post-feminist generation is suddenly taking a renewed interest in these traditional pursuits, is a matter open to speculation. Or perhaps these born-again domestic goddesses are simply having fun with an ironic smile, because they do not have to do those sorts of thing day in day out, as their grandmothers did?

But something is definitely going on with respect to the changing levels of happiness in our society. A poll conducted in 2006 by GfK NOP for a BBC Two programme *The Happiness Formula* suggested that the proportion of people saying they are 'very happy' had fallen from 52 per cent in 1957 to just 36 per cent at the time of the poll.[12]

David Cameron, then the leader of the Conservative Party but still some years away from becoming Prime Minister, told *The Happiness Formula* programme:

We should be thinking not just what is good for putting money in people's pockets but what is good for putting joy in people's hearts. When politicians are looking at issues they should be saying to themselves: 'How are we going to try and make sure that we don't just make people better off but we make people happier, we make communities more stable, we make society more cohesive.'[13]

In fact, governments have begun to prioritise the calculation of happiness over the calculation of material wealth only relatively recently. The concept of Gross National Happiness (GNH) was developed in Bhutan in 1972 by the country's former king in an attempt to define an indicator that could measure quality of life or social progress in terms other than gross domestic product (GDP). In Bhutan, this approach was rooted in the spiritual and non-material values of Buddhism, but Westernised versions of the concept have subsequently developed in other countries. What was considered bizarre in 1972 is gradually moving into the mainstream. And the reason is not difficult to see: our growing need to measure and understand happiness is caused by the current near-epidemic of depression, combined with the increasing sense that the endless pursuit of wealth may in itself be a bit pointless unless it has some kind of social purpose.

So happiness is becoming more important socially, even though the science is as yet very inexact; and the idea that governments have some kind of obligation to care for and indeed to foster the happiness of their citizens is spreading – a concern that goes way beyond a government's usual responsibility for security, rule of law and provision of public goods and services. Of course, some cynics might argue that happy citizens are going to be easier to govern than dissatisfied ones. Indeed, Roger Scruton has argued that there is value in 'humane pessimism', and that unrelenting optimism and idealism can lead to appalling chaos and harm.[14] For instance, the argument goes, if a banker is unrelentingly optimistic and thinks that a risky investment will somehow come out all right in the end, there is an increased chance that he will risk large amounts of money, perhaps leading to banking problems – and even, if his is a group behaviour rather than an individual one, to a banking crisis. That is an oversimplification, but illustrates the general principle.

There is a related argument that says happiness should be about grabbing opportunities for joy when we can, but without needing to be relentlessly upbeat, smiling and optimistic and thereby denying ourselves the comfort of our natural cynicism, self-doubt and caution.

Levels of happiness don't seem to be the same across different countries and different cultures. Drawing on the 1999–2001 World Values Survey, Michael Bond of the *New Scientist* examined this topic in 2003.[15] He found that the most satisfied people at the time of the survey tended to live in Latin America, Western Europe and North America, while the least satisfied people were from Eastern Europe. Britain was twenty-fourth in the league table. Looking at other strands of research, running from 1946 to 2006, many countries show clear trends towards rising levels of happiness. Of the countries for which there is long-term data, nineteen of the twenty-six polled countries show rising happiness levels. India, Ireland, Mexico, Puerto Rico and South Korea show steeply rising trends of public happiness, whilst Argentina, Canada, China, Denmark, Finland, France,

Italy, Japan, Luxembourg, the Netherlands, Poland, South Africa, Spain and Sweden all show some increase. The US, Switzerland and Norway show flat trends from the earliest to latest available survey, with only four countries – Austria, Belgium, the UK and West Germany – showing downward trends.

That all looks interesting enough, and the downward trend polled from Austria, Belgium, the UK and Germany is a pretty hard piece of evidence. However, the value of such results is somewhat undermined by the problem of distinguishing satisfaction from happiness, not to mention the many different definitions of happiness. And, if these considerations aren't enough to confuse the results, researchers have pointed out that people in different countries tend to understate or overstate personal happiness in keeping with their own society's cultural norms on how to answer such questions.[16]

The thorny issue of nationality aside, it's interesting to speculate whether age has anything to do with happiness. As we have seen, there are some indications that it does, with older people tending to be happier than younger people. A new study undertaken for the bank First Direct looked at the happiness and financial health of people grouped in ten-year age brackets.[17] They found that over fifty-fives were the happiest and that it was only in the over fifty-five age group that a majority of people (53 per cent) described themselves as happy and content. Middle-aged people between forty-five and fifty-four were the least happy. Indeed, in contrast to the happy 'baby boomer' generation, the so-called 'baby gloomers' face enormous financial pressures, with mortgages to pay and children to fund, as well as in many cases having to look after their elderly parents.

Perhaps our happiness increases as we mellow with age

and learn to appreciate the simple things in life more. That's what many of us have always have suspected, and now modern brain-imaging techniques are beginning to suggest we may be right. In a study published in September 2007 in *Psychological Science,* neuropsychologists recorded the brain activity of sixty-three adults from a range of ages, who were shown a series of negative and positive images.[18] The results showed that older adults were about 30 per cent less reactive to the negative images than younger adults.

One of the scientists involved in the study is quoted as saying: 'Why people regulate emotions better as they age may be due to school-of-hard-knocks experience. The later stages of life offer more opportunities to avoid those parts that are stressful.'[19] That may be so, but there is plenty of evidence to suggest that older people do suffer from some age discrimination, and are likely – just as younger people are – to be happier when fully occupied with something that gives them a sense of meaning and self-respect. It is clear that older people want to make a contribution to society, and that they do best, and are happiest, when that is not only possible but actively encouraged.[20] Above all, older people want the chance to pass on their skills and experiences to younger people in some way that makes sense. Nevertheless, despite these and other obstacles to their happiness, they seem generally more content than the young.

Perhaps this is because older age brings with it the bittersweet realisation of the shortness of life; as the saying goes: 'Nothing focuses the mind so much as the threat of execution on the morrow.' Either way, it looks as though old age – contrary to the fears of many young people – may be a time when we can actually increase our happiness. A wonderful poem by Elaine Feinstein called 'Getting Older' makes just this point:

The first surprise: I like it.
Whatever happens now, some things
that used to terrify have not:

I didn't die young, for instance. Or lose
my only love. My three children
never had to run away from anyone.

Don't tell me this gratitude is complacent.
We all approach the edge of the same blackness
which for me is silent.

Knowing as much sharpens
my delight in January freesia,
hot coffee, winter sunlight. So we say

as we lie close on some gentle occasion:
every day won from such
darkness is a celebration.[21]

Since so many of us today are living for longer, one of the keys to increasing our total sum of human happiness may lie in preparing to meet old age in a new way, without fear – regarding it instead as a potential time for happiness in its many forms, from excitement to contentment. This change in attitude might make us rejoice in old age, whatever its downsides, because to our great surprise we find that contentment comes with increasing years.

It is not only the case that levels of happiness vary across the age spectrum; studies suggest that it is possible that men and women are not equally likely to be happy. That is not to suggest any innate differences between the sexes, but rather that men and women experience different pressures in life, including those factors that may lead to happiness.

In the United States it has been claimed that women's happiness has declined over the years.[22] Every year since 1972, the United States General Social Survey has asked men and women: 'How happy are you, on a scale of 1 to 3, with 3 being very happy, and 1 being not too happy?' According to the results, women's overall level of happiness has dropped since 1972, both relative to the level forty years ago and relative to men. This is regardless of whether or not they have children, and it is irrespective of health, wealth, marital status and ethnicity – although, interestingly, the one exception in the US is that African–American women are now slightly happier than they were back in 1972, although they remain less happy than African–American men.

Other sources come to slightly more nuanced conclusions, taking age and different expectations into account. Research by Anke Plagnol of the University of Cambridge and Richard Easterlin, an economist at the University of Southern California, concludes that women are less able to achieve their life goals and tend to be unhappier than men later in life, even though they start out happier.[23]

While there is a lot to support the view that women experience particular pressures, and in many cases lack a reasonable level of support from men, the sad fact seems to be that both men and women experience gender-related pressures which get in the way of happiness. Employment pressures may prevent both women and men from establishing a happy balance between home and work, while subtler pressures such as gender-stereotyping continue to result in women having to do the lion's share (perhaps that should be the lioness's share) of work on the domestic front, as well as working hard outside the home. And all too often, just to add insult to injury, that work can still be for less reward and with fewer opportunities than men receive. Equally, men who wish to share parenting duties and domestic chores with a partner often meet with a distressing lack of understanding at work, so that their good intentions are seldom realised in actuality.

So it is not simple. Indeed, novelist and journalist Geraldine Bedell argues that women may now have too much choice about what they do, leading to their not doing anything properly, and that they are suffering from a huge increase in depression, ten times what it was fifty years ago, and twice as high as the levels experienced by men. She argues that life really has become quite hard for women, as expectations of them have changed so dramatically. But she also claims, interestingly, that a happy woman is '... probably in a romantic, generous relationship, is surrounded by a family she's fond of, or by friends; works part-time for herself and has plenty of autonomy and control over her time; is involved in the community; has activities and projects outside herself which are consuming and which provide her with a sense of flow; is physically active and has a more or less spiritual sense of something valuable beyond herself.'[24] She is convinced that the key to happiness is not to examine your innermost self, but to be involved in something bigger than yourself: 'Happiness, it seems, is losing yourself in something, or someone, else.'

Intuitively, most of us feel that having a loving family, in particular children and grandchildren of our own, contributes to personal happiness. But we should never assume that single people or those without children cannot be happy, as of course there are many ways to be fulfilled. Nor should we ever assume that family life can only mean heterosexual, nuclear families. Many people aspire to a long and loving relationship with another person, but the extent to which that union takes place in marriage has varied over time. In England and Wales, 2008 saw the lowest marriage rates since they were first calculated in 1862.[25] In fact, the number of first-time marriages in England and Wales peaked in 1940 at 426,100 when 91 per cent of all marriages were the first for both partners. This number fell to 147,130 in 2008 (provisional figures), accounting for 63 per cent of all marriages.

There has also been a falling-off in the rate of civil partnerships in the UK since 2006.[26] (The Civil Partnership Act 2004 came into force on 5 December 2005 in Britain, the first day couples could give notice of their intention to form a civil partnership.) However, that may suggest little other than that the large number of gay men and lesbians who had waited many years for the opportunity to enter a civil partnership have now done so, and the backlog of waiting couples has been dealt with; and perhaps some of those who enter civil partnerships today are choosing to do so at a somewhat earlier stage in their relationships.

I've found that people hold wildly different views on whether marriage and civil partnership make us happier. In fact, it's quite difficult to know what is the cause and what is the effect: whether we marry because we are already happy, or become happy because we are married. For example, many of us in the West choose to have children and then marry, so it could be argued that we have already decided that we are happy enough with our partners to marry them, rather than assuming that marriage will bring increased happiness.

Nor is it entirely clear whether having children increases people's happiness. Kate Devlin argued in the *Daily Telegraph* that having children can raise a woman's self-esteem;[27] and it has also been claimed that having children reduces the risk of a woman committing suicide, with the risks of suicide falling further the more children she had. But others have suggested that growing children tend to decrease parental happiness, at least until they leave for college – although in terms of a broader life narrative, the opposite may be true.[28] This is another way of saying what many of us know: that a screaming baby at three a.m. or a door-slamming teenager at any time of day or night does not usually feel like the height of joy. However, the highs of caring for children are unimaginably high and tend to outweigh the lows – or at least make the lows fade in our memories. So, in sum, bringing up children (or being involved in children's lives if we don't have them ourselves) can be wonderful.

Of course, it can be terribly hard work, but it is usually worth the effort in the end: it is not for nothing that babies are referred to as bundles of joy! One moment of pure joy that I feel strongly we should celebrate to greater effect as a society is the birth of new babies. Most of us feel huge pleasure at the birth of a child, something made very clear by the Channel 4 documentary series 'One Born Every Minute', which followed everyday life in a maternity ward in Southampton.[29] In the UK, we are increasingly willing to copy the American idea of baby shower parties, and we are generally happy to celebrate new births privately, with families and friends. But why do we not do more to celebrate the arrival of these 'little bundles of joy' communally, be it with a party thrown in honour of local newborns once a month, or through neighbourhood centres inviting all new mothers to meet on a regular basis to welcome the child into the community? Like christenings and baby blessings, such celebrations could be occasions for the whole community to come together – and quite separate from the bureaucracy of National Health Service weight and health checks!

∞

As we have seen, there is no end of theorising about happiness – what it is, who has most of it, when and why we are most happy. This theorising is all very well and actually quite important if we accept that societies can be organised in ways that maximise or minimise happiness. But it is really only half the story.

If life is to have meaning, for most of us, it must also have pleasure. Although there are those who can find meaning exclusively in prayer, contemplation or in selfless devotion to others, they are rare. Most of us choose – and need – to strike a balance in our lives between hard graft and pleasure. After all, doing things for enjoyment is a source of enrichment for our own lives, and also increases our capacity to be there for others.

Not that it is always easy to make time for fun. Some of us are incredibly lucky as our daily routines include activities we would do anyway for the pure enjoyment they bring us, such as meeting others, reading interesting material or making beautiful objects. But, sadly, for many people work is not necessarily pleasurable and the need to do other things for the simple enjoyment of them may be all the more essential.

Pleasure doesn't seem to come easily to everyone. People who for whatever reason suffer from low self-esteem may not think they are worthy of having pleasurable experiences. Those of us who are busy as carers, whether as parents or looking after relatives or friends, may simply be so exhausted that we have neither the time nor the inclination to have fun. And not having fun is a hard habit to break. If your world seems like it is always grey, it may not occur to you to seek out bright colours. And yet we should, because that in itself will lift the spirits.

Human beings need to feel joy. I have even come across a day-course in rejoicing at a retreat centre in the Peak District in Derbyshire: 'To rejoice means to appreciate and celebrate our own and others' happiness, good qualities and good fortune. It is a powerful and simple way to develop a happy and positive mind.'[30] So, it seems that some people believe we can learn to rejoice, and I certainly think we can learn to exercise the muscle that allows us to enjoy and celebrate.

All too often, it becomes a habit to be cynical or to moan. But the act of celebration, of deliberately exercising the muscle of enjoyment and grabbing pleasure, can provide additional meaning in our lives. For instance, celebrating a new job, anniversaries and birthdays can lift the spirits even if these are done, initially, with a heavy heart. In this respect, the expression 'because you're worth it' has some real currency. Celebrating the good things that happen, however simply and inexpensively, can in fact make us feel happier!

We need to keep our antennae on the alert for joy: sometimes it will come across us totally unexpectedly, such as the sense of great wellbeing we experience at a particular stunning view, for instance. Creating the capacity for enjoyment by celebrating the good things (there is enough bad stuff around) is a very valuable exercise. A celebration will make you feel loved and treasured if it's in your honour. Or it will give you an extraordinary sense of pleasure if you are organising it for someone else. Celebrating together helps weave us into the fabric of our communities and step beyond our own lives.

Whether it is going for a family picnic (some families I know do this on New Year's Day, all huddled up in boots and waterproofs, and have huge fun) or another kind of group activity, it is clear that being part and parcel of the family, the group, and doing things together brings a kind of happiness. In my own Jewish tradition, some families will go for a ramble at some point during the seven days of Passover. As we eat unleavened bread called Matzah during Passover, these walks are commonly referred to as 'matzah rambles' because the one thing you cannot eat is the standard picnic sandwich made of bread! On the theme of shared meals, French families often have kitchen tables that are expandable, so that the whole extended family can eat together on Sundays or on high days and holy days.

Parties do not necessarily mean drunkenness, but an opportunity to eat together round a table and enjoy a sense of fellowship. And at the very beginnings of Christianity, in the first century AD, table fellowship – eating with people – was extremely popular amongst Jews and early Christians alike. They understood something fundamental about the contentment and happiness that can be gained from eating together as a group, linked by family, friendship or a common purpose.

If we work on exercising enjoyment in our lives, we may find that we even discover it in the company of elderly parents who are getting frail. Instead of thinking of them as a burden or a responsibility, we will begin to find pleasure in spending time with them and taking life more slowly in their company, enjoying the fact that they are, hopefully, content – and learning contentment in turn from them.

We do not always need to be in a rush. Older people move more slowly and often react more slowly, but there is such pleasure to be gained from including them in our activities, and encouraging that special relationship between grandchildren and grandparents. At best, it is wonderful to witness. Having heard grandparents teach their grandchildren about the Second World War, rationing, the petrol shortages of the Suez crisis or other events that have shaken the world, I know that when these relationships have been fostered and all works well, the special connection between grandparent and grandchild can be a source of completely irreplaceable joy.

There are many things we can do for ourselves which will contribute to our happiness and also to the happiness of others. This idea has become so important in modern thinking that today there are even enjoyment assessment quizzes![31] Rather bizarrely, it seems as if getting tattooed (now a mainstream activity with a fifth of the adult population being 'inked') is also a source of joy and meaning for quite a lot of people!

According to Sean 'Woody' Wood of Woody's Tattoo Studio in High Wycombe: 'Tattooing is a genuine popular art form, and people are only now beginning to realise what it can bring to their lives.' He explains that having a tattoo has in some respects given him something 'to live for' and a reason to get up in the morning. He is clear that he doesn't want his to be a dull life ruled by train timetables and routine. Rather, he – like many others, he implies – is looking for a way to make life seem more 'personal and fun and exciting', in a world that can all too often seem over-whelmingly 'drab and grey'. Woody argues that, for him, tattoos supply this sort of life-enhancing colour and are an important vehicle for self-exploration and self-expression. He believes they can even help people find out more about themselves, as well as offer a means to connect with other like-minded individuals. What's more, he says that when he gets up in the morning and looks in the mirror, he doesn't just see his own reflection staring back at him: he sees a 'work of art, in progress'.[32]

So what are the things that bring happiness, if not money *per se*, children necessarily, relationships, or a good standard of living? Tattoos? Retreats? Volunteering? Being involved beyond oneself, having lots of friends? David Halpern, who advised the previous UK government and is busy advising the present one on these subjects, has strong views on the subject, and regards the way we treat each other as key to the whole picture: 'When you look at wealthy nations, GDP is less important than the measures of institutional freedoms.'[33] Ultimately, according to Halpern, our happiness relies on those closest to us: 'The way in which people treat each other is really, really important. Acts of consideration and kindness loom very large.' In other words, to do yourself a favour – first do a favour for someone else. It could just save your life.

Political journalist Gaby Hinsliff, quoting Halpern in an article on happiness, has other ideas too. Listing the advice that she has gleaned from Halpern, she suggests that if we are to be happy we should think about moving closer to the office, rather than buy a big house further out of the city. While many of us may think that living in a large house in the countryside will make us happy, our contentment is bound to be compromised if we subsequently find that we spend most of our lives commuting to and fro between work and home, which has 'a proven negative effect' according to Halpern's findings.

Similarly, Hinsliff says that while the evidence suggests that marriage is good for increasing our levels of happiness, we won't necessarily find that having children will enhance our enjoyment of life. She notes that: 'Happiness peaks in people when they are in their twenties and declines through their thirties and forties, the child-raising years.' Halpern's research shows that it doesn't peak again until we retire. And, while there are many rewards to be found in bringing up children, it seems that the pressure of combining work and family can cause our levels of happiness to dip.

However, while raising children may be stressful, it appears that the same cannot be said of growing plants: cultivating a garden is one way to find happiness. 'Flow activities' such as gardening can be shortcuts to happiness in that they occupy our brains to such a degree that they enable us to switch off from our daily worries.

Another way to increase our levels of happiness is simply to get out more. Hinsliff notes that Scandianvians are amongst the happiest nations in Europe, who tend to spend their increased wealth on socialising more, whereas Anglo-Saxons (such as the English) tend to become more insular as their wealth increases, 'for instance by buying children televisions in their bedrooms which separate the family'.

Halpern's most controversial suggestion is to ditch public service targets in favour of targets to ensure clients are satisfied: 'Do we say to health professionals, "We will scrap 95 per cent of those targets and the one thing we want you to worry about is whether your users are happy with what you do"?' He argues that what patients actually say they want most is respect and dignity.

If we were to follow Halpern's thinking, a pro-happiness government might also treat public servants differently. In one of Halpern's studies doctors who were asked to make a diagnosis from X-rays did so faster and more creatively when offered sweets while working, which boosted their mood.

This attitude to happiness is now part of government thinking: it is the new science and the new politics. It will continue for the foreseeable future to influence public and private life in modern Britain. Perhaps this is the reason why so many people seem to be trying to make us happy today, sometimes in a rather forced manner. We are offered 'happy meals' and cheap drinks in 'happy hour'; magazines – particularly women's magazines – are full of quizzes about happiness; and if you were to type 'find happiness' into Google as I have done, you'd unearth a truly terrifying array of happiness options, from 'timeless tips' on how to find happiness, daily exercises, tips from 'happiness coaches', to complete 'toolkits on happiness'. It might all sound a bit desperate, if examined too closely.

However, if this is what it really takes for people to learn to enjoy themselves, then so be it. But I can't help thinking that it would be a better situation all round if we were to grow up with a sense of entitlement to pleasure in life, alongside the inevitability of sadder or challenging times. If we are to take pleasure in what life has to offer, we may need to think about how to use our precious time carefully so as to have the good experiences we would like. Some enjoyment can be very passive, such as listening to music, looking at beautiful scenery or reading a good book, but much of what gives people pleasure requires a considerable investment of time and energy. If we develop a sustained interest in seeking pleasure through leisure activities we tend to call those occupations 'hobbies'. However, Carolyn Clark, an acquaintance who was interviewed for this book, would take issue with the word 'hobby', as she explains:

> 'Hobby' is interestingly often used or seen as quite a dismissive term, possibly because it suggests something quirky or small-scale in the grand scheme of things. Also, the working class has 'hobbies' such as car booting or darts and the upper class has 'pursuits' such as art collecting and clay pigeon shooting! Maybe it is better to say 'interests' or 'leisure pursuits', although 'pastimes' (as in pass time?) is also an interesting word.

Carolyn is a person whose many interests include Tai Chi, collecting and researching early plastics such as bakelite jewellery (she is a member and treasurer of the Plastics Historical Society), collecting eggs (all kinds, but not birds' eggs), researching and collecting ephemera from the 1939 New York World Fair, local history – and singing! Many of these interests are very long-standing and Carolyn managed to find time for them even when she was employed full-time in senior posts in the NHS, charities and community organisations. She has always had a wide range of interests outside work and sees these as adding meaning to her life.

The enduring popularity of radio and TV programmes that educate us, fascinate us and inspire us to explore things further, such as Melvyn Bragg's 'In Our Time' on BBC Radio 4 or the Director of the British Museum Neil Macgregor's 'History of the World in a Hundred Objects', also on Radio 4, suggests that many of us need this kind of stimulus – and enjoy it. These sorts of programme push us to learn more, gain more, experience more – and basically enjoy life more and all the opportunities it gives us for expanding our horizons. Academic studies have come to a similar conclusion. Studies by Kennon M Sheldon and Sonia Lyubomirsky found that new, enjoyable activities have more potential – possibly fourfold – for making us happy than improvements in our circumstances.[34]

To return to Carolyn Clark: she argues that hobbies and interests press lots of the buttons connected to what it means to be human. She thinks that, as well as simply being enjoyable, for many people, their interests reflect our human tendency to be hunter-gatherers. This trait may manifest itself as trainspotting, bird-watching, climbing mountains, collecting or in any number of different ways. She also sees human beings as having a deep need to be creative, a need which having a whole range of interests will fulfil. Also, as she points out, most people who have a serious hobby want to learn more about it. Hobbies can provide a challenge, exposing us to new people and taking us outside our comfort zones. Indeed, many people find that their leisure interests extend their social life and bring them into contact with a wide range of other people. However, although hobbies and interests can give us a sense of identity, what they cannot do is to meet that other important human need – for love, unless pursuing the hobby leads to romantic encounters. At the other extreme, if people become totally immersed in a hobby, this may become a substitute for nurturing personal relationships.

For Carolyn, as for many of us, what we do for our own interest and amusement, rather than to earn a living, is hugely important and Carolyn argues strongly that these activities can bring joy and give meaning to life. As she says: 'There are millions of people over time, and to expect yourself to be the special one may lead to disappointment to many – but there is the possibility of joy in the minutiae of life, and in simple things, that brings happiness.'

Yes, simple things can bring happiness. Although they can't necessarily make life joyful in the face of serious problems such as grief, loss, pain or destitution, I suspect that they can make any life feel more worthwhile in the long run. Knowing how to have fun, how to make time – and allowing others to make time – to enjoy doing, making, seeing or experiencing something outside our usual day-to-day activities: these are important skills for all of us, and we need to cultivate them in ourselves and in others.

I grew up in a household in which both my parents had lots of interests outside their working and family environments: they collected art, they read voraciously, they sat on committees, they volunteered and they studied new things. My father even became an amateur historian of considerable distinction, as well as indexing books and researching into archives. Those activities did not make my parents happy in the sense of family contentment, but they did bring them real pleasure, interest, fun and new friendships – and they meant that, even in old age and physical frailty, both of my parents had plenty to keep them busy. They wanted to do lots of things before they died, which others helped them to achieve as they became older and frailer.

Maybe the pursuit of personal happiness is a goal that needs testing out, so that it does not become a simplistic, hedonistic 'laugh and the world laughs with you' exercise. Maybe we need to explore in greater detail how sport or taking risks gives some people real happiness (see Chapter 5). Maybe the quest for happiness is about being busy, yet also content and serene, serving others as well as ourselves.

Perhaps if we are fortunate enough to be happy, a duty to help others to be happy comes along with our own contentment. This duty can often be fulfilled simply, such as by spending time with friends and family, giving the parents of young children or carers a break by looking after whoever they are responsible for from time to time; or in any number of other ways that we know will make someone feel happier than they would be otherwise.

It could be that the search for true happiness may involve our spending time voluntarily in the service of others, trying to make the world a better place for other people as well as ourselves. This has already proven to be a tried and tested way for many, including myself, offering a sense of pride and purpose in life. And, in the end, it seems to me as good a way as any other for most of us to give our lives meaning.

CHAPTER 4

BELONGING AND FEELING NEEDED

In all our contacts it is probably the sense of being really needed and wanted which gives us the greatest satisfaction and creates the most lasting bond.

Eleanor Roosevelt

My mother was a genius at needing other people and being needed. After my father's death, she was unwilling to spend the night alone in her flat and had a succession of people live with her, all of whom fell for her charm. But she also managed to make friends even into late old age, partly through her hunger for companionship but also because she was exceptionally easy company and a very good listener. Her need for connection meant that there was never a day when she didn't have at least three or four visitors, often far more; nor was there a day when someone had not entrusted some great secret, confidence or embarrassment to her. She needed people, but she also carried on being needed by others until the end of her life.

It's a rare talent to achieve that level of interaction for so many years. Yet we know that feeling needed in one way or another brings meaning to almost all of our lives. In spite of our occasional resentment at the demands that are placed on us, it seems to me that human beings fundamentally need to be needed, which is why isolation or a lack of a sense of purpose in our lives – except preparing to die – is what leads to so much depression amongst older people in care homes. Being needed by others helps to anchor us in a network of people whose lives would perhaps be poorer without our help – and thereby offers a way to give meaning to our own lives.

Need permeates our lives, from cradle to grave. As babies, we need our mothers and fathers, although our physical need for food usually makes our mother the first bond. In a connection that is as unexpected the first time as it is fascinating, mothers often find they have a physical need for their babies too, as their milk starts to flow when they hear the baby cry. And as children we need friends – pity the child who cannot be part of the group, who is not needed or wanted in a gang or even at home. Later, as teenagers we need to be desired and loved – for our bodies, for our characters, for our wit, for ourselves.

A healthy self-respect and self-image grow out of our being needed. This is as true at work as it is at play: if we are told we are no longer required in a job, when we thought we were essential to the smooth running of the organisation, we are devastated. We habitually behave as if we are needed at work – and so cannot believe it when we are not. 'No longer needed', 'surplus to requirements' – phrases that will drive an ice pick through most of our hearts, because we so need to be needed. But we worked our socks off, we protest, and that is all the gratitude we get, especially when we were so necessary!

As we settle into adulthood, we may marry, divorce, remain single, begin relationships; we will have spouses, partners, parents, friends, children, nephews and nieces by whom we need to be needed – and to whom we also often feel we are tied by a sense of duty. And sometimes that sense of duty can become conflated with needing to be needed, and we cannot tell the two apart, so that what we do for others ends up being more about what we need to do for ourselves and not, in fact, about what the other parties really want at all.

Sometimes the search for a new relationship all of our own, in which we are desired and needed by one special person more than by anyone else out there, does not happen for us. We may turn to the lonely hearts columns and intro-duction agencies without much success. And so we find ourselves putting even more energy into being needed by our family members, friends, or even some organisation or other in which we can find a role to play either as a volunteer or employee. We need to care and be cared about.

Although 'caring' in a philosophical sense is seen as important by most of us, physical caring can often be thought of as a burden, perhaps because it is believed to entail a certain loss of personal freedom. Yet most of us will have to provide a degree of physical care for parents or children, or disabled friends or siblings, at some stage in our lives. And if we organise this properly, which means taking breaks from it and having really excellent respite arrangements in place, it can be hugely rewarding to provide support and care to someone beloved who needs a great deal of help. Despite the strain that looking after others can bring, and regardless of the other complications that this sort of caring may bring in its wake (such as exhaustion, isolation and even poverty if we have to give up work to assume the role of carer), caring often satisfies the strong human desire we have to be needed.

Many of us will feel strongly driven to care for the frail and vulnerable – partly because of social expectations, of course, but also because this sort of caring can give us a role in life, a role that we may often feel we alone can fill.[1] Others of us will believe that we are the best people to care for our sick husbands, wives, partners, parents, children, friends and acquaintances. Although it was exhausting, I loved providing care to my mother for five years, during which she had different levels of need as she became increasingly ill. What can be more fulfilling, in many ways – despite the exhaustion – than being needed for what we can give to someone we love?

Youth, middle age, old age and even older old age are no barrier to offering someone else physical care (though some physical aspects of caring become harder as one gets older). Instead of regarding the provision of such a care as a monstrous burden, I believe that we really should celebrate the satisfaction people achieve from caring with real skill and devotion for someone they love.

Nevertheless, the satisfactions of caring for others can often be outweighed by problems. A number of studies have shown that over a third of those providing care for a relative with dementia suffer from high levels of stress, depression or general psychological morbidity themselves. They also report more daily hassles than non-caregivers of a comparable age. They have poorer physical health on self-report measures and they also take more prescribed medication than age-matched samples.[2]

The care recipient's behaviour can occasionally be so challenging that it causes the caregiver to withdraw and sink into depression. As withdrawal happens, the relationship becomes less mutual; the carer may have increasingly low levels of satisfaction, as the care recipient's appreciation of what is being done for them diminishes rapidly.

It seems that spouses generally have a more wholehearted commitment to giving care to their ageing partners and report more satisfaction in doing so than adult children report when caring for parents with similar conditions. This may be to do with a stronger sense of duty, of 'till death us do part', or simply be to do with a lifetime's emotional investment in the wellbeing of the care recipient, making spouses feel more involved, less burdened and less likely to seek institutional care for their partner as a solution to the situation than are adult children.[3]

Similar patterns emerge with respect to caring for relatives with mental health problems. In Healthtalkonline's discussion of reasons for caring, many of the same things were said about caring for someone with severe mental health issues as were said about caring for older people.[4] When discussing caring for a son or daughter with mental health issues, it was noted that many of the parents made comments such as 'I am his mother, I should take responsibility and care for him'. One mother joked: 'I have told him that if I was his wife, I would have left him.' Some said that 'giving up' on a relative would be 'like I disowned him'. Others said it was part of their culture to feel responsibility for others.

It seems that some people are simply more able to find meaning in these challenging circumstances, which enables them to keep going and to continue to gain satisfaction out of caring. However, there are various different approaches to caring that can help everybody. The nine most popular include such obvious strategies as: realising that the person you care for is not to blame for his or her position; taking life one day at a time; finding out as much as you can about the problem; keeping a little free time for yourself; realising that there is always someone worse off than yourself; realising that no one is to blame for the situation generally; keeping one step ahead of things by planning in advance; getting as much help as you can from professionals and service providers; and, finally, talking over your problems with someone you can trust.

Despite the challenges of caring for others, it seems that it is possible for some people to become almost addicted to caring. In Mary Larkin's academic research on people's experiences after the end of caring, she makes the point that people who have cared for someone they love (most often a partner) undergo something different from, and beyond, grief.[5] There are the standard emotions of bereavement, such as bitterness, guilt, regret, loneliness and loss of confidence, self-esteem, sense of purpose and identity. But for many former carers who are of an age still to be in paid employment, there is also the sense that they have lost skills and work experience. In Larkin's interviews, she found people describing 'a sense of a loss of purpose; many reported feeling "lost" and "at a loss" when caring ceased because their purpose in life had gone ... Bob felt that caring for his wife had given him a "purpose" which was now gone. Ted went one step further and said he felt that "all the reason for living had gone" ... Clive explained, "It [caring] becomes part of your identity."'

What is most striking is that many former carers try to fill the gap left in their lives by undertaking new activities, such as voluntary and paid work. Former carers will surprisingly often take on yet another caring role, which has led to some scholars coining the term 'vocation carer'. It is as if the experience of caring makes these people feel that they need to care for others on an ongoing basis, even though the initial recipient of their attention has died.

Of Larkin's sample case studies, several people were 'undertaking voluntary work associated with caring. This included work with disabled groups, volunteering at hospitals and hospices, membership of carers' groups.' But her most significant finding was:

> ... the way that post-caring involved further caring activities where the relationship with caring was strongest; half did caring tasks for friends and neighbours such as 'a bit of washing and ironing'. There was no obvious explanation as to why this group undertook these tasks but three said they felt that they wanted to continue 'to look after people'. More significantly, for many of them, post-caring life involved or had involved being a carer yet again; over half (twenty) had undertaken their most recent unpaid caring role following the cessation of a previous episode of caring. Another six were now caring once more and two of these had also cared prior to their most recent unpaid caring role.

This suggests two things to me: that the experience of caring, however exhausting, satisfies some very deep need within the carer. Losing that role leaves them bereft, and so the only way to 'cure' that bereavement is to care for someone else – to recreate that sense of being needed and regain the satisfaction of being indispensable.

The only hesitation in all this is the question about how much these addicted carers, needing to be needed, are looking after themselves. We probably also ought to take into account that the appreciation of the person for whom one is caring and the intimacy of the carer/recipient relationship may in themselves become addictive factors. These become so necessary, so central to the carer's self-image and self-esteem, that he or she cannot do without them – and if things go that far, it is probably worth seeking professional help.

Conversely, it's all too common to hear widows and widowers, and people who have lost partners or close friends for whom they were caring, lament the fact they no longer feel needed. This is all the more so if they do not feel especially close to their remaining family. Or they find that they are needed, but not necessarily in the ways they would like to be: they are pressed into doing lots of babysitting or collecting the grandchildren from school, as if they are seen by their own children as having no lives of their own. This is when our need to be needed can sometimes become complicated by a sense of duty or obligation which ultimately conflicts with our own fulfilment.

∞

Many of us will find ourselves caring for others out of a sense of duty – a sense of obligation towards parents, children, siblings, neighbours, even compatriots. The extent of that obligation may be unclear, or loosely defined by the society in which we find ourselves or by our natures as individuals. Whereas some of us may barely be moved by it at all, others will feel keenly that their obligation to others reaches wide. They will feel bound to distant neighbours as well as close friends; to members of, say, the same faith group or community as well as to the immediate family.

There will also be those of us who believe that the public services or authorities, for example, try to make us feel we have certain obligations to others, such as caring for older or vulnerable relatives, even when we do not recognise those duties personally. This passing on of responsibility may be a hangover from the age of serial monogamy, and can entail those in public services attempting to get a former daughter-in-law or former mother-in-law to take responsibility for someone who is no longer within the family framework.

We may well ask ourselves whether our sense of obligation or duty should extend beyond our immediate communities to those who may be anything but like us: people with different attitudes, who come from different communities or even different countries. Are our obligations only to 'other human beings like me' or to 'those not like me' as well? Indeed, do our obligations extend beyond human beings to animals and even to the environment (although we may well reason that caring for the environment will benefit our great-grandchildren and generations beyond, and that therefore we have a duty to protect it)?

Yet, for all that the parameters of our obligations to others may be vague, there is something at the heart of these connections that sits strongly with us. We are bound, albeit sometimes unwillingly, by ties of kinship. We know we have a duty towards our parents, siblings, children, cousins, aunts and nieces. It is also clear that these ties can offer us the opportunity for personal reward – the buzz we get from doing good; from, for example, being an exceptional grandmother or a superb aunt to a difficult teenager.

But service to family members is not the same as finding a role in the wider community. It does not, for many of us, satisfy a desire to serve which goes beyond personal duty and obligation, which anchors us in wider society and encourages us to play a positive role in society because we want to experience a sense of a wider societal gain.

A few years ago, when I chaired – as a volunteer – the independent Commission on Volunteering in Britain, we looked at who was volunteering, how they did it, where the barriers to volunteering lay, what was needed to improve the facilities for volunteers, and why so many people in our society do in fact volunteer. It provided a fascinating glimpse into the psyche of the British public.

The most recent figures from Volunteering England, the organisation that set up the Commission, show that one-quarter of the adult population of England volunteers with an organisation at least once a month. Findings from a recent citizenship survey (whose headlines were published in July 2010) show a very small decline in rates of volunteering from the peak figures of 2005; apparently, some 40 per cent of adults volunteered formally at least once in the twelve-month period prior to interview in 2009–2010. The figures also show that women are slightly more likely to volunteer than men, and that younger people are less likely to be regular volunteers with organisations but more likely than older age groups to have taken part in regular informal volunteering. No great changes, then, in the first decade of the new millennium, despite significant government efforts to get more people volunteering.

The concept of 'The Big Society', launched in the Conservative Party's manifesto in 2010 and now part of the coalition government's programme in the UK, encompasses some of the current thinking about creating a social environment in which volunteering and the notion of duty play important roles. The idea is that each of us will have a sense of obligation to others as part of a wider community framework, because we feel interconnected in a society in which relationships go beyond the immediately local or familial. In that view of society, everyone stands to gain, with society as a whole benefitting considerably from people's willingness to play an active part in it. If this sort of thinking catches on, we may even see people volunteer in 'rolling' sets of voluntary activities, in which they do something themselves for the wider good, but also receive services from others who are making their voluntary contributions in turn.

There are some wonderful examples of rolling volunteering. In certain US cities, when an individual has more or less recovered from a serious operation, she is often asked if she would be willing to volunteer to talk to the next person down the line, who is going to have the same surgery; and then to keep an eye on that person when he leaves hospital, until he no longer needs support. At that point, the recipient of the volunteer's care is asked to volunteer in turn, and to offer support to the next patient down the line. This seems to me to be an ideal way of providing care beyond that which professionals can give, and also offers to the recovering patient a sense of being needed the minute the person is capable of doing anything – an admirable scheme.

Back in 2007, there was a lot of interest in the UK in ideas such as 'community credits', which would be given to those who do good works, somewhat similar to time-banking schemes in which time credits are exchanged for activities performed by one member of a community for another. Originally an American idea pioneered by the great social reformer Edgar Cahn, time banking has begun to find acceptance in the UK and other European countries, though progress has been astonishingly slow. However, these sorts of schemes appear to be on the rise internationally.

In Japan, schemes of this nature fund community care for the elderly. Japanese couples who live too far from their ageing parents to be able to look after them 'adopt' an elderly stranger locally and care for them instead of their own relative, earning credits that their parents can use to 'buy' similar volunteer care near by. The US state of Minnesota has established a similar system of 'community service dollars', in which the act of volunteering to care for someone earns the caregiver a variety of care or other services in return.

I believe that if we were to organise society so that time-banking schemes could play a greater role and the concept of public happiness were to become a truly prized quotient, then more value would be placed on informal care such as that provided by the many people looking after elderly relatives, and volunteering would also benefit. But the idea of rolling volunteering, or exchanging kindnesses for the communal good, is not only about getting a reward personally (even if indirectly). There is also evidence that, besides experiencing considerable stresses and strains, those who provide such care gain huge satisfaction from doing so: 'Satisfying aspects within their caring role are identified by 55 per cent to over 90 per cent of family carers.'[6] In 2010, the ideas of 'rolling' volunteering and community credits have become very much in vogue in Britain as the coalition government wrestles with finding ways to encourage 'The Big Society'.

No other country has used the term 'The Big Society' in quite the same way as the British coalition government, although President Kennedy famously said in his inaugural address in January 1961: 'And so, my fellow Americans, ask not what your country can do for you; ask what you can do for your country.' With respect to other countries, Anna Pierce, from the market research company Ipsos Mori, decided to analyse 'how big (or not) UK society already is, and how we compare to other countries around the world'.[7] She focused on the example of shovelling snow from the pavement outside a house; her findings revealed that a considerable number of British respondents expected local councils to provide the shovels for them, whilst people in Germany expected their fellow citizens to clear away the snow as a matter of course, as they would in the United States, and they would certainly expect to use their own shovels rather than require the council to provide them. This response suggests that the Germans displayed much more willingness to take responsibility for their locality than most British people felt, and that they were prepared to take simple yet direct action to make things better for the community as a whole.

Before we become too focused on these results, it's worth bearing in mind the fact that the world values survey of 2006 ranked Britain as twenty-fifth out of the fifty-one countries surveyed for agreeing with the statement 'it is important to this person to help the people nearby'. Sixty-eight per cent of the British residents who responded said that the statement sounds 'very much like me' or 'like me'. According to Pierce, 'We are ahead of the USA, Australia and France by around ten percentage points. Of course, this is a self-defined metric, and there's a myriad of reasons why you probably shouldn't draw too many conclusions from this comparison, but it does suggest some cause for hope.'

During my involvement in the Commission on Volunteering, we encountered some mixed views on whether volunteering means the same thing to people from different backgrounds, faiths, cultures and communities. It was clear from our research that the desire to help others transcends differences between communities, yet most people told us that they felt that social and cultural contexts shaped the interpretation and organisation of volunteering. In particular, many of our respondents thought that volunteering was more formalised in the UK than in some other countries.

International research suggests that this is true, though an emphasis on volunteering is becoming a strong theme politically in much of the developed world. In Australia, they have been collecting statistics on volunteering for many years. Back in 1996, 24 per cent of adult Australians had taken part in voluntary work; by 2000 the figure was 32 per cent; and by 2007 it was 34 per cent and continuing to rise.[8] With its strong tradition of volunteering going right back to the beginning of the nineteenth century, Australia shows how encouraging volunteering as a deliberate political strategy can lead to significant increases in participation.

The sense of feeling needed, however universal, nevertheless means that in some (particularly Muslim) communities, volunteering is seen more as an expression of 'who you are' rather than as 'something that you do'. In our research, we found it was not that people in particular communities did not volunteer; it was just that they volunteered within their own communities without labelling their involvement as such, since their actions were simply an expression of their faith and community identity.

An example springs to mind of the large and wonderful Nishkam Sikh community centre in Handsworth, Birmingham, where there are hundreds upon hundreds of volunteers who do everything from running physical fitness classes to cooking in vast vats to feed the hungry. A volunteering spirit of goodwill is essential to the whole enterprise and the endeavours of the participants have transformed the local area. Now, the Sikh community are happy to use the word 'volunteering' in their literature. However, the traditional word, used by both Hindus and Sikhs, is sewa. Therefore, taking their inspiration from Jewish Mitzvah Day (a day of volunteering and social action), the Sikh community joined with the Jewish community to celebrate the first ever joint 'Mitzvah and Sewa Day' in November 2010.

When communities come together like this in voluntary work, there is a benefit to society for all of us, as people at the Nishkam centre would be the first to agree. It is the wider gain that results from our contributing on a broader stage, rather than confining our supportive actions to our immediate families.

It's also clear that any form of volunteering brings huge benefit to the volunteer. And in some cases, it may even benefit the volunteers more than it benefits the recipients. Some of the motivation seems to lie in wanting to find ourselves in the sort of society in which it becomes the norm to volunteer – to give, to be part of something bigger than ourselves.

So why do people volunteer? The evidence received by the British Commission on Volunteering makes for rich reading, and I am grateful to Volunteering England for allowing me to plunder it.[9] For some, volunteering is about developing confidence and increasing self-esteem. In the research compiled by the Commission, one person explains: 'After a period of ill health, it was volunteering that gave me back my confidence. I certainly would not be doing the job I do now, if I hadn't had the opportunity to volunteer.' Another states: 'It taught me so much about myself and others. It gave me confidence, self-esteem, self-respect. I felt valued. Ultimately it gave me the confidence and skills to move into paid work, but this wasn't my motivation for volunteering. I wanted to give something back and use my experience to help others a bit, having had help myself.' And that is a common theme – wanting to give something back, having had help oneself.

Another theme that came through strongly was how for many young people, and for people who had been or still were in prison, the fact that volunteers are unpaid is of critical importance. Some young people who have led chaotic lives will come into contact with professionals from a variety of backgrounds and disciplines. For them, the volunteer relationship often seems extraordinary and it may well be the only relationship they have with a responsible adult who is not paid to be there, who is there for them purely because they want to be. That changes the nature of the relationship dramatically, and allows the young people to realise that there are those who are willing to carry out activities simply because they think that they are worth doing – even for free!

There are social reasons for volunteering: 'I love it! You meet different people ... living on my own, it's good to share the same thoughts and talk with people with a different view on life.' Or: 'It gives me some purpose in life, and I enjoy being part of a team. I am happiest when I am busy.' Gaining a sense of purpose, of meaning, is perhaps the key reason why so many people go out and seek volunteering opportunities in retirement, or because they are unemployed or have been ill. All this suggests that the volunteers gain as much from the relationship as those for whom they are volunteering: they are needed; they have a role; they befriend others and are befriended in turn. Volunteering gives them something to do and makes them happy.

Whatever the conclusion to the question of quite why giving service to others within society, beyond our immediate families and communities, is such a good thing for us and the population as a whole, most of us will ask ourselves at some point what, as unique human beings, we have to bring to the table that will really make a difference. For, as I have already argued, I believe that most of us *need* to be needed. And planning our lives in such a way that our need to be needed is recognised and realised is an exercise worth undertaking. That way, pious though it may sound, we can bring something exceptional to the world, to our community and to our families and friends.

We do not necessarily have to have any special talents to become volunteers, beyond a willingness to commit to the work at hand. Sometimes it is enough simply to be there for someone else and to share our personal experience with them, as is the case in the buddy system created in response to the AIDS epidemic that hit New York and San Francisco in the 1980s. Affected people offered to 'buddy' each other, and social circles arranged to be available for friends with AIDS whenever they might be needed.

In the UK, Andy Jackson is a good example of the benefits of the buddy system today. When he was diagnosed as HIV-positive eighteen years ago, he thought he was going to die: 'I had my bags packed, waiting for the Grim Reaper. In a way it was a relief to know what direction I was headed – even if it was into the jaws of death ... It took me a long time to realise I needed a buddy, as I'm not somebody who easily asks for help. I spend lots of time on my own not talking to anybody, but with my buddy I have found somebody I can talk to very easily ...'[10] Whereas it was once seen as a death sentence, AIDS has in recent years become regarded as a chronic illness, but it remains a tough one at that. Jackson says: 'The thing my buddy did for me was blow fresh air back into my life, just by being with him ... Now I feel absolutely secure and able to explore the friendship. It's a great place to be.' And to make the point, Jackson has himself become a buddy for others. He has gone on to found Waverley Care (a large Scottish organisation for people with AIDS/HIV, their families and carers in Edinburgh).

Today, student volunteering sites around the UK advertise for volunteer buddies and the demand for such buddies is increasing in all walks of life. The buddy system is so successful that it has become a much more generalised way of providing help, thereby satisfying both the buddy and the person who needs the support.

Buddying has become a significant component of cancer support as well. The Cancer Buddies Network (CBN) was set up by Jan Rutter following her own diagnosis with breast cancer in 2001. She buddied up with another woman who was being treated at the same time and says she wants everybody to have the positive experience that she had: 'It is wonderful having family and friends, but nobody knows what it feels like unless they have been there … It suddenly occurred to me though that there was nowhere out there that you could go and talk to people.' So useful has the system become that today all the major cancer charities in the UK support buddying, and the movement has grown internationally.

Although the support she received from professional health carers, her family and friends was excellent, my old friend Barbara Pollock regretted deeply that she didn't really know anyone else who was going through the same process as her, with whom she could share her feelings and struggles. Sadly Barbara eventually died of breast cancer a few years ago and I cannot help feeling that she would have had a better experience of her illness, treatment and ultimately death had she had a buddy. It's therefore a great comfort to me that the buddy movement is growing, offering a combination of volunteering and self-help that is extremely powerful.

Despite the hard physical grind, not to mention the often tough emotions of the relationship, people report huge satisfaction from buddying, from volunteering and caring for others. Indeed, there is considerable evidence that our happiness and sense of satisfaction with life is pretty closely connected with those who are closest to us and how we conduct ourselves in those relationships. According to David Halpern, whose insights into happiness we considered in Chapter 3, the question is simple: does somebody love you? He says, 'Those who can confidently answer "yes" are significantly more likely to be alive for the next ten years than those who feel all alone. For love is a more accurate factor than smoking in predicting life expectancy.'[11]

While we may not yet completely understand the biological relationship between happiness and health, research has already shown that happy people tend to have lower blood pressure and are less likely to abuse drink or drugs. Apparently, being shown kindness can even produce a measurable surge of oxytocin – the bonding hormone released by breastfeeding mothers and couples during orgasm – which makes people less stressed. This was the evidence that led the Downing Street strategy unit to look at how possible it is to stimulate kindness towards others in wider society, by encouraging volunteering and other good works.

So, given all the benefits to society and to individuals, why does volunteering often have such a bad press? And, as I discovered from my work with the Commission on

Volunteering, why does it have such a strong association with little old ladies sorting out clothes in a charity shop? (Not that there's anything wrong with little old ladies, I hasten to add, as I'm on the way to becoming one myself!)

For although lots of people do indeed work in charity shops, and get a great deal of satisfaction from doing so, this is just a tiny part of the world of volunteering. Every hospital has its volunteers, from the people who provide 'meet and greet' services, to those who play the organ in the chapel and visit people without relatives. Many courts have volunteers who look after people who are upset or nonplussed by what is going on. The Citizens Advice Bureaux that exist nationwide in the UK, and increasingly around the world, are largely staffed by volunteers who advise the public on a whole host of different problems. Similarly, hospices are staffed by volunteers and professionals working alongside each other.

In the case of one organisation I came across during my time at the Commission, a professional volunteering development manager argued that they used the services of volunteers in order 'to share personal knowledge of specific disabilities, issues etc. Our volunteers are well placed to spot need before we do. They can usually – and do – act quicker than us in trying to fill the gap ... Our volunteers are successful campaigners, fundraisers, innovators and supporters who care passionately. We could not provide the services we do without volunteers.' Most of the services provided by volunteers are different from those provided by paid employees: they are more personal and their value is more difficult to quantify. And that is, of course, the answer to those who argue that encouraging people to volunteer will simply provide a cheap substitute for paid jobs, and risks undercutting wages.

However, volunteering is by no means a completely free good. Volunteering requires managers, training, recognition and organisation – everything, in fact, paid employment requires, but without the contract and salary.

To my mind, the benefits of volunteering will always outweigh any potential drawbacks. One of the most moving examples of volunteering as a way of gaining skills, meaning, employment and joy resulted from the four-year Capital Volunteering Programme paid for by the British government and run by Claire Helman of Community Service Volunteers (CSV). The programme tackled issues of mental health and social inclusion through volunteering, and over 5,000 people with severe and enduring mental health issues were helped to become volunteers. This involved their making new friends, learning new skills and improving their levels of confidence; so volunteering became a chance for them to feel part of the wider community once again. The project ended in 2008, but the evaluation by the Institute of Psychiatry demonstrated that considerable savings in the use of mental health services had been made, as well as huge personal benefits accrued by the participants and those they worked with – as good a demonstration of the human need to be needed as one could possibly hope for.[12]

But, as we have seen, people volunteer, and give their money, time or other contribution, for many different reasons. Dame Stephanie Shirley is a classic example of this. Once one of the UK's richest women, she has given most of her fortune away in order to fund education and research into autism, which scarred the short life of her son.

'Steve' Shirley was a child refugee from Vienna who started a cottage industry, employing women tied to the home, and who built up a business that became the £1 billion technology group Xansa. In an interview with Mary Greene, she describes herself as 'driven by [her] early childhood': in the summer of 1939, five-year-old Stephanie was one of only 10,000 Jewish children who escaped to Britain from Nazi Europe.[13] She left on a Kindertransport train from Vienna, with her nine-year-old sister Renate and 1,000 other child refugees, on a journey which took two and a half days.

Stephanie and her sister were taken in by a Mr and Mrs Smith from Sutton Coldfield, who treated them like the longed-for children they had never had. Later, she felt that she had to live her life in a way that would justify having been saved when so many died: 'It's called survivor's guilt. I don't think I have it now. But I have a need to make the life that was saved worth living. I know it sounds a bit pious, but that still drives me today. At the end of each day, I need to feel that I've helped somebody, achieved something, that I haven't frittered the day away in shopping.'

Talking of her charitable work, Steve Shirley also explained: 'But I gain much more than I give. I have a wonderful life, I work with young, bright people, I'm part of a move to do something really worthwhile. What more could one want in one's seventies?'

Just as much of Steve Shirley's giving has been in the area of autism for personal reasons, so most people have a reason for doing what they do – however generous, however remarkable. Amongst the most generous forms of giving must surely be those who give of their physical selves, from blood to – at the other extreme – organs to those they do not know. There is a major tradition in the UK of giving blood, in what British sociologist Richard Titmuss (1907–

1973) called 'The Gift Relationship'. Although insufficient blood is collected via the blood donation system, it is still by far the largest component of the blood used generally in healthcare in the UK, and is symbolic of altruism.

And there are those who go beyond the giving of regenerative blood, which the body can replace relatively easily, to the giving of organs – an act which to my mind requires greater understanding. Take, for instance, the case of Chris Kendall, who decided to donate a kidney to a total stranger as the result of a television programme. He said, 'I had a classic lightbulb moment: I thought, here's something I could do. It was something that could transform someone's life.'[14] He became one of the 'twenty-three people in England, Wales and Northern Ireland who in 2009 voluntarily, even enthusiastically, allowed part of their body to be removed for the benefit of a total stranger'.

Most live organ donors go through with the procedure in order to enhance or save the life of a sick relative, partner or friend. But the altruistic donors, few in number, do something else. For forty-nine-year-old civil servant Kendall it 'wasn't like putting a fiver in a collection box or giving a pint of blood. It was me at last making a personal contribution to a cause, which I'd never done before, and helping someone in a positive way and doing something worthwhile for society.'

It involved being needed through what must be one of the most extreme forms of giving, considering the significant risk of health problems later on for the donor. Because of the potential dangers, the process involves stringent psychological testing as well as health testing before the organ is removed. There is also the need, of course, to make sure that the giver's nearest and dearest agree to the procedure. Kendall's wife Rachael had to give her blessing to the donation: 'If she had been against it,' he explains, 'it wouldn't have happened. They won't allow you to donate unless you have family around to support you.'

Many altruistic donors will never know who has received their gift of life. But Kendall exchanged letters with his recipient, and the two men finally met in June 2010. Kendall explains: 'He looks incredibly fit and well, given that before the transplant his kidney function was down to 9 per cent and he was on ten hours of dialysis a day every day.' And that is what matters to Kendall: 'I have given him his freedom; I have given him his life back, and his wife too. They can now do things they previously couldn't, like go on holiday and plan ahead. I have got enormous satisfaction from it.'

Others have also gone through the process of organ donation and gained immense satisfaction from it. Another donor interviewed by Denis Campbell argues: 'Sharing the healthy life that I was blessed with, with another person who's not that fortunate is not only a noble gesture on my part but also uplifting philosophically and spiritually. It has given me immense inner happiness. More people should come out and do this.' The happiness experienced by the donor is a wonderful reward for such generosity.

These extreme forms of giving probably yield even greater personal satisfaction and happiness than do the philanthropic actions of millionaires and billionaires, who can often afford to make huge donations at little personal cost. Organ donation literally entails giving a part of ourselves so that someone else can live. Kendall, though, insists he is not a hero: 'I don't consider myself altruistic because I have got so much out of it too. It transformed someone's life, but it also made me feel really good about me.'

The sociologist Titmuss once argued that people who give blood are simply enacting a 'fundamental truth' of human existence, that 'to love oneself one must love strangers'. In Titmuss' view, the good society is one built on this truth, and welfare systems should be based on the recognition that all people are dependent creatures needing each other for support and comfort. Conversely, a bad society is one which, in the name of freedom and independence, denies people 'the right to give'.

Read any number of younger writers today, and increasingly we see them aver that giving to charity makes them feel good. 'Giving to charity is one of my favourite things,' says Caitlin Moran in *The Times*: 'My coins are bullets in the war on awfulness.'[15] It is as though she needs to give for her own sake, not the recipient's.

According to Marcus Aurelius, the Roman philosopher emperor, kindness is humanity's 'greatest delight', although modern society as a whole seems to believe that such thinking is somewhat suspect. In spite of the good deeds of individuals and organisations, we have created, as authors Phillips and Taylor put it, 'an image of the self … that is utterly lacking in natural generosity', because we emphasise autonomy and independence in our Western society. They suggest we have taught ourselves that 'as a species … we are fundamentally antagonistic to each other.'[16]

Phillips and Taylor, however, regard such thinking as manifestly ludicrous and try to show how it came about. They start from the premise that in our modern Western society 'kindness … not sexuality, not violence, not money, has become our forbidden pleasure'. Kindness is seen as unfashionable, as a weak manifestation of care – and only the incapacitated, children and old people ought to have kindness shown to them, whilst the rest of us need to stand on our own two feet!

Personally, I do not believe we have gone that far, but there is undoubtedly a desire in society to believe that we can sit within our own isolated worlds and look after ourselves. Yet the teachers of old knew better. The great twelfth-century Jewish philosopher Maimonides argued that giving anonymously, his second highest order of charity, is a wonderful thing to do: 'We are required to take more care about the mitzvah [religious duty] of tzedakah [charity] than for any other positive mitzvah.'

According to Maimonides, there are eight levels of tzedakah or charity, each greater than the next. The greatest level, above which there is no other, is to strengthen the name of another person by giving him a present or loan, making a partnership with him, or finding him a job in order to strengthen his hand until he no longer needs to beg from others.

Below this are those who give tzedakah to the poor, but who do not know to whom they give; nor does the recipient know his benefactor. For this is performing a mitzvah 'for the sake of Heaven'.[17]

Exactly. There seems to me to be compelling evidence that we benefit personally from giving our time and money to those who need it, and from finding a place in our hearts for others, whether close to us or those whom we may never even meet, yet whose lives are touched by our actions. We gain from being needed and wanted and appreciated. So what's to stop us volunteering more, being needed more, and finding more pleasure, satisfaction, and benefit for us, and those we help, in what we do? Surely the rewards of giving far outweigh the risks?

CHAPTER 5

TAKING RISKS AND FEELING ALIVE

'To boldly go …'

Star Trek

T he other day, a friend described to me her experience of doing the Cresta Run: hurtling headfirst down an icy track at great speed on a toboggan seems like one of the most terrifying things anyone could possibly want to do! Technically, women are not eligible to compete in the 'real' Cresta Run, but many go round the track to prove to themselves that they can – which is dangerous in itself, requiring great skill; but, as my friend told me, it's an 'amazingly exhilarating' experience.

Over the years, I have found that some people seem to need to take risks in order to find some meaning and purpose in their lives. For such people, the idea of building a secure nest, working in a stable environment and living a fairly predictable life feels either insufficient or deeply unattractive. It leads them to ask the question that is the title of this book: 'Is that all there is?' And for those individuals the answer comes, fairly pat: 'Surely not … I'll do something to give me a sense of being more alive, more challenged …' Those of us who feel like this seem to need to prove ourselves, often physically and sometimes emotionally, against the odds. We need adventure, thriving on daring, on pushing ourselves to the limit physically, or risking everything for the sake of our relationships, however unsuitable these may appear to others.

It's not clear quite why some of us should be so drawn to taking risks, although it may have something to do with ideas of 'the Sublime' that are described later in this chapter. The dramatic experiences of mountain climbing or great exploration, or of losing oneself in passionate love, may also be a part of it. Risk-taking can be associated with a great romanticism, such as travelling to the ends of the earth and seeking faraway places; or it can be simply a need for thrills (and probably the associated spills), giving us a sense of physical or emotional danger that heightens our self-awareness and sense of connection with all that is around us.

Meanwhile, some of us, without doubt, remain overcautious. I'm certainly in that camp as far as physical challenges are concerned, and cannot personally really see the point of climbing mountains or achieving great heights of physical prowess. Even though most of us are conscious of only having the one life (or, at least, only the one we know about), some of us nevertheless seem unable to take the sort of emotional or intellectual risks that others of a different turn of mind would hardly describe as risky at all – such as throwing in the job we hate, going on that journey over treacherous terrain, travelling alone in risky areas, or just doing the things we really want to do, rather than staying timidly where we are. If the spirit of adventure in all its guises – physical, emotional, intellectual – is worth cultivating and exercising, then the question remains as to why we do or do not take advantage of it. If it lies dormant within all of us, then why do we not all decide to take risks and seek adventure at least occasionally?

Although I am wary of physical challenges, I do think it is important to take some risks in life. Many of us ought to exercise that muscle of adventure before it is too late – and we wake up to find that we have wasted much of our lives in the humdrum.

We automatically take risks in very different ways throughout our lives. A baby learning to walk is taking risks, but cannot see them. And children are not necessarily risk averse, but often cannot appreciate what risk there might be in a situation. When it comes to young people, adolescence is often regarded as the peak time for both girls and boys to take risks, motivated by a variety of factors such as simple experimentation, defiance, thrill-seeking and even immaturity of judgement.

Lynn Ponton has explored adolescent risk-taking in her work.[1] She argues that, rather than simply being a turbulent time emotionally, adolescence is a period in which risk-taking is mostly positive and healthy. In her view, 80 per cent of young people manage this developmental period without significant difficulties, engaging in the kinds of risks that will allow them to develop their potential as they mature. The other 20 per cent are the ones for whom risk-taking causes trouble.

In her book *The Romance of Risk*, Ponton presents the case histories of fifteen troubled adolescents who could not get through their teenage years without taking unhealthy risks, from becoming pregnant to cutting themselves. Although she concludes that the factors that trigger unhealthy risk-taking behaviour are many and various, Ponton suggests poor parenting may be partly at the bottom of it. This can be either through the parents' over-involvement in their children's lives as 'peers' rather than as responsible adults, or through the parents' own issues which create distance in the relationship. She argues that adolescents need adults to be properly adult instead of trying to be like them; they need adults to help and guide them in making choices and to give them examples of healthy risk-taking. In her view, adolescents definitely do not need parents who take the wrong kind of risks, or in the wrong kind of way.[2]

She may be absolutely right, but the years of adolescence are precisely when most of us do push boundaries and take ridiculous risks. Happily, the majority of us will survive relatively unscathed – suggesting the world is in fact a relatively safe place. Moreover, adolescent risk-taking is not, usually, about finding meaning in life or looking for a sense of nearness to death. After all, most adolescents believe themselves to be immortal on some level. It is more likely to be about experience and thrills, about seeing what the world has to offer. It is about setting their own boundaries on the world, rather than heeding those set for them by parents and teachers.

There is something in adolescent risk-taking that is about exploring and finding a world that makes sense to them, and which is not a million miles away from using risk as a means of establishing meaning and feeling alive and immersed in existence. Now, it may be that those who continue to regard risk-taking as normal after their teenage years are also the individuals who find that the actual experience of risk and the sense of adventure it affords are what gives their lives meaning. In some cases, the thrill of actually taking risks may count for more than any achievement those risks lead to.

As this book is primarily about finding meaning in our lives, it would be foolish to pretend that a sizeable section of the population don't get their sense of meaning through pushing themselves to achieve amazing physical or intellectual feats. Some of them enjoy the sense of danger and the closeness to nature that physical challenges can entail. Others like testing their own limits, or are attracted by the fame that can come with success in their chosen field. Still others believe that, ultimately, these sorts of extreme challenges give them a glimpse of God's presence on earth. They might, for instance, succeed in reaching a summit in the Himalayas, like British woman Bonita Norris, who conquered Everest in April 2010 at the age of twenty-two; or they might beat an athletics record; or ride in the Grand National and come fifth despite not being a professional jockey, as Sam Waley-Cohen did in 2007; or win the Gold Cup at Cheltenham, still an amateur; or manage any other remarkable sporting achievement like these. If these forms of activity, and the acknowledged risks that go with them, are what give people a sense of meaning in their lives, then we have to recognise this as an integral part of what makes them tick.

More interesting, and perhaps more difficult, is the process of understanding a thirst for risk-taking, or having any empathy with it if we are not hard-wired in the same way and find ourselves disapproving of the level of danger to which our nearest and dearest are willing to expose themselves. For a thirst for risk is not part of everyone's personality, even though we all take risks some of the time. From crossing the road to getting on a plane, from going for a swim to walking on rough paths, a degree of risk-taking is inevitable, healthy and necessary for us in life.

As we grow older, we may find that the younger people around us begin to cosset us, telling us to 'be careful' – not to fall on the ice, for example (as if we would do so deliberately) – and perhaps even suggesting we go into a care home to avoid risks in our own home. If we do stay in our own homes, occupational therapists may try to make them risk-free, and we find ourselves being treated as individuals who should no longer be taking any risks – because we will only be causing trouble for everyone else. Yet I hear all the time of grannies going paragliding and jumping out of balloons, of grandfathers driving fast cars (provided their eyesight is good enough!) and setting out on challenging expeditions.

Whatever our age, we have to ask ourselves whether the risk involved in a particular activity is reasonable or simply too dangerous: are we being adventurous in wanting to explore the Amazon basin on foot, or are we being foolhardy, potentially causing other people trouble and anxiety on our behalf?

In my opinion, being totally risk averse (as public policy in the UK has increasingly led us to be in recent years) is not healthy. The more we are told not to do particular everyday activities because they are dangerous – or might just be – presumably the more driven many of us become to take risks. We may decide to travel into danger zones or push ourselves to the limit at sport, simply to regain the sense of adventure in our lives that has been taken away from us by the officious notices that seem to exist everywhere today – from warning us not to swim out of our depth to not going nearer the cliff edge.

Today, many children and their parents appear to be frightened that, as soon as a child leaves the house on his own, he is likely to meet a child molester. This level of anxiety suggests to me that we are in danger of becoming a completely risk-averse society. According to a survey conducted by Demos and the Green Alliance: 'Beliefs about the inherent hostility and danger of public places is commonplace.'[3] Children in our society walk to school less and less, and really believe that there are bad strangers out there in the guise of sexual abusers and kidnappers, waiting to get them. Gillian Thomas, co-author of the Demos Green Alliance report, writes: '... on the crime front, my worry is that, because it's turned into a fantasy, they imagine what a stranger looks like and it's always a man with nasty eyes and horrible clothes. It makes them unreal, and they might not be able to recognise real danger.'[4] So children grow up feeling it's a dangerous world, whilst their parents worry about who out there might have an unhealthy interest in their children.

When parents become unreasonably risk averse, the resulting over-protectiveness of their children makes it unsurprising when some kids kick back and indulge in serious risk-taking behaviour through drugs, sex and gang warfare. These young people will sense that they have been unreasonably held back from assessing for themselves what a reasonable risk might be.

Our Western attitudes to risk appear to be changing – and not necessarily for the better – although I suspect they are still very culturally specific. And they also appear to be largely gender specific – remaining rooted in society's definition of masculinity, in spite of the growing numbers of young women today who are willing to take risks in the pursuit of adventure.

Our current attitudes to risk-taking have clearly developed over time. Nineteenth-century ideas about risk continue to influence our present-day attitudes very strongly, but they in turn were pre-dated by eighteenth-century thinking –

in particular the political theorist and philosopher Edmund Burke's notion of the sublime:

> Whatever is fitted in any sort to excite the ideas of pain, and danger, that is to say, whatever is in any sort terrible, or is conversant about terrible objects, or operates in a manner analogous to terror, is a source of the sublime; that is, it is productive of the strongest emotion which the mind is capable of feeling ...[5]

So pain and danger, horror and beauty come together in the notion of the sublime – reaching towards a sense of transcendence. In more recent years, author and academic Francis Spufford has demonstrated how the thinking of Burke found its way into Gothic novels.[6] Notions of the Sublime also became inextricably linked with the particular set of experiences sought after by privileged young men (and a few women) on eighteenth-century Grand Tours, during which they travelled around the ancient and Renaissance sites of Europe. The quest for these sorts of experiences, in which landscapes were connected with stirring emotional responses, influenced the ambitions of later travellers and explorers.

A sense of the Sublime found its way into the thinking of explorers such as the blacksmith C J Sullivan on HMS Erebus. He kept a diary of the British Antarctic Expedition of 1839–43, in which he wrote:

> Beholding with Silent Surprize the great and wonderful works of nature in this position we had an opportunity to discern the barrier in its Splendid position. Then I wished I was an artist or draughtsman ... We set aside all thoughts of Mount Erebus and Victoria land to bear in

mind the more imaginative thoughts of this rare phenomena that was lost to human view.

As is clear from his diary entries, Sullivan enjoyed the vocabulary of the Sublime, which he in all probability picked up from the sailors and officers he heard talking on board – suggesting that ideas of the Sublime, although changing, were solidly present in everyday conversation on those great nineteenth-century explorations – and remain with us to this day.

Based on the book of the same name by Joe Simpson, the 2003 film *Touching the Void* directed by Kevin Macdonald depicts Simpson's and Simon Yates's disastrous and nearly fatal climb of the 6,344-metre (20,813 foot) Siula Grande in the Peruvian Andes in 1985.[7] The film makes the enduring connection between the Sublime and our current attitudes very clear, as it combines scenes of extraordinary natural beauty and amazing physical prowess with extreme danger. It manages to convey the fiercely cold temperatures and beauty of the place, and the excruciating pain after the accident as well as the miraculous survival. It is a remarkable account of survival against the odds, and imprints an interpretation of the Sublime, twenty-first-century style, on the viewer's visual memory.

At a more extreme level, the urge that inspires us to experience the Sublime may also feed our fixation with space exploration. In this instance, exploration really is about the wholly unknown, without any sense of what might be encountered. Space exerts an enormous fascination for many people and yet, just as our explorations in the field seem to be reaching new heights and offering us fresh knowledge, the space industry is being scaled back, presumably largely for financial reasons in a time of public spending cuts the world over.

We certainly need to take risks in order to advance our knowledge – and in order to become richer people materially, mentally and spiritually. For risk-taking is inevitably bound up with progress and the discovery of new things. Examples that spring to mind include those experiments in which scientists have injected themselves with their own blood, or tested drugs on themselves (thereby taking risks themselves rather than experimenting on others); the desire for new markets and new riches that made the great explorers set sail in the Elizabethan period and earlier; and even the early story of evolution, in which individuals first left the cave at great risk to themselves to hunt and find food. On some level, many of us will take risks in order to improve our lot in life; and these endeavours are very much a part of what it means to be human. They embody ambition, greed, intellectual curiosity and the drive of sheer basic necessity, such as when it comes to feeding the family. Most of us possess those qualities in one combination or another, but how they fit together and precisely what pressures make some of us and not others exercise them and take risks are far from clear.

When it comes to the positive aspects of risk, we are probably influenced by a whole series of apparently unconnected ideas and philosophies which, along with the concept of the Sublime, came together in the nineteenth century and contributed to our present-day ideas. The development of capitalism itself, with its emphasis on individual risk-taking and entrepreneurship, is one significant influence. It is, after all, fairly usual these days to equate risk-taking with entrepreneurship. Many successful businessmen, such as Richard Branson, are as well known for their risk-taking in sports such as ballooning as they are for their business activities. Another businessman, Mike Belitz, the owner of two audio-related businesses in El Segundo, California, climbed Kilimanjaro alone and also likes to hang-glide, skydive and fly stunt planes. He says: 'Entrepreneurs are typically risk-takers ... I think we like to see if we can overcome challenges.'[8]

In his fascinating book on the social history and significance of mountaineering, *Mountains of the Mind*, Robert Macfarlane makes a similar point when he reminds us that Samuel Smiles used mountain climbing as a metaphor to illustrate the character-building benefits of encountering difficulty.[9] Smiles's book *Self-Help* became a bestseller when it was published in 1859 and turned its author into a celebrity. In it, Smiles describes how the process of overcoming entrepreneurial challenges will make us better people. Widely quoted in later works, he enjoins his readers: 'Let us help one another up the mountain ...'[10]

Despite Smiles's mention of mountains, mountain climbing as a metaphor for exalted human experience is quite a recent phenomenon. As Macfarlane points out in *Mountains of the Mind*, three centuries ago 'risking one's life to climb a mountain would have been considered tantamount to lunacy'. (And some people today would still hold that view!) Indeed, as we know from Capability Brown and his contemporaries, the eighteenth-century fashion in landscapes was for fertile rolling grounds with formal gardens, rather than for wild, craggy and mountainous terrain. Even the Victorians, who came to love mountains, really idealised the wild garden with rhododendrons and camellias rather than mountain flowers, and delighted in ferns, shades, glades and grottoes rather than in high and precipitous ascents.

Although mountain climbing became more popular in the late Victorian age, it was fraught with risks, as Edward Whymper's ascent of the 14,780-foot Matterhorn in 1865 demonstrated all too clearly: only Whymper and his two guides, the Taugwalders, survived from a party of seven. When the news hit the British press, the public was horrified. 'Is it life? Is it duty? Is it common sense? Is it allowable? Is it not wrong?' thundered *The Times*, quoted by Jim Ring in *How the English Made the Alps*. In his book, Ring considers the fact that '... underlying those questions was the larger question of what drew these Englishmen to the Alps. What was it that possessed these men to throw themselves with such courage, not to say recklessness, at these mountain ranges far from home?'[11] Yet throwing oneself at mountain ranges soon became standard, the Alpine Club having been founded in 1857 and Thomas Cook's first tour to the Alps following soon after in 1863.

There is a sense of purpose behind setting up a new enterprise, and in experiments and explorations that ultimately benefit others, which seems to offset the risks involved. However, dicing with death through extreme sports remains more difficult for some of us, including myself, to come to terms with. Although I believe that an element of risk is needed for us to function as a society, I also believe that the argument put forward by some – that risk-taking can simply make one feel 'more alive' – needs testing. There may well be those who will always feel unsatisfied unless they take risks, regardless of the detrimental effects that their risk-taking may have on their nearest and dearest ones – something these people may find somewhat challenging!

I have always felt extremely ambivalent about this kind of extreme behaviour and, indeed, about some of the high-risk sports in which natural risk-takers indulge. The family joke goes that my husband does not have to tell me he wants a divorce: all he has to do is go hang-gliding! I see that sport as so dangerous, wilfully putting life and limb at risk, that it could lead to my divorcing him on grounds of the agonising worry such behaviour would cause me.

It seems to me that there is confusion for some of us between finding a sense of purpose and meaning in life (which we all need to do) and taking extreme risks in order to feel that it is worthwhile our being alive at all. As we have seen, risk-taking can clearly be positive in its goals, but equally there is a danger of it becoming a means of shutting others out when it entails the single-minded pursuit of a personal goal, such as climbing a mountain. As a society, we can afford for some people to become obsessed enough to dedicate themselves to a single goal in this way – and maybe we even need a number of individuals like this – but we also have to ask what kind of selfish society we would have if we all chose that path.

With respect to the habit of taking risks making people – particularly sportsmen – 'feel alive', I believe that it ought to concern us that, somewhat paradoxically, it seems to be the increased possibility of death which contributes most powerfully to this feeling of 'being alive'. This struck me when I came across an article on a rock-climbing site that states: 'So, why are you taking risks? If you look deeply enough, you'll realise you take risks to grow and growth gives you experiences that make you feel alive.'[12] It seems to me that it's all too easy to romanticise risk-taking behaviour and to forget that, while risk-taking may lead to a feeling of enhanced aliveness for some people, it can also result in a person's not being alive at all!

Carl Hiebert from Ontario was in a hang-gliding accident in 1981, which left him a paraplegic.[13] He now makes a living as a motivational speaker, talking to business audiences about risk. However, he asserts firmly that the risks he took were calculated ones, in which he did everything possible to reduce the danger involved: 'Risk-taking to me should be an extremely prudent exercise … If the only way you can feel alive is to push yourself close to death, then I think something's wrong,' he says. Hiebert also says that compulsive risk-takers should ask themselves whether they're engaging in daredevil activities instead of exposing themselves to more meaningful emotional or spiritual risks.

Hiebert is not alone in his view. The journalist David Rose wrote a fascinating article in the wake of a Scottish mountain tragedy, in which he considered the life-enhancing aspects of risking death through activities such as mountain climbing. In his piece, he challenges simplistic explanations of why people risk death unnecessarily:

> It isn't simply danger, and the adrenalin charge
> of fear, but something more profound: a desire,
> not to court death, but to countenance it. As the
> American writer Robert Reid puts it, 'climbing
> is a way of studying the ultimate unknown …
> [climbers] go not to die – that is very important
> – but far from the tumult of the valley below
> to linger in safe communion with death, to feel
> the exquisite tension that separates it from life'.
> And also, in a world where any one of us may
> die from involuntary causes such as Creutztfeldt-
> Jakob disease, to feel the existential power of
> influencing one's ultimate destiny. [14]

Hence, presumably, the reasons why people get involved in all sorts of activities – potholing, climbing, conquering the mountain, sailing across the Atlantic – in which contemplating the vastness of creation and feeling in 'safe communion with death' play a major part. The language that is being used verges on the religious, yet this is not what we might ordinarily call a religious experience that is being described – although profound contemplation, a sense of awe, and a sense of being near the possibility of death are involved. In his article, David Rose seems to capture what makes people today do these extraordinary things: these activities give them a profound sense of being alive in the face of the tenuous barrier between life and death.

The religious connection with risk is explored in the writings of Reverend Neil Elliott, an Anglican clergyman who wrote his PhD thesis on the spirituality of snowboarding.[15] He argues that God can be found in deep powder snowboarding: 'I was both in and out of time. There and not there ... I was very close to God at that time.'

In *Where the Mountain Casts its Shadow*, Maria Coffey (the former girlfriend of Joe Tasker who disappeared on Everest in 1982) has written about this sense of needing to leave partners and children; of the urge to explore; to achieve the unachievable; experience the unknowable and to have experiences of the sublime or the otherworldly in the process.[16] Her thesis is that part of the need to face extreme physical challenges may be the urge to recapture a closeness to nature and an ability to engage with our surroundings which modern humanity has lost. She praises the sense of peace and emptiness that can be achieved after a long trek or difficult kayak journey. Although she somewhat sheepishly suggests that these activities may offer a 'sense of spiritual transcendence' found nowhere else, she never really nails down what it is that moves some of us to keep leaving the safety of our homes to go climbing and exploring.

Sadly, it is not only the physical thrills afforded by mountain climbing and polar exploration that get people hooked. On a much more mundane level, many of us may find ourselves caught up in all sorts of addictive behaviours, from gambling to drug-taking, alcoholism to eating disorders. These are also forms of risk-taking, but the ways in which they affect people are very complicated. We do not fully understand the neurological and psychological wiring which allows some of us to enjoy the occasional flutter whilst others become seriously addicted to gambling. We do not know why some people seem able to drink in a controlled way all their lives while others become alcoholics. Nor do we wholly understand other addictive substances or what makes it so hard for some people to give them up. Perhaps some of us are adrenalin junkies and, whereas climbing Everest might not be feasible, risking our lives through illicit drug-taking is an option that is open to us – however tragic it may be.

Given the history of risk, with its connection to exploration and physical challenge, it is perhaps not surprising to find that risk-taking behaviour has typically been regarded as a profoundly male characteristic. However, it is equally striking how many adventurers have not only been dependent on their wives' active support, but have married women who are risk-takers in their own right. The Antarctic explorer Captain Scott's wife, Kathleen, and more recently Ginny Fiennes, the late wife of Ranulph Fiennes, were both willing to take risks of their own, as well as putting up with their husbands' risk-taking propensities. Kathleen Scott took risks in both her art and in her somewhat risqué personal life, whilst explorer Ginny Fiennes was a recipient of the Polar Medal for exploration. Meanwhile, Scott's sister Grace saw nothing strange in her brother's being drawn by 'the call of the vast empty spaces; silence; the beauty of the untrodden snow; liberty of thought and action; the wonder of the snow and seeming infinitude of its uninhabited regions whose secrets man had not then pierced, and the hoped-for conquest of raging elements.'[17] Risk-taking seemed a normal part of life to her generation of women; indeed, as we have seen, a fascination with empty spaces and with conquering the raging elements, with all the risk that that entailed, was a mainstream reinterpretation of elements of the Sublime.

But in our contemporary society, I suspect that we see risk-taking as a more fundamental part of men's characters and of masculine behaviour than of women's. This is how it has been portrayed since the Victorian era, despite the prevalence of women travellers and explorers, many of whom had to wear men's clothes in the eighteenth and early nineteenth centuries in order to find a way to take risks at all.

Jeanne Baré was a member of Louis Antoine de Bougainville's expedition on the ships *La Boudeuse* and *Étoile* in 1766–1769, and initially joined the expedition disguised as a man. According to the Wikipedia article about her, her 'true gender remained undetected by the entire company of the expedition until they reached Tahiti'. However, Mary Wortley Montagu, one of the best known of the early female explorers, was renowned (amongst other things) for wearing women's clothes throughout her travels. Another, slightly later example is the Viennese explorer Ida Laura Pfeiffer (1797–1858), who was a member of the geographical societies of both Berlin and Paris, but not of the Royal Geographical Society in London because she was a woman. She started exploring once her two sons had homes of their own, and in 1846 she embarked on a journey round the world, visiting Brazil, Chile and other countries of South America, Tahiti, China, India, Persia, Asia Minor and Greece, before returning home in 1848.

Yet, the obvious presence of women in the worlds of exploring and mountaineering does not appear to have impacted significantly on our current association of risk-taking with men. Even worse, it would seem that any weakness in a male climber or explorer has traditionally resulted in that individual being regarded as effeminate – as being like a woman. In *Mountains of the Mind*, Robert Macfarlane quotes the art critic and social thinker John Ruskin's discussion of the moral effect of danger in a letter to his father of 1863, which makes just this point:

> … if you come to a dangerous place, and turn
> back from it, though it may have been perfectly
> right and wise to do so, still your character
> has suffered some slight deterioration; you
> are, to that extent, weaker, more lifeless, more
> effeminate, more liable to passion and error
> in future; whereas if you go through with the
> danger, though it may have been apparently rash
> and foolish to encounter it, you come out of the
> encounter a stronger and a better man, fitter for
> every sort of work and trial, and nothing but
> danger produces this effect.

'Stronger', 'better', 'less effeminate' – clearly, here, the idea of taking a risk is bound up with masculinity, with male strength and moral worth. Being 'sensible' and risk averse are seen as being like a woman. This fits well with Adam Phillips's and Barbara Taylor's examination of our modern attitudes to kindness, which we considered in Chapter 4, and how this trait is regarded as a female attribute in modern society – one that men should not display, for fear, presumably, of being thought effeminate.[18]

Even though more women have become involved in dangerous sports in recent years, they are less frequently associated with high-risk activities such as car racing or mountaineering, even though they take part in them. Often, women who become involved in dangerous activities such as mountaineering are rendered invisible, or treated with disapproval, thereby feeding into the received belief that women do not take risks.[19] Indeed, it may be that risk-taking women have been written out of the sporting and exploring records because, culturally, we simply do not think they should be there. For somehow we believe that women should not be taking these sorts of risks.

When women do take risks, they are often subjected to intense criticism for putting themselves at risk, particularly if they have children. Alison Hargreaves is an excellent illustration of this; she was the first woman to reach the top of Everest alone and without oxygen in May 1995. Three months later, aged thirty-three, she was blown off K2 while descending from the summit. Her body was never recovered. Her widower, Jim Ballard, was always supportive of her decision to climb:

> She didn't look like a climber. She was small,
> pretty, compact ... I don't know why she
> captured the world's imagination. People need
> adventure in their lives. Maybe Alison showed
> them it was possible. I wanted my kids to know
> that there are wild places on earth where Nature
> is still king or queen or even dictator.[20]

Her widower may have understood and, indeed, supported her. But much of the press she attracted was extremely critical of her, sometimes vitriolically so, and usually on gender grounds as she was a mother. Yet her son Tom Ballard is now following in her footsteps, and in 2010 he announced that he was planning to climb the 28,000-ft peak of K2, the second highest ascent in the world, which only 300 other people have managed to climb and which is far more dangerous than Everest. Ballard has been climbing since he was a child and he told a BBC film crew in spring 2010 that he was undaunted by the fact that the peak had claimed his mother's life, explaining that it was no different to her having died in a car crash: if she had, he would still travel around by car. He described the deep-seated urge he had to climb mountains, which he felt that his mother would have understood. Although she might not have approved of his climbing initially, he believed that she would have soon realised that he was only doing something that she enjoyed herself and that she would have been pleased by the parallels between them. Ballard thought that she might still have been nervous on his behalf, but also proud and happy that he was doing what he had always wanted to do. He said: 'I am following in her footsteps, they are already there so I can just step in them and carry on.'[21]

And so a woman who was criticised for putting her two young children at risk of losing their mother, and who did indeed die in her love of mountaineering, has left a legacy that continues in her son's deep fascination with mountains and desire to match her mountaineering achievements.

Little is written, by contrast, about fathers who take risks, potentially rendering their children fatherless. It is as though this is just 'normal' male behaviour, which illustrates all too well the extent to which this risk-taking business is a social construct, and suggests that if there is a capacity for finding meaning in life through risk-taking, then it may be a licence given only to men. Robert Reid's rather beautiful explanation of why people venture up the most dangerous of mountains – 'to linger in safe communion with death, to feel the exquisite tension that separates it from life' – is presumably therefore only applicable to men. To my mind, either it is possible for both men and women to feel 'more alive', and to find a sense of communion with nature, of nearness to death, in these behaviours – or perhaps it really is a form of gaining meaning that genuinely does belong more to the sphere of men than to women.

Some might argue that there is so much risk inherent in women's everyday existence that they hardly need to feel 'more alive' by exposing themselves to additional dangers. After all, bearing children, then rearing them and protecting them may be enough to fill most women's risk-taking quotas. Yet in Western societies childbirth is hardly seen as dangerous at all these days (although an element of risk is still involved), and the protection of children is clearly not perceived as an especially risky business – with the notable exception of society's current preoccupation with the risks of child molestation presented by strangers. However, it's a fair bet that more women will risk their lives protecting their children from danger in one way or another than will face danger on a mountain slope. And there are also other sorts of risks that women face, such as sexual predation, domestic violence and financial insecurity. These considerations may go some way to explain why fewer women feel the need to take risks beyond those that are already ever present in their lives and near the forefront of their consciousness.

Taking risks is an inevitable part of being alive. And yet, if we find ourselves drawn to chasing risks, I think we need to keep our eyes open to the link with adolescent behaviour. Teenagers tend to be very self-absorbed, taking risks as a means of pushing at boundaries and maturing. Adults should have completed that stage, which is why risk-taking in adulthood needs to be assessed and weighed in the context of the potential benefits and harm that may come of it. As adults, we have to guard against the selfishness that can be inherent in this kind of behaviour.

We should not be immune to how our risk-taking may affect others. Feeling more alive, being close to nature, communing with God, realising how transient life is, and treading the thin line between life and death – all these are admirable, or comprehensible, things for us to want to experience. But we have to count the cost – to ourselves and to others.

We may admire the risk-taking grandmother, but we may also – consciously or subconsciously – feel she should make sure that her appetite for risk doesn't result in others having to change their own lives in order to cope with the consequences of any accident she may have. When it comes to others, there must be a calculation as to whether our risk-taking is ultimately worth it. And only individuals, families, and close friends and partners can decide on that.

There may come a time in life when there is much to be gained from thinking carefully about slowing down, and about going into old age 'all passion spent', at peace with ourselves. While taking risks may give us meaning when we are younger, there is much to be said for taking stock as we grow older and appreciating the rewards that may be found in going slow.

CHAPTER 6

WHEN TO GO SLOW

We are always getting ready to live,
but never living.

Ralph Waldo Emerson (1803–1882)

Assaulted on all sides by twenty-four-hour news; hourly messages from Facebook and Twitter updating us on our friends (and to which we are expected to respond immediately); shops open dawn till dusk: that's the world we live in. And it's speeding up faster and faster. They say New York is the city that never sleeps, but it's now the case that most cities never rest. In fact, these days we probably need to get out of the city to find any peace and quiet at all!

Now, I'm an inveterate list-maker and I was making one of my customary lists at my desk the other day when I realised that I hadn't looked at the news for over an hour: these days that felt almost like not keeping up, like not being in the picture. Not much changes in an hour usually and in fact most of the twenty-four-hour news bulletins are packed with gossip, repetition and often rather dull opinion, for want of anything else. But I'd found myself caught in the twenty-first-century trap – got to keep up, got to know what's going on, got to keep the news on all day, just in case.

This sense of haste may have been expressed by Ralph Waldo Emerson in the 1830s, but it reached its peak in the lyrics of 'Fifty-Ninth Street Bridge Song' by Paul Simon. That seems all the more appealing today than when the track was originally released. 'Slow down,' it says, as if we're all going too fast. When it appeared on one of Simon and Garfunkel's hit albums, *Bridge over Troubled Water*, back in 1966, it captured the mood of the era, when – at least in some parts of society – slow was the default setting. When the happy, hippy days of the Sixties passed, life sped up (although it was always faster for those not involved in the counter-culture) and has continued to do so ever since.

Perhaps unsurprisingly, the slow, dreamy times of the Sixties were followed by a fast, acquisitive era: if the lyrics of 'Feelin' Groovy' embody the spirit of the Sixties, the line 'Lunch is for wimps' from the 1987 film *Wall Street* captures the life-in-the-fast-lane, greed-is-good culture of the Eighties. That go-getting pace has in turn then been followed by a resurgence of interest in slowing down, although the hectic pace of life itself doesn't appear to have lessened. It all makes me wonder what the 'right' speed might be for living the good life.

If we make the assumption that the pace of modern living somehow reflects our current attitudes to life, then I believe that we ought to examine the emergence of the Slow Movement in its many guises over the last couple of decades, and see whether it has anything to tell us about engaging with time in a way that yields satisfaction. A global phenomenon, the Slow Movement wishes to promote a cultural shift towards slowing down the pace of life. And it has a definite appeal: many of us feel that slowing down would benefit our lives hugely, both in terms of how we treat our children, parents, partners and friends, and in how we ourselves might use our time to reflect and grow spiritually – to simply be.

There is something peculiarly depressing about the way in which the furious speed of our lives destroys the chance for the contemplative. We might occasionally do well to consider the example of older people who've been left behind in the rat race; they have all the time in the world, and yet that time is to be treasured because, in some respects, they have little else. The abundance of time they have on their hands can appear very attractive to the rest of us (and we should certainly help them make the most of it). But perhaps much of its attraction lies in the fact that we ourselves appear to have so little of it.

Even if we do have plenty of spare time, we have become culturally attuned to filling it up with yet more phone calls, emails, more dealings with the online banking system that was supposed to make life simpler, more attempts to get reception on our BlackBerry when we are in remote parts of the world. (I've even watched holiday makers wade into the sea to get reception!) The further we travel to remote parts, the more we will be inclined to make great efforts to stay in touch with the hubbub we have left behind. It seems we cannot let go.

And that is where I believe the Slow Movement has something to teach us. Slow says we have to get personally involved: email is not enough. Slow says we need to slow down in order to appreciate the beauty of nature, or hear the music, or savour the lushness of the fruit or vegetables. Slow says that cities can be harmonised to represent all the groups within them. Through Slow, we can begin to find inner harmony by listening to ourselves and acknowledging our competing needs, wants and desires.

There is a voice within and beyond us. Some of us might regard that inner voice as an expression of the divine. Others would see it as the voice of conscience. And there are those who would simply see it as a warning light, telling us to stop the headlong rush. It does not matter which. What is important is that we all occasionally find the time to be quiet and still, to hear our own inner voice tell us what matters to us. I believe that slowing down is an important message for all of us.

However, each of us has to discover our own way of slowing down, of finding downtime and of stopping ourselves from imposing huge speed on everyone else. In fact, that's the truth that peace activist Satish Kumar has been telling us for decades. Kumar originally trained as a Jain monk, the Indian religious order that in some respects is the progenitor of what has become the modern Slow Movement.

For Kumar, all the talk of targets for carbon emission reduction, carbon footprints and climate control miss the point. He wants to see us reinvent reverence for nature and rediscover our respect for the natural world and its rhythms, instead of focusing on short-term economic targets and making decisions based on fear. He believes that 'economics should be put in its place. Imagination should be at the forefront'; and argues that scientists must acknowledge that the relationship between humanity and the natural world contains an element 'that cannot be quantified but is crucial to our species moving away from the prioritising of economic concerns over qualities of love and compassion'.[1]

Much of what Kumar says is what the Slow Movement is also trying to say. In my view, neither is wholly right: economic concerns need to be taken together with love and compassion if we are ever to create a more comfortable and sustainable world. But Kumar's note of spiritual concern has been left out of much of our current attitudes to slowing down – and that is a shame, for he has something important to say, even if we do not necessarily agree with all of it.

Some of the tenets of the modern Slow Movement can be traced to the 1960s, when Transcendental Meditation (TM) and Buddhism influenced a whole generation of young people. But long before hippies were ever thought of, there was the great pastoral movement of nineteenth-century Romanticism. This movement influenced art, literature and music with the notion that contemplating pastoral scenes might help calm us down, connect us with our inner selves and enable us to see beyond the everyday – providing respite from our duties and the usual speed of living. Reacting against Enlightenment ideals of logic and science, the pastoral romantics wanted to reconnect humanity with nature, which may have modern parallels in the way in which the Slow Movement is a response to classical monetarist or Keynesian economic theory. Whether it was admiring nature in the form of ferns, grottoes and natural landscapes, or listening to music with birdcalls and alpine horns conveying the pastoral idyll, our nineteenth-century ancestors knew that calming ourselves down, and slowing down, were important.

When we want to slow down now in the twenty-first century, it still makes perfect sense to listen to a violin sonata or to one of Beethoven's great works, such as his Pastoral Symphony. And we can hear the glory of the pastoral in some of Schubert's songs, see it in the paintings of landscape artists such as John Constable, or read about it in the Lake poet Wordsworth's poems 'The Prelude' or 'Daffodils'. The pastoral images in art are their own form of 'slow', and they still make me slow down, stop, think and connect with my inner self in a way I can't when the phone keeps ringing, or there is another meeting to chair.

The twenty-first-century Slow Movement, advocating life in the slow lane, comes in many guises, a sense of connection with nature being among them. Although, as with all social movements, it is difficult to pin down its appearance to an exact moment in time, it is widely acknowledged that the Slow Movement's first big public outing under that name came in Italy, when Carlo Petrini protested against the opening of a branch of McDonald's in the Piazza di Spagna in Rome in 1986. It was this initial protest that spawned the growth of the Slow Food Movement, which has its head-quarters in Turin. Over the years, its many offshoots have extended the Slow 'concept', with its characteristically witty snail motif and logo, to other areas of life. For example, there is now a Slow Money movement, which attempts to mobilise investment by donors into small food enterprises and organic food, and which has been moderately successful.

Another movement to be inspired by Slow Food is Cittaslow (Slow City), founded in Italy in 1999 but which has now travelled way beyond that country. It aims to encourage the creation of a new kind of city (although quite small ones, as Slow Cities' membership is for urban developments with under 50,000 inhabitants):

> Instead of encouraging speed and strictly
> functional and most often commercial exchanges,

a slow city would allow its inhabitants to take
time to enjoy their living space, to create new
spaces for human interaction, for reflection,
for all different kinds of ideas and actions
that cannot be pursued quickly or under time
constraints and stress.[2]

One of the movement's main concerns is the promotion
of a more leisurely pace of life. However, the Cittaslow
manifesto consists of at least seventy recommendations and
obligations in total. Its key ideas are profoundly influenced
by the ecological concerns of the Green movement, which
advocates protecting the planet and preserving it for future
generations – a very different objective from simply living
at a gentle pace, and arguably a more proactive one.

Cittaslow is also motivated by the desire to support
small local businesses. Although Cittaslow's founders do not
mention the influence of British economist E. F. Schumacher,
their philosophy appears to have its roots in his theory
that 'small is beautiful'; an idea that represented a significant advance in thinking in the 1970s on how to live the
good life.[3] Popularised by Schumacher, the phrase 'small is
beautiful' in fact originated with his teacher, Leopold Kohr,
an Austrian economist and philosopher: both Schumacher
and Kohr propounded smaller, more appropriate technologies (intermediate technologies) which they believed
would empower people and thereby improve their lifestyles
– in contrast to the ideology embodied in phrases such as
'bigger is better'. They wanted to give individuals a greater
sense of belonging and involvement in their communities,
connecting them with their environment. Translated into
the Slow City movement, this also means a way of life that
is more in tune with nature.

Cittaslow's manifesto also includes: conserving urban heritage; reducing energy consumption; promoting environmentally-friendly technology; increasing the number of green areas, pedestrian zones and recreational spaces; keeping cities clean; prioritising public transportation and other non-polluting forms of transportation; and reducing waste and developing recycling programmes. It also wants to develop the collective infrastructure of cities, providing facilities that are suitable for people of all ages and for those with physical disabilities. Perhaps most empowering of all, the movement is keen to develop a genuine participatory democracy in urban environments.

Many of Cittaslow's aims would fit neatly into any run-of-the-mill, environmentally conscious programme (apart, perhaps, from its passionate opposition to genetically modified organisms, which springs from its origins in the Slow Food Movement). However, the empowerment element of its manifesto gives it a unique appeal; for most of us, being able to affect our environment and the circumstances in which we live is one way of finding meaning in our lives.[4]

If Slow and small bring empowerment and meaning, then there has been a particularly interesting political offshoot to the Slow Cities movement in the United States. Particularly strong in impoverished, post-industrial cities, 'Degrowth' is an environmental, anti-consumerist and anti-capitalist movement, which shares some of the philosophy of the Slow Movement. Degrowth is a call to action, rather as the Slow Movement has been, asserting that we need to redress the balance in relationships between cities, communities, individuals and the environment.

Although by no means part of the Degrowth movement, the Obama government in the United States has asserted that urban growth is not the only option to remedy the social and economic problems of cities in deep financial crisis. This thinking has led to a new approach to urban planning under the slogan 'Shrink to Survive'.

One of those in charge of the new government policy is Dan Kildee, treasurer of Flint, Michigan – one of the poorest cities in the country. He has applied the new system in Flint, demolishing deteriorating housing stock in residential neighbourhoods and buildings on industrial sites that had been abandoned owing to the financial crisis and changes in industrial economies. These crumbling buildings were replaced with parks. At the time of writing, the Obama administration is planning to implement this system in fifty other cities, former industrial areas which have been particularly badly affected by various crises, and where there are neighbourhoods that have been completely abandoned.[5]

But is this really the right way in which to live – transforming the environment by pulling down derelict buildings rather than rebuilding them, and forming parks, green spaces and other community resources for anyone who still happens to be left in the area? Do these kinds of actions truly give people a sense of meaning, a reason for being in those deeply depressed towns at all?

To my mind, the destruction of unoccupied houses makes a mockery of what is the real tragedy: the abandonment of neighbourhoods where families once bought homes (thereby indebting themselves for many years) and put down roots, but where they were unable to continue making the payments on their mortgages because of unemployment, consequently losing the properties into which they had put so much. Those families – the ones forced to move from the area – are no longer in a position to participate in deciding what is to replace their old neighbourhood. Yet might they feel better, seeing something good coming out of what has happened to them?

Could they see some meaning rise out of the ruins of their dreams, hopes and expensive investments?

⚭

There is an alternative model that is loosely related to the principles of Cittaslow and Degrowth, which is currently giving many people renewed hope and a sense of purpose in life. Project H.O.M.E in Philadelphia is the work of Sister Mary Scullion. Through it, great tracts of uninhabited houses in marginal and abandoned neighbourhoods are being reclaimed: the project helps homeless families to restore the buildings themselves and then move in, creating pride in the houses and in the neighbourhoods once again.

Sister Mary shows that there are real choices to be made in how we live our lives; through her own life's work (clearly not spent in the slow lane), she has transformed the lives of thousands of others.[6] Her approach to urban regeneration is in keeping with many elements of the Slow City philosophy, but is not confined by that movement's ideal size limit of 50,000 people.

Indeed, Cittaslow's equation of small with beautiful makes me wonder what relevance some aspects of their philosophy have to the majority of us who live in larger towns and cities, particularly those rapidly expanding cities in Africa and in China, where the populations of former villages such as Shenzhen have increased to millions over a decade or so. Such thinking represents an admirable attempt to revisit the ways in which we coexist and to revive the worn-out social fabric in cities where neighbours do not even know each other (where social interaction is sometimes confined to superficial relationships with storekeepers and service providers), but it simply does not apply to the massively expanding metropolises around the world.

The Slow City philosophy states:

> We are looking for towns brought to life by people who make time to enjoy a quality of life. Towns blessed with quality public spaces, theatres, shops, cafés, inns, historic buildings and unspoiled landscapes. Towns where traditional craft skills are in daily use, and where the slow, beneficial succession of the seasons is reflected in the availability of local produce, in season. Towns where healthy eating, healthy living and enjoying life are central to the community.[7]

Whilst that all sounds delightful, it is not your average city. The same applies with respect to the Slow Movement's dislike of the homogenisation of shops and communities, and its revulsion towards chains of shops or cafés. Of course, there is a lot to be celebrated and enjoyed in difference; and it's wonderful to be able to stroll around without feeling each high street is just like every other one. But we somehow need to find a way to sustain those differences without losing sight of some of the advantages that modern stores, for instance, have to offer us. Small, local shops are great, but they often can't pay or train their workers properly, or do not have the means to allow them to take parental leave or carers' leave. Small may be lovely when selecting a beautiful artichoke for a special dinner, but most of us simply want to have the option of dashing into somewhere convenient which sells all the basics.

Some of the thinking behind Slow Cities looks to me as though it may contain a counterproductive element of nostalgia — a romantic harking back to a form of expanded village life, in which everyone can become involved in the community because it is small enough. In relation to this, I was struck by the tone of an article written by novelist Jeanette Winterson, in which she describes the fruit and veg shop in Spitalfields of which she is the proud owner:

> My shop is right opposite Spitalfields market, now full of chic shops and funky stalls, but formerly the fruit and veg market for London.
> ... When I first came to Spitalfields in 1990, the Ten Bells pub was still an all-nighter, and about four in the morning, when the market was in full swing, loading up for the coming day, the place would be packed with night workers. Tarts off shift used to come in for a gin and a bag of veg. Market porters had a pint of beer and a round of figs ...[8]

These short extracts seem to describe not the 1990s, when she first arrived there, but a much more distant era, so it's not surprising, given this hankering for the past, that Winterson adds: 'The shop front had been restored by me back to the original, but with the 1930s signage above the door.'

Now, there's nothing wrong with looking back, and the past can be a great source of inspiration, but nostalgia shouldn't blind us to progress. This is also an important consideration with respect to the way in which the Slow Movement's emphasis on 'small is beautiful' means that it is very much bound up with localism. Exhortations to buy from local producers and to encourage the spread of farmers' markets, for example, are appealing, but there are downsides too. If we British citizens, for example, support the East Anglian farmer or the owner of the small orchard in Kent, that's all to the good. But if we only buy local, we may be condemning the grower of green beans in Kenya or the mango grower in Pakistan to poverty. Wherever we live, isn't our responsibility just as great to the global community of human beings as it is to those we can reach on a bicycle?

I wonder too whether the emphasis on localism isn't a badge of conspicuous consumption worn by the rich. For as long as local organic food is so much more expensive than the produce offered by the supermarkets, it will only be readily available to the minority of people who don't need to count their pennies. If we are collectively to reap the benefits of the Slow Movement, we all need to be able to enjoy that which is currently the privilege of the few.

Moreover, buying local, being green (and thereby perhaps regarding ourselves as ethically superior to our less affluent neighbours) are not actions that necessarily make us behave well in other ways. Apparently, if people feel that they have been morally virtuous in saving the planet, they are more likely to act badly in other ways through a mode of behaviour known as 'moral balancing' or 'compensatory ethics'. In one recent study, it was found that those who had bought green were less likely to share a set sum of money with others than those who had not. Similarly, when green consumers were given the chance to cheat on a computer game and then lie about it they did so, whilst conventional purchasers did not.[9] That may be, of course, a one-off but perhaps there should be at least a suspicion that going green and slow may not always make us behave as well as we should!

If the message of the Slow Movement is to be more than a gimmick, we need to get our heads around the wider moral implications, as well as the difficult question of how to assert some control over the pace – and quality – of our lives without descending into an unattainable (and, for most of us, undesirable) trip down memory lane to a bucolic era that simply does not fit with the modern world.

In some respects the Slow Movement, and Slow Food in particular, may be an attempt to live out a retro fantasy in which all is calm and peaceful, and we (mostly women) have little to do other than shop for exquisite vegetables and cook wonderful meals for the family. There may well be a thesis waiting to be written about the implicit sexism in much of this nostalgia: just why can't we go back to an era in which women stay at home and have the time to prepare meals from scratch and bake cupcakes, etc? Like all the best fantasies, it has little to do with reality: even in days gone by, most people of both genders had to work extremely hard and may not have been anything like as happy in their supposedly slower, gentler era as we would like to believe they were.

Nevertheless, there is an argument that says rediscovering forgotten skills and old-fashioned ways of doing things – be it slow cooking methods, keeping a few hens (almost a national obsession in the UK), or the art of knitting – can bring huge satisfaction, even if it also brings the realisation that these labour-intensive tasks kept our ancestors in a state of perpetual busy-ness. Speaking from experience, as someone who normally sits at a desk or goes to endless meetings, I have to say that there is something enormously satisfying about making jam from fruit you have grown yourself, or sewing curtains yourself, or even simply baking a cake. It's not purely about nostalgia for an age in which, for instance, convenience foods didn't exist; it's also about the profound satisfaction to be found in making something yourself (and finding it often tastes better too!). Making things for ourselves can be immensely rewarding for both men and women, as Matthew Crawford describes brilliantly in his book *The Case for Working with Your Hands*.[10]

Some of the old skills can in fact help us save time, allowing us to become more self-reliant and make better use of the resources we have to hand. Darina Allen, the inspirational cook and founder of the Ballymaloe Cookery School in Ireland, suggests that by no means all of the traditional cooking methods are time-consuming; indeed some, such as using up leftovers, may be positively time-saving.[11]

In our time-obsessed society, the rise and rise of convenience foods, convenience stores and of a 24/7 lifestyle means that we do not have to plan, shop for or cook meals, or do many of the chores that our grandparents would have regarded as the norm. However, imposing a routine whereby we carefully plan what to eat, shop only for what we need and freeze leftovers, for example, can have the curious effect of anchoring us into the rhythm of life. Routine and planning can connect us with the seasons, allowing us to enjoy them and ground ourselves in the process.

The very idea of slowing down and the whole concept of the Slow Movement should make us stop and ask ourselves some serious questions: *am I doing too much? Going too fast? Do I have time to stop and stare? Do I reflect? Spend quality time with family and friends? Do I believe that doing nothing might be good for me, even if the idea terrifies me right now?* At the Slow Movement's heart is a reaction to the runaway train of the goal-oriented society in which we have lived ever since the Industrial Revolution. It questions whether speed and always rushing on to the next task (or the next source of fleeting pleasure) is compatible with a happy and satisfying life. To that extent, the Slow Movement is undeniably a helpful focus for all of us, encouraging us to look at the way we live and to think about whether there are ways to do things differently and enjoy a better quality of life.

After all, many people give up life in the fast lane in order to do something different – more slowly, more satisfactorily. These are the downshifters, discussed in greater detail in Chapter 8. Among them are the bankers who become teachers, the lawyers who become cabinet makers and the doctors who become artists. Those people make particular lifestyle choices to downshift because, for them, living in a perpetual rush, with no time to think, becomes increasingly unbearable. But it is not true for everyone.

As I have already suggested, when taken to excess the concept of Slow may merely substitute one flawed way of life for another. And, in asking ourselves whether we should go Slow, we could sometimes be posing the wrong question: perhaps 'going slowly' should not be our aspiration, but rather doing things at an appropriate pace. Sometimes slow is just right, but sometimes slow is both inefficient and frustrating.

When taken to extremes, slowing down can become absurd. There is a glorious website entitled SlowDownNow. org created by the ludicrously named 'International Institute of Not Doing Much'. It too has a 'Slow Manifesto':

> There are those who urge us to speed. We resist!
> We shall not flag or fail. We shall slow down in
> the office, and on the roads. We shall slow down
> with growing confidence when all those around
> us are in a shrill state of hyperactivity (signifying
> nothing). We shall defend our state of calm,
> whatever the cost may be. We shall slow down in
> the fields and in the streets, we shall slow down

in the hills, we shall never surrender![…]Some
are born to slowness – others have it thrust upon
them. And still others know that lying in bed
with a morning cup of tea is the supreme state
for mankind […]Infectious multitasking is on the
increase. If you're attempting to eat breakfast and
floss at the same time, or if you take phone calls
during your meditation practice, you could be in
trouble …[12]

This is the witty brainchild of Christopher Richards, an
Englishman who now lives in the United States. Although
it is highly tongue in cheek, there is a serious message as
well. Richards writes:

It's a common mistake to think that other
cultures are like your own. Only after working
in the corporate world and running a company
did I understand what Josef Pieper referred to
as 'The Total World of Work' in his book,
Leisure: The Basis of Culture. It was this book that
was my impulse (if impulse is not too strong a
word) for writing about slow[…]Pieper's point
is that one can become so immersed in work
that nothing else matters. Total work destroys
culture. Total work saps our energy. There
is no time for interiority. This led me to
investigate the subject. I started to write about
work–life balance, but at first found my tone to
be preachy. There's a big difference between
knowing what to do, and actually doing it.
Slowdownnow.org became a place to find my
voice as a humorist.

Slow is a serious subject, even if the treatment of it isn't always. Yet humour opens us to being receptive: the world is in constant flux; change is rapid and we don't know what will happen next, so we need to challenge our assumptions. We need wisdom to cope with change, and wisdom doesn't arrive overnight. We need to work at finding it.

On one level at least, Richards is making a serious point. People today are working too hard, leaving no time for reflection, for an inner life or for creativity. They are suffering, as some German psychologists have suggested, from a new condition of *Freizeitstress*.[13] Many of us fear free time; we become sick when we go on holiday (a syndrome I recognise all too well); we feel stressed if our diaries are overbooked for two weeks, but just as anxious if they are empty; and whenever we have finished our 'to do' lists, we feel we should be doing something else – such as writing another list of things to do. All of which suggests that we don't really know how to slow down, do nothing and simply enjoy spending our free time hanging out, chilling, thinking, reflecting, enjoying the countryside and our children and friends.

Idealistic though some of it may be, thinking about how to live the good life at a pace that works for us individually and collectively seems to be here to stay. In fact, you name it and somebody probably thinks it ought to be slowed down! There are calls for Slow Parenting, which seem to me to be quite understandable in a society in which some parents organise every second of their children's time, steering them towards ever greater accomplishments and leaving little time for play or rest; or rushing them out of the door to the childminder every morning, leaving little time just to be together with them, idling around. There are also calls for Slow Shopping, at least in part to do with eliminating plastic bags.[14] And there's a movement advocating Slow Travel, with an emphasis on travellers engaging with local communities. In fact, there's a movement for slowing down just about everything.

What these movements have in common is a sense of dismay about the harmful effects of living in a society in which many of us may be well-off financially, but where we are nevertheless time-poor. As I have already suggested with respect to the Slow Food Movement, what they also seem to have in common (and much less attractively, to my mind) is a preoccupation with the problems of the better-off rather than those of the poor: slowing down travel for people who are cash-poor and possibly time-rich does not make sense; people who are financially struggling need the cheapest means of travel, and if that means Ryanair, so be it. After all, a bus fare may be difficult to find too.

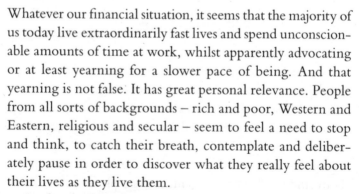

Whatever our financial situation, it seems that the majority of us today live extraordinarily fast lives and spend unconscionable amounts of time at work, whilst apparently advocating or at least yearning for a slower pace of being. And that yearning is not false. It has great personal relevance. People from all sorts of backgrounds – rich and poor, Western and Eastern, religious and secular – seem to feel a need to stop and think, to catch their breath, contemplate and deliberately pause in order to discover what they really feel about their lives as they live them.

In the course of its development, the Slow Movement has absorbed some of the contemplative traditions of Eastern religions (albeit unconsciously), from the popularisation of meditation through the hippy counterculture to Buddhism's search for higher truth in all its manifestations.

And we need time in which to stop and breathe. We need the space in which to think about our day, our week, our month, our year. Physically, we need to give our bodies the opportunity to relax from stress and tension, whilst keeping fit. If we are continuously overstretched mentally, our minds will become exhausted and, tired, we will make faulty decisions. Rushing through our days in the fast lane will deny us any spiritual life at all: the life of the spirit requires time, calm and quiet, and a pace that slows us right down to allow us to think, hope and pray.

That is why meditation, increasing in popularity, has been such a powerful force for good worldwide. It can sometimes be poorly taught, sloppily practised and therefore of little effect. But, at its best, it allows us to slow down and apply a form of psychological and spiritual discipline that is enormously beneficial. Clinical psychologists worldwide have been advocating the use of a technique called 'mindfulness meditation' for decades, after evidence emerged that using the mindfulness technique properly was as effective as the use of antidepressants amongst people in remission from major depression.[15]

The rise in the use of cognitive behavioural therapy(CBT) for depression and other mental disorders has also been significantly influenced in recent years by meditation techniques, particularly those of mindfulness. It seems as if the combination of forcing the brain to slow down and focus; practising being still mentally and physically; learning how to keep body and mind in alignment; and simply thinking differently – allowing the spiritual to come to the fore – does, in itself, give people considerable relief from stress, pressure and depression. It is as if what many Eastern gurus have known for centuries has suddenly demonstrated its true value in the Western world.

Mindfulness meditation does not require special equipment, particular rooms or any unusual facilities, although beginners may benefit from finding a teacher or joining a class: although the practice seems simple, it is not easy to do. But it does slow you down. It also appears to boost immunities, to increase a sense of wellbeing, and, if done properly, help people keep on a plane of reasonable calm.

But mindfulness meditation is not a panacea for all ills – although the present enthusiasm for it across the world of psychology might sometimes suggest it is. As Florian Ruths, the director of a mindfulness meditation programme at London's prestigious Maudsley Hospital, makes clear, it is important that it does not become seen as a cure-all: '... there is a danger of saying it works in psychology so why not use it for almost everything in life? And suddenly having a bit of pleasure, or seeing something beautiful, becomes an act of mindfulness.'[16]

Yet slowing down has something to teach us: I know it when I sit and look at the sea; when I decide to make a cake or casserole rather than email; when I allow myself downtime. And the question for all of us is how we can slow down enough to reconnect with what is inside us; how to slow down so that we can think, contemplate and relax without losing the impetus that keeps us connected to others. We should not become so slothful that we have nothing more to contribute.

Slow is about trying to decide what the right pace is for us as individuals, for us as parents, children, carers, friends, and workers. Slow is good for us, but it is not enough and it is not always right. While going at full speed – New York style – may be exhausting, it is also exhilarating, and the fast and hard pace can lead to our getting things done. Going more slowly may be better for us in some respects, but the old adage 'if you want something done, ask a busy person' still stands up to scrutiny – and that can involve the person who is not only efficient in their use of time, but who also rushes about, working at a breakneck speed, and who regards life in the slow lane as a waste of time. As a philosophy, Slow is full of contradictions. And yet, as we hurtle towards acquiring ever more possessions and leading even busier lives, it says to us: 'Stop. Listen!' And that's a call worth heeding.

Of course, the future may develop in ways that will change the pace of how we live whether we like it or not. In his book *In Praise of Slow,* Carl Honoré fully accepts that while Slow may not be the appropriate pace for every aspect of our lives, the concept has become a shorthand for a better way of doing things.[17] He thinks that recession and environmental threats may necessitate a slower pace and that, as he puts it, 'most of us are yearning to reconnect with our inner tortoise'!

So the issue should not be whether Slow is 'good' or Slow is 'bad'. Sometimes we will need one pace and sometimes another. To my mind, the problem is that elevating Slow as a force for good in its own right in all areas of life simply doesn't play to the real world. If we're not just going to talk the talk, then we must be honest about what we'd be happy to give up in order to walk the Slow walk.

I am happy to admit the benefits of slowing down a bit and indeed would like to do more of this in some areas of my life. But if I had to go back to shopping daily in half a dozen shops, and then slowly cooking a meal that we'd all sit around eating at leisure every single day, there would be a huge downside in terms of what else I would have to give up. Would it be work? Seeing friends? Volunteering? And if local shopping afforded me nicer carrots at the price of increasing third-world poverty, then the cost would surely be too high.

We should certainly be asking ourselves the question about how fast or how slow life should be, but we should not be too glib or too assured about the answer. As with so many things, a happy medium may be preferable. And simply becoming more aware of the pace at which we lead our lives may make us take some conscious choices about slowing down or, indeed, speeding up! The process of making those choices, and being aware we are making them for a particular purpose – be that for greater spiritual awareness, a better lifestyle, to care for our children or ageing parents, or simply in order to reclaim an inner life – requires a level of self-discipline, of personal effort, that people rarely discuss or even understand at the outset.

Indeed, it may be that pacing our lives so that they flow harmoniously has far more to do with imposing a form of discipline on ourselves than with whether our cities are large or small, where our carrots come from or whether we cook a full meal every day. Self-discipline may involve doing things 'properly' – from cooking to crafts to our daily routine – but it is also about making ourselves try harder, about giving up unproductive behaviours and about establishing a workable pattern to our lives, even when outside forces seem to be destabilising us. Fast or slow, what our lives do need is to be stable.

CHAPTER 7

THE BENEFITS OF BEING TOUGH (ON YOURSELF)

'The first and greatest victory is to conquer yourself;
to be conquered by yourself is of all things most shameful
and vile.'

Plato (429–347BCE)

My mother used to say whenever I visited her: 'Take it easy', or 'Be good to yourself'; but my father was quite different. He said you should be tough with yourself. Whenever we met up to mark the secular new year in January, we'd sit together with a glass of wine and mull over our New Year's resolutions, and he'd say 'OK, give me three things that you are going to make yourself do this year … How are you going to be tough with yourself?' This was a man who, late in life and desperately addicted to the habit, gave up smoking. This was the man who loved his food but gave up all butter and fatty things for the sake of his heart. And this was the man who, lover of his car and experienced driver that he was, decided as soon as he had one minor car accident after the age of seventy – a bump at that – to stop driving, which had been one of his great pleasures in life. He certainly knew how to be tough with himself, for his own good and the good of others; and it was a discipline he tried, to some extent successfully, to pass on to me.

Based on my own experience, it seems clear to me that being self-disciplined and tough with ourselves, in the right way, can help to make us more resilient to problems and more capable of achieving the things we think are really important in life. So what precisely do I mean by this? Self-discipline is an attitude of mind and implies a firmness of character. It also involves having the intellectual rigour to work out just what it is we need to be tough about in our lives. It is not just about physical toughness; it is not the boot-camp approach to making ourselves fit. Rather, it involves taking an analytical approach to what needs to be done, how best to do it, and then sticking to those decisions, however diffi-cult we find them. This can apply to dieting, to finishing a piece of work, to using our time productively, to giving up smoking or drinking; or it can be about getting fit physically and mentally. It can be about imposing a period of reflec-tion on ourselves; or it can simply involve organising our day and allowing the time in which to be good to ourselves, as well as meeting the demands that we and others place on us.

For self-discipline means not over-extending ourselves either. Over-extending ourselves is a recipe for disaster, whereas there are great benefits to be gleaned from valuing ourselves and being good to ourselves. But being good to ourselves is only really productive when combined with being really tough on ourselves as well. This means having the discipline to keep fit, eat a balanced diet and get enough sleep, for example – the pros of which every media outlet reminds us of all the time. But it also means having the toughness of mind to examine whether what we are doing is worthwhile or whether we could or should do it better. Just like assessing our physical wellbeing, this sort of rigorous self-examination is something we can all do regularly – and it includes not letting ourselves get away with a job poorly done, or a state of mind half-achieved. It's not for anyone else to do. It's for us personally, and it's about our individual pride. Good enough is often just not good enough, when we could have done better. And only we ourselves can tell if that's the case.

There are many reasons for undertaking this sort of self-audit, one of which is simply to enable ourselves to do better than we have been doing at whatever it is we are undertaking. More profound is the sort of self-examination that asks the question of whether what we are doing is, in fact, what we want to do or even worth doing at all. Creating a bit of distance, standing back, thinking, even meditating or – as many of the world's great religions suggest – going on retreat and absenting ourselves from our usual routines for a day or a week may be one way of finding some perspective.

Self-discipline can be an end in itself – presumably to prove we have what it takes to endure the experience, however tough. This links with the ascetic philosophy of self-denial that is found in some of the Eastern religions and which is assumed to lead to a form of spiritual gain. Being tough with ourselves can, however, be a means to achieving a defined end or a personal goal (e.g. to lose weight, become fitter, or pass an exam), as physical self-criticism and being tough with ourselves often are.

Then there are those who make the assumption that self-discipline in one part of a person's life will automatically lead to better behaviour in another part, which is of course the theory behind boot camps and other forms of 'character building' or 'tough love' punishments and training camps. The argument goes that the experience of simply imposing discipline upon ourselves, in whatever way and for whatever reason, is beneficial and will help us function better as human beings.

There are also some schools of child rearing which argue that firm discipline and clear boundaries are very important to children: for example, that letting a baby cry is good for him and will lead to his learning not to make a fuss unnecessarily. There is obviously plenty to debate around that school of thought. However, to my mind, the idea of imposing a degree of discipline on ourselves as adults (as opposed to a baby) has considerable attractions.

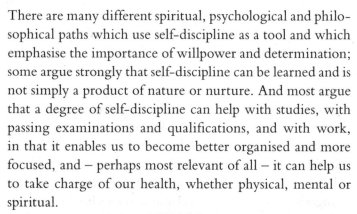

There are many different spiritual, psychological and philo-sophical paths which use self-discipline as a tool and which emphasise the importance of willpower and determination; some argue strongly that self-discipline can be learned and is not simply a product of nature or nurture. And most argue that a degree of self-discipline can help with studies, with passing examinations and qualifications, and with work, in that it enables us to become better organised and more focused, and – perhaps most relevant of all – it can help us to take charge of our health, whether physical, mental or spiritual.

In my experience, when taken to an extreme, some of these different paths can look more like self-punishment or even a rather desperate display of power over others (a bit like some anorexics use their illness, often terrifying as they fade away, to exert power over their parents, relatives and friends), rather than a genuine desire for discipline and self-knowledge to lead to a greater good. Self-discipline and self-knowledge are not necessarily the same thing at all, which is why some clarity about all this would come in handy.

In the process of researching this chapter, I came across a huge amount of material about the pros and cons of acquiring life coaches and spiritual masters. And this, in turn, led me to some areas of what seemed to me to be particularly cloudy thinking. Some of the material I came across seemed to confuse purposeful with pointless self-denial; for example, ideas about manifesting willpower in order to improve our lives or overcome great difficulties would be combined with pretty obvious and banal health tips, such the benefits of not eating ice-cream for a day or getting off the bus a stop earlier and walking more. In other words, eat less fat and get more exercise! All too often, I found life coaches who seemed to be making rather extravagant claims about what they could help with, leading me to suspect that we need to take a much more discerning approach to their claims and the techniques they use, be it neurolinguistic programming, hypnotherapy or, amongst the counselling community, increasingly, CBT.

Many life coaches offer services to help tackle issues as diverse as stage fright, exams, fear of flying, losing weight and building confidence. While increasing a person's overall confidence may help her tackle her fears, a very specific phobia may require a more targeted intervention – and the danger here is if a life coach claims to offer a blanket panacea, when all too often what can be improved is only a relatively small section of the whole canvas.

In considering how to be tough with ourselves in ways that will benefit our lives, I believe we need to look beyond modern life coaches and counselling, beyond self-help books and the advice of our friends, however well intentioned, to the ways in which religions have approached this subject over several millennia – from Buddhism to the Quakers (the Religious Society of Friends). For instance, Buddhism makes it clear that the 'liberation of self' is an individual's own responsibility, and places heavy emphasis on the importance of self-reliance, self-discipline and individual striving. It becomes clear that we have to be prepared to be tough with ourselves if we are even to begin to become good Buddhists. The practice of meditation in Buddhism is similarly very important. Whilst various religions teach some form or variation of meditation, only Buddhism emphasises Vipassana (Insight) Meditation as a powerful tool in seeking enlightenment, a meditative discipline that can be taught to Buddhist adherents.[1] Buddhists are, moreover, expected to live disciplined lives in order to verify the Buddha's insights for themselves:

> The Buddha intended his philosophy to be
> a practical one, aimed at the happiness of all
> creatures. While he outlined his metaphysics,
> he did not expect anyone to accept this on faith
> but rather to verify the insights for themselves;
> his emphasis was always on seeing clearly and
> understanding. To achieve this, however,
> requires a disciplined life and a clear commitment
> to liberation; the Buddha laid out a clear path to
> the goal and also observations on how to live life
> wisely. The core of this teaching is contained
> in the Noble Eightfold Path, which covers the
> three essential areas of Buddhist practice: ethical
> conduct, mental discipline ('concentration'; or
> 'meditation'), and wisdom. The goals are to

cultivate both wisdom and compassion; then
these qualities together will enable one ultimately
to attain enlightenment.[2]

As I am fascinated by the concept of getting to grips with
a teaching in this way, I asked my Buddhist cousin how he
viewed self-discipline in the Buddhist tradition. Like many
young people in the 1970s and 1980s he became a Buddhist
at university, but he has continued his Buddhist practice
with varying levels of enthusiasm over the years. And he
was quite clear with me: Buddhism is all about self-discipline. It is about possessing a degree of self-awareness which
makes us realise who we are and the ways in which whatever
we say and do affects others. Although he was a little less
clear about the Eightfold Path of Buddhism, my cousin was
absolutely adamant that his teachers had taught him that self-
awareness brings the need for action, action brings increasing
awareness, and that this leads to a form of enlightenment and
ultimately a higher stage of spiritual knowledge.

As a Buddhist, you have to see yourself clearly and,
having seen, you must act. So, if you know that you talk
too much you will be obliged to keep silent – a form of
self-discipline that my cousin explained he hated. Similarly,
if you do not work hard enough, your exercise would be
in very hard work – perhaps in the kitchen of a Buddhist
centre, washing up, serving and working so hard you can
barely think, imposing the discipline on yourself to do so
much that you are nearly dropping with fatigue.

Christianity takes a somewhat different approach. An
anonymous essay on the Jesus College, Cambridge website,
states:

Christianity has often been understood as
demanding not self-knowledge, but self-

abandonment. The self has been understood
as necessarily imperfect, so corrupt that it is
worthless: in seeking Christ, Christians may
abandon themselves, condemning the self and
attempting to discard its influence. They may
feel that it is impossible both to express the
individual self and to emulate Christ.[3]

This seems to me to be in complete contrast to the Greek
instruction to 'know thyself', and the author may not have
realised just how strong the emphasis on self-knowledge
and indeed self discipline is in some Christian traditions.
For instance, amongst the Religious Society of Friends
(Quakers), there is strong guidance on how to be tough –
and indeed honest – with oneself:

Be honest with yourself. What unpalatable truths
might you be evading? When you recognise your
shortcomings, do not let that discourage you.
In worship together we can find the assurance
of God's love and the strength to go on with
renewed courage. [4]

A friend who is a member of the Society of Friends agrees,
saying: 'You have to recognise the weaknesses in yourself.
Quaker meetings help you to find strength, both to recognise
the weaknesses and deal with them – indeed, the fellowship
of other Friends makes it possible to go the extra mile, do
the extra things.' I think she is right. I am always struck
by the extent to which Quakers examine what is going
wrong in our world and, instead of praying for those who
are afflicted (although they do that too), they examine their
own 'weaknesses' and then act accordingly – with practical
measures such as delivering clothes to abandoned children
in Kosovo, helping Afghan child refugees, assisting people

who are 'failed' asylum seekers to find somewhere to lay their heads at night, or feeding homeless people. They do not sit around waiting for someone else to do something – and it seems that the self-discipline inherent in their faith, combined with the support of the members of the Meeting, make it more likely that Quakers will volunteer to help when others do not.

Achieving set objectives is an inherent part of other religious paths too. Hinduism, Buddhism and Sikhism all share the concept of *Sadhana*, which is defined as spiritual exertion towards an intended goal: 'Stern self-discipline is absolutely essential. Self-discipline does not mean suppression, but taming the brute within. It means humanisation of the animal and spiritualisation of the human.'[5] Or, as the Hindu spiritual leader Sri Swami Sivananda puts it:

> Good intentions alone will not do. They must be backed up by good actions … During the period of Sadhana, do not mix much; do not talk much; do not walk much; do not eat much; do not sleep much. Observe carefully the five 'do-nots'. Mixing will cause disturbances in the mind. Talking much will cause distraction of the mind. Walking much causes exhaustion and weakness. Eating much induces laziness and sleepiness.

A Hindu friend explained to me that the discipline of *Sadhana* makes one find other things one needs to do – not only good intentions, but good actions. And, having found them, she argues, we then have to carry them out: we cannot abrogate responsibility.

It seems that religion and spirituality have much to teach us about the virtues of self-discipline. Yet, given the distractions of our daily lives, we may need to take time out from our usual routine in order to digest those teachings – and this too can require self-discipline. We may need to go on a retreat.

Although many young people still head to the ashrams of India (even if not in the numbers who did so in the late 1960s and early 1970s), today Christianity leads the retreat movement in the West. As a student rabbi and young pastoral rabbi I adored going on retreat – usually, but not always, to Charney Manor, a Quaker retreat house in the Oxfordshire countryside. Comfortable but not luxurious, good but plain food, no alcohol (although we rabbis often snuck out to the pub!), and with simple but elegant furnishings, Charney Manor had a wonderful atmosphere which made me feel instantly more comfortable in my skin, and taught me – coming from a religion that does not have a strong tradition of retreats or even much space for silence – to be alone, to think, to assess, to work out what it was I wanted to do. Although I rarely go on retreat now, I still savour that sense of freedom with discipline; the awareness that the environment has been especially designed to allow you to think and meditate, but that it also expects you to work out whatever it was you went there to think about, rather than spend your time reading thrillers or simply sleeping a great deal. A good retreat allows the personal space for reflection and self-audit, and indeed it offers the chance to involve others in our self-audit, if that is what we desire.

One of my fondest memories of Charney Manor is of a small inter-faith Jewish–Christian retreat and dialogue that I took part in there over a decade ago. During it, I realised how different we Jews and Christians were: the Christians lapsed comfortably into silence straight away, whereas we Jews immediately jumped into any conversational hole that appeared – something I had been brought up to do, like many of my co-religionists. Not only that, but the Christians would listen respectfully to each other before asking questions or disagreeing with what had been said; whilst the Jewish members of the group would not let another Jew say much more than a couple of sentences before jumping in and disagreeing with them, or, at best, putting a gloss on what had been said!

Happily, the wonderful surroundings of Charney Manor encouraged silence and reflection as well as honest debate. Places like that, which allow us to breathe, to think, to stop and stare, and to reflect on the past as well as the future, are truly valuable if we have the self-discipline to make use of them. A retreat should be exactly what it sounds like: the chance to step aside from everyday life for a while, to rest and just 'be' in welcoming, peaceful surroundings. Most retreat houses are in beautiful buildings with gardens, although the accommodation may vary. The majority are owned by religious foundations, but they are open to everyone in most cases. All retreat centres aim to give their visitors the opportunity to find space and time for reflection.

The Retreat Association gives full details of retreats available in the UK, where they appear to be mushrooming in popularity.[6] Some are deeply religious whereas others are 'religion-lite'. Where some may be highly contemplative, there are many that simply provide an opportunity to recharge mental and physical batteries at a spa or a country house hotel. There are also quiet days, one-day retreats, organised by Churches up and down the UK. Retreats can offer everything from quiet time to the chance to develop specific interests, such as painting or needlework.

In addition to providing a refuge from daily life, many

retreat houses offer the opportunity to talk to someone in complete confidence about any experiences that a person may need to process during the retreat. Almost all retreats run by Christian foundations offer spiritual direction as well, similar in my view to the sort of guidance often offered by life coaches, but provided with greater clarity in the retreat context. Partly, this may be because spiritual direction is broadly about faith and there is a clear focus when meeting with a spiritual director or guide on sharing thoughts and reflections about faith. But it is also because a spiritual director is probably (although not always) specifically trained in this area. In addition to being available during retreats, spiritual directors may agree to see individuals every six to eight weeks for about an hour throughout the year. In my experience, they come from a wide variety of ages, denominations and traditions, but they are always there to make the path of faith clearer, more straightforward and often more disciplined than it might otherwise seem.

Retreat and spiritual directors can be very helpful to those who have no specific religion, as well as those whose faith they share. Sharing our thoughts with someone who is there to help us express our inner selves, and firm up our self-discipline in the process, can genuinely enable us to deal with issues concerning work and play, study and exams, health and spirituality. The experience can give us the wherewithal to become fitter emotionally and mentally. Somehow, through discipline from within and without, we can learn to do things differently, live differently, savour life differently, and stick to our exercise regimes and our new health plans. New Year's resolutions are all very well, but most of us abandon them all too quickly. Having someone such as a spiritual director with whom we can share them can be immensely valuable.

If we are not lucky enough to have a spiritual director with whom we can work through our thoughts and establish a degree of self-discipline in our lives, we might turn instead to books or films for guidance. The trouble is that books, even the best of them, do not encourage direct debate or bring a reassuring presence in our lives, as a good spiritual director might do. And, in my view, some are also just plain bad, such as Rhonda Byrne's books *The Secret* (2007) and *The Power* (2010). *The Power* begins with the immortal words: 'You are meant to have everything you love and desire.' Really? Really truly? Surely not – the whole point of being ambitious, determined and tough with ourselves is that we do not believe in that simple a form of personal empowerment.

As social commentator Joan Smith points out, Byrne's ideas are actually based on a form of late nineteenth- and early twentieth-century 'New Thought', which encapsulates what we might now call visualisation techniques.[7] Byrne was apparently given a book by Wallace Wattles, a Christian socialist from Illinois, who was an early advocate of visualisation. The writer and philosopher Alain de Botton has suggested that Byrne's writings, and others that are similar, are in fact a form of neo-religion. So, although there's no spiritual direction here, we have a form of new religion. But he says – and here I would agree – these forms of writing lack two essential ingredients of real religion: humility and pessimism.

Byrne clearly believes that we can achieve what we want by the power of thought alone, and dresses this 'secret' up as a form of ancient and arcane wisdom. In fact, I am tempted to go so far as to say that this is dangerous claptrap, which preys on the minds of 'gullible, disappointed, and negative people'.[8] There are other, better self-help books out there which show how to live with a degree of discipline; the trouble is that, unlike a spiritual director, they cannot help us to stick with whatever it was that we said we would or would not do!

There are various self-help schools which offer different forms of self-discipline, some more effective than others – from 'de-cluttering' (for which endless notices are pushed through my letterbox at regular intervals), to 'laundry days', in which the idea is to sort through thoughts and actions rather than material possessions.

So-called 'de-cluttering' appears to have become a profession, with de-cluttering experts advertising in September and October and using lines such as 'It's a new school year and the perfect time to de-clutter!'[9] They promise to organise us so that we can enjoy life more: 'Cluttergone provides an expert, experienced and practical de-clutter and organise service. You can change your life! Book a session now!' Of course simply getting rid of the clutter in our houses, offices or garden sheds is not going to change our lives in any serious way. But one of the reasons these de-clutterers may have a role to play (if they are any good at what they do) is that they can impose on us the discipline so many of us lack within ourselves.

'When did you last wear that?' one of them asked me as she riffled through my wardrobe.

'About five years ago,' I replied.

'Then you're not likely to wear it again – give it away!' My lame excuses were treated with the polite contempt they deserved. And quite right too.

But most of us should be able to do this sort of de-cluttering for ourselves: tidying, getting rid of stuff, spring or autumn cleaning are never stupid things to do. Around the Labor Day weekend at the end of the summer in the United States, there is yard sale after yard sale as people have a good clear out to mark the end of summer. It is similar to Freecycling in the UK, and also to taking stuff to charity shops. All we need is to make it an annual end-of-summer exercise, so we do it ourselves. And, of course, in the thinking of the American yard sales, or 'tag sales', as they are called, one person's clutter is another person's treasure. Help yourself!

What is more worrying about some of the de-clutter websites and advertising is that they claim to be able to help people whose lives are somehow 'out of control'; as if getting rid of stuff, however much it is no longer needed or wanted, will somehow clear one's head. We might well feel better once we have got rid of a lot of junk, but it does not usually represent a major improvement in our lives. It may not, however much the de-clutterers like to say it does, resolve stress. It does not automatically give one more space in which to move emotionally, only physically; nor will it help everyone to think more clearly or improve their self-esteem. Moving stuff is, often, simply moving stuff.

More interesting to me is the idea of a life laundry day: 'Life Laundry Day: Get Your Affairs in Order Each Week to Clear Your Mind.'[10] The website that caught my attention on this subject cites Count Vronsky in Tolstoy's novel *Anna Karenina*: every now and then, the Count has a 'laundry day' during which he puts all his affairs (financial, career, personal) in order, and completely clears his mind. As the website says: 'And when he's done "doing his laundry" (he doesn't actually wash his clothes), he feels like a new man. His friend says it always looks like he just got out of a bath.' The idea of a day for putting our affairs in order seems sensible to me. This is not just about de-cluttering ourselves from rubbish; it could involve dealing with financial paperwork and personal administration, cleaning, errands, repairs and maintenance, or other practical things.

A Laundry Day can also involve taking a good look at your career and your relationships: looking, for instance, at whether you're spending enough time with the people you love the most, or dealing with the idiocy of there being anyone in your life with whom you aren't talking because of some silly grudge or another. If so, the best advice is to phone them straight away: 'life is too short for grudges'. Along with this, a Life Laundry Day allows us to review our life goals, and see whether we are doing anything to make achieving them more likely. It also allows us to celebrate our achievements, and that is no bad thing either.

There is some similarity here to the Day of Atonement – Yom Kippur – in the Jewish tradition. The Day of Atonement involves a twenty-five-hour fast. During the day, we think about all the sins we have committed against human beings and against God, and we ask for forgiveness. But that is as nothing compared with what we are expected to do in the preceding month – and especially the preceding ten days, from Jewish New Year onwards – when we have to start thinking about what we have done wrong over the past year. If we have offended any person or sinned against another human being, we are asked to see whether we can somehow apologise and put things right; and only then can we really ask for forgiveness from God.

Yom Kippur is a challenging day to be spent in the synagogue, thinking, praying, and somehow putting ourselves in order through prayer. It allows time for personal contemplation, as we are free to move in and out of concentration on the service. And, although there is no celebration at the end of the day, when the fast finishes there is a sense of completion, even elation, as the result (it is hoped) of a job well done, having atoned for the past year and having wiped the slate as clean as possible. And although this is a specifically Jewish way of doing things, Christian Lent and Muslim Ramadan have some similarities, offering a form of discipline that is physical as well as emotional and intellectual to help put ourselves in order.

In addition to sorting out our physical possessions and our relationships, we would do well to bring a measure of self-discipline to our general attitudes – in particular, ostentation and false pride. Judaism does not disapprove of wealth; indeed, it thinks wealth is a good thing provided some of it is used for charity. But there is a strong tradition against ostentation, which means not going with the bling and not showing off, although lots of people disregard this tradition entirely. Nonetheless, it is about exercising a measure of self-discipline.

The emphasis on avoiding ostentation may be in order not to embarrass those who cannot compete, say, with the glamour of a truly glitzy wedding, or it may be because the money could be better spent elsewhere, such as on charity. Take funerals, which can cost an enormous amount of money. In the Babylonian Talmud (dating to around the fifth century AD) we read that certain changes were made to funeral ceremonies so that poor people would not be embarrassed by being unable to keep up with the rich:

> Our Rabbis taught: Formerly, they would bring
> food to the house of mourners in following
> manner: to the rich, in baskets of gold and
> silver and to the poor in wicker baskets made
> of peeled willows. And the poor people were
> ashamed. The sages therefore instituted that all
> should be provided with food in wicker baskets
> made of peeled willows out of deference to

> the poor ... formerly, they would carry out
> the rich [corpse] in a state bed and the poor
> on a common bier. And the poor people were
> ashamed. The sages therefore instituted that all
> should be carried out on a common bier out of
> deference to the poor ...[11]

As a result, to this very day Jews bury their dead in the simplest of coffins when coffins are required. Otherwise the body is simply wrapped and put into the grave: there is no distinction between rich and poor in death. And that is a form of self-discipline which has become common practice. Originally, many of the rich wanted to do the best they could for their dear departed. But, for the best of reasons, this form of self-discipline prevented them from doing so and resulted in cheaper funerals and more money being available for giving away to good causes.[12]

Similarly, there have been sumptuary laws at various periods of Jewish history which have limited personal expenditure on religious grounds. The Jewish rabbinic conference of the Rhineland decided during the thirteenth century that: 'No child of the Covenant shall dress after the fashion of the gentiles, nor wear sleeves nor shall have long hair.' And, likewise, in the fifteenth century in Italy: 'In order that we may carry ourselves in modesty and humbleness before the Lord our God ... no one may possess cloaks of any other colour than black, sleeves may not have silk linings ... so too cloaks of sable or ermine or expensively dyed material are forbidden.' It all started as a form of self-discipline, of course, and ultimately became a form of discipline imposed upon a whole community. But it had exactly the right effect: less show, more thought and more consideration for those who cannot afford the expense. This sort of thinking represents a slightly different version of being tough with ourselves, maybe, but an important one nonetheless.

Which is not to say that there's been no celebration, no excitement, and indeed not to say a lot of bling, furs and satins since in the Jewish tradition. The tabloid newspapers all too frequently describe how the wedding celebrations of wealthy members of the Jewish, Greek and Indian communities can last for three days; or how the latest rock star has been flown in to perform for a bar-mitzvah party. I definitely believe that celebration can be good for us; it can be uplifting and offer a sense of extreme wellbeing. But I also believe that if you are going to put on a bit of a show, then there is an even greater reason to give more to those who could not even dream of having such a party or enjoying such a celebration themselves. And that is where a measure of self-discipline comes in.

As we have seen, there are many different ways in which we can impose some discipline upon ourselves: through retreats, exercising moderation, dieting, exercise, self-examination, laundry days. All are good. But there is more.

When I was a much younger woman, the redoubtable Barbara Hosking (who has been a mentor to me over many years) asked me to sit down with her and work out what it was that I really cared about – what was at the core of my life. I have used her technique many times since with others. But it requires a bit of time. It requires a certain amount of self-discipline. And it certainly requires some thought.

What *is* it that we most mind about? What, if we were to draw a circle with the core at the centre and rings and rings around it, centres us? What issues, beliefs, people motivate us the most? Our children? Our parents? Our relationships?

Are we moved by the idea of justice? Integrity? Honesty? Is the righting of wrongs important to us? Or is it being rich? Becoming famous? What is it? If we can spend enough time thinking through and then writing down what we care about, either by ourselves or with the support of someone such as an official mentor or an older, wiser friend, I believe we will discover what really matters to us and how that fits with everything else in our lives.

If our friends come close to the centre of the circle we have drawn, we may wish to consider whether we have been good friends ourselves. If righting wrongs lies at the centre, we might reflect on what we regard to be the most glaring injustices around us and work out what, if anything, we have done to counter them. And so on and so on. Of all the techniques that people use to clear the mind and start the process of discovering what matters most to them, this kind of tough discipline – of sitting there till you have drawn your circle, entered what matters and puzzled out what, if anything, you can do about it – is the one that works best of all for me.

Each of us will find our own most rewarding form of self-discipline. Suffice it to say that I do not believe that you can live a good life, nor indeed a happy or successful one, without occasionally spending some time looking at what you are doing, assessing how far you have come, and realising that there are steps you can take to bring your goals nearer. But it is neither an easy process, nor is it necessarily a pleasant one. It can even be quite shocking when you realise how little you have done of the things you said you would do the last time you conducted the exercise.

All the same, it is an immensely valuable form of personal audit, and it is one way (albeit among many) of imposing a regular discipline on your life and helping yourself grow.

In my view, this form of self-awareness helps sow the seeds of a way in which to live wisely, with the knowledge that while life should be enjoyable, it takes plenty of self-discipline to achieve our potential and obtain the true rewards that are out there for us. And those rewards are not necessarily physical possessions.

CHAPTER 8

HAVING IT ALL?

Vanity of vanities, saith the Preacher, vanity of vanities; all is vanity.

What profit hath a man of all his labour which he taketh under the sun?

One *generation passeth away, and* another *generation cometh: but the earth abideth forever.*

Ecclesiastes, 1:2–4

The support of physical possessions is an illusion. I grew up in what seemed to be a very small flat in northwest London. Two years after my mother died in 2001, when we had finally finished clearing the flat of my parents' enormous number of belongings, I came to realise it was in fact a very large space – it was just that my parents had filled it up with so much stuff. But that's not really surprising. My mother was a refugee from Nazi Germany. In Germany, she had been prevented from fulfilling her dearest ambition of attending art school because she was Jewish. A paid-up member of the Communist Party, she worked instead for a couple of years in a left-wing bookshop in Frankfurt. However, in order to protect his father, the son of the owner of the shop joined the Nazi party and advised my mother that she had better leave straight away; he explained that she could do so as a domestic servant. As a result, she left with virtually nothing – a few clothes, a suitcase, a couple of knick-knacks and that was all. This may begin to explain why she became so wedded to her possessions and to belongings in general. Indeed, as her story is part of my own, it may explain why I appear to have inherited her inability to get rid of stuff!

My mother eventually succeeded in getting her much younger brother out of Germany in late 1938, after the pogrom of Kristallnacht. She got her parents out only three days before war was declared, at the very end of August 1939. Then the most remarkable series of events unfolded. My grandparents went to live in one room in a big house on Wimbledon Common, which had been made over to the new, penniless and desperate refugees by the well-known banking and military Seligman family. In this one room my grandparents tried to put back together the pieces of their lives. They were already in their fifties and learning a new language was going to be hard for them. But, only a few weeks after their arrival, their stuff – masses of it – began to arrive from Germany.

My grandfather had been a prisoner of war on the German side in the First World War. Although they were careful not to visit my grandfather in the months leading up to his departure, his German army friends from the POW camp in France (where it seems they had spent their time drinking and playing cards) had gone to my grandparents' flat in Germany after they had left and, instead of looting the place, which is what usually happened, they packed everything up, took it across the border into France just as war was about to break out, and had it sent by carrier to London.

I am not quite sure how they managed to get everything out from France, given how quickly the country became involved in the war. Presumably it reached a channel port just in time. Whatever the case, my grandmother was overjoyed. She got her dinner service, her huge (and to my mind very ugly) wardrobes, rugs, pictures, tables, beds, chairs, silver, glass – and everything else that went to make up the household of the Jewish bourgeoisie in small-town Germany. There it all was. And, a vast accumulation of possessions though it was, my grandparents crammed it all into their room, where they lived on top of it for months.

Those possessions came to have a significance in excess of their actual value, which was pretty low (as I came to find out when I tried to sell some of the stuff in 2002–2003, only to find that no one wanted it and I couldn't even give it away). But this was home sent from home. These items symbolised my grandparents' lost home and my mother's childhood. My grandmother keened over the stuff, as she never really got over leaving Germany, and my mother could never bring herself to get rid of it either, although much of it remained in capacious cupboards that were built all over the flat for precisely this purpose: to store these unused belongings.

Perhaps my mother's experience in her early twenties gave her what people call a 'refugee mentality', making her frightened of losing everything again. Is that pathological? Who knows, but she then became the collector of art that she would probably never have been had she been allowed to become an artist. At her funeral, her great friend Frances Carey talked of her as 'the collector', searching everywhere and tirelessly for the things she wanted, and then being unable to let anything go. And indeed that was what she was; and it was understandable. But, although she loved those things so much, I was never convinced that they gave her any more than an illusory sense of security. And it has left me, an only child, with huge amounts of stuff that I cannot bear to throw away; for it meant so much to my mother and grand-mother, and someone might want it, surely, some day …

Today, it seems that we are constantly being encouraged to buy more, acquire more, have more, and be more and more spendthrift – to keep up with the Joneses. The financial news reports describe how various store groups are doing less well, as if this is all down to our not buying enough from them. Our acquisitions, or lack of them, affect the market. The argument goes that there should not be stringent cuts which will result in the public having less money in their pockets; if there are, people will spend less, which will be bad for the economy. And that, in turn, might suggest that we as a nation are becoming pathological acquirers; or perhaps it is simply a publicity stunt to get us into the shops – as if what we do individually will make an enormous difference to keeping the economy afloat.

Not so very long ago, obtaining credit was easy – all too easy – and we were encouraged to pile up debt and to acquire more and more stuff. And yet to what purpose? Is the acquisition of stuff simply being used to make us numb, so that we fail to recognise the need to acquire something else, be that wisdom, a sense of purpose or meaning in life? After all, we are largely judged by the clothes we wear on our backs and the furnishings we have in our homes, the cars we drive and whether we have gym memberships or personal trainers, and the level of grooming we pay for in the way of haircuts and facials, for example.

We in the West enjoy a standard of living that would be unimaginable even to the wealthiest of our ancestors only two generations back. The rich among them may have had staff to look after their homes, but they would have been cold if they went from room to room; they had fewer clean clothes (until dry-cleaning came along) and their means of communication with friends and acquaintances would have been far less efficient. They too would have been judged by appearances, which has been the case for generations, if not for ever. And they too would have wanted the latest furniture, the latest pictures and books, the best clothes, and the finest schools for their children. Many nineteenth- and twentieth-century writers – from Henry James to Edith Wharton, from George Eliot to Charles Dickens – were quick to point out the superficiality of all this and to recognise that all this stuff was a mere veneer.

In fact, we might just be beginning now, in the early twenty-first century, to recognise that, provided we have the basics, things do not really matter very much. We may be beginning to realise that we need affection rather than things; that a sense of purpose is more important than gizmos and gadgets; and that we need a sense of meaning to our lives rather than endless superficial communications on the internet, which of themselves give us no sense of purpose.

All the same, so many of us seem driven to acquire the latest mod-con. Even those on really low incomes want the latest flat-screen TV, for instance, or the newest iPhone. It's as if this new stuff conveys status and, even though many of us are no happier with our new flat screens than we were without them, the latest devices bring with them a form of satisfaction, in that we can say 'we've got it' when asked.

Whoever we are and however much we already possess, it can take a considerable effort to get rid of that sense of needing more stuff. While it may be clichéd in the extreme to say that 'you can't take it with you when you die', the fact that most of our belongings are impermanent, not memorable nor heart-stoppingly beautiful, should make us pause in our tracks. It's just stuff. Yes, we may love it. Yes, we may peer longingly into shop windows at a particular item. And of course it's comforting to be able to leave treasured possessions to others when we die – but just how much do we need to own in order to live a happy life? Although it may be a reward for hard work, does having enough money to buy whatever we want really make us happy?

We should not underestimate the value of some possessions, however. Even though the constant advertising, the constant pressure to buy something 'new' may irritate – and indeed lead to unnecessary acquisitions – certain belongings do have meaning. I still use the old electric citrus squeezer that my parents once owned and which my father glued together with his own fair hands whenever it fell apart. I treasure it; it makes me think of him.

Similarly, I still use my mother's large, square, continental, linen pillowcases, which were prepared for her trousseau in the early 1930s by my grandmother and used by my mother all her life. Although they have been laundered almost to bits, I still like knowing that her head lay on that same linen. And my mother-in-law's pepper grinder sits on our table in Leamington Spa. It's of no value, but I like the fact that her hands once twisted it.

Possessions can bring back happy memories of loved ones. In some cases, they can even bring back the smell of those we have lost, such as my father's prayer shawl which, although it has been dry-cleaned twice, still smells a little of him after fourteen years. These sorts of memories are important, and the fact that 'mere objects' can evoke them most powerfully is one reason, amongst many, not simply to jettison all possessions for the simple life.

As I have already mentioned, possessions can take on immense importance for people whose lives have been turned upside down in one way or another, either as refugees, for instance (as was the case for my mother), or by serious illness, for example. The photographer Mary McCartney took pictures of people with cancer for a show in aid of Maggie's Centres, which provide support to people with cancer. She portrayed them with their treasured possessions.[1] For Anu Guatam, it is a small golden Buddha; for Peter Clark, a radio-controlled glider; for Isobel Allen, a wedding scrapbook, because in spite of her bowel cancer she was due to marry – and did so in all her glory in September 2010. For Gordon Kirk, it is a bicycle, because when he read about Tour-de-France-winner Lance Armstrong's brush with testicular cancer he was inspired to get fit, take up cycling and study sports psychology. All these people were not simply wedded to possessions because they were possessions, but because the possessions had come to mean something special to them. They symbolised the different ways in which these people coped with suffering, illness and fear, and found a space in their lives for laughter, creativity, hope, energy and strength in spite of their illnesses. So possessions can mean something quite profound; although all too often I'm afraid that they do not.

I remember visiting an old man and hardly being able to get inside his door for the amount of stuff that was stacked there. I asked him what it was all for. He explained that it gave him pleasure to think about who in his extensive network of family and friends he was going to leave it all to. But even he had to admit that there was little of intrinsic value there. He began to talk to me about his first ventures into Eastern religion, when a Hindu teacher told him that *sannyasa* in old age meant getting rid of physical possessions and going out into the world with a begging bowl, as a means of putting one's mind and spirit in order before death. And yet he seemed to me to be doing much the opposite.

However, I was pleased to see that his fixation on how he was going to leave his possessions did not overrule his readiness to acquire new insights; he was at least willing to try to abandon his obsession with belongings. Easy enough for him, you might say, as he was approaching death. Yet any twenty-five-year-old ought to be able to see that acquiring possessions isn't the answer to life's problems – that more stuff simply will not satisfy, and that thinking through our desire for possessions is essential. We need to understand the true purpose of our acquisitions, rather than get caught up in the act of acquiring them. And yet we still talk of the benefits of retail therapy and our national pastime does seem to have become shopping.

In my experience, many older people find it terrifying how much younger people acquire and then simply throw away. The wartime attitude of 'make do and mend' is something that older people can teach younger people; I for one would be happy to see it become a multi-generational activity or campaign. By that, I don't mean setting up formal search parties to find firewood on the beach or establishing darning circles for mending socks. But I think we need to listen to the voices of those who can challenge us about whether we really do need to acquire the latest gadget for its own sake, or whether we could reuse items in different ways.

In the *New York Times* bestseller *The Case for Working with Your Hands* (mentioned in Chapter 6), Matthew

Crawford points out that learning how to mend things is deeply satisfying. After all, the sheer waste of unwanted items, which are disposed of in ways that pollute the earth, is enough to prick the conscience of all but the most hard-hearted anti-Green. Happily, in the UK these days, items are often recycled by local authority dumps and internationally there are websites which enable the free exchange of unwanted possessions.

Today, there are plenty of examples of people who are making a concerted effort to reduce their dependence on material things. A major BBC series in the UK in late spring 2010 focussed on Anglican priest Peter Owen Jones as he attempted to live without money for eight months.[2] He begged for food and shelter, bartered his skills for scraps and lived off his own produce. He wanted to follow the teachings of St Francis of Assisi through living a life of 'voluntary poverty' as a key to acquiring a deeper spiritual understanding and fulfilment. Like many of us, he felt he was caught up in a pointless frenzy of spending. But his response to that feeling was rather more extreme than many of ours would be: 'All the great religions say don't rely on money – it is too much the measure of a life. And I'm addicted to the stuff. I want to see if I can wean myself off it and live a different life.'

Most of us would not be able to emulate Peter Owen Jones, and nor would we necessarily want to, but he was serious in challenging our dependence on 'stuff', and showed that it is possible to live a different kind of life without money. And we do not need to emulate St Francis of Assisi to do it. There are plenty of others doing similar things, less dramatically maybe, but with the same thinking to drive them on.

Take Richard Cannon, a friend of a friend. Richard is a classic downshifter. He made the decision to downsize because he was fed up with what he was doing – a not unusual phenomenon. He explains: 'In 1999 I'd been watching the first TV series of *River Cottage* and, in the space of six or seven weeks, my second marriage broke up, I had a minor heart attack and my eldest daughter was killed in a motorbike accident. It said to me that the boundaries between life and death are a very thin line. You start to realise you don't see the family sufficiently. It's a short life, so why be someone's slave?' He is pretty clear he would have done it even if circumstances had been different. Earlier, he had drifted though jobs in advertising and marketing: 'You could categorise the working side of my life as being a drifter. But since I have downshifted I am now self-reliant (not self-sufficient). I am eleven years into it and there is nothing that I would change. You find even if you are leading a simpler life, any other job you have done helps you.' He is also quite clear that one of the best parts of downshifting is that he does not have to do anything he really does not want to do. Apart from a short season working at Kent Cricket Ground in the summer, he can do whatever he likes.

Nor is money a problem. He has developed a pretty straightforward view of money (and there are striking similarities here between him and Peter Owen Jones): 'I have a simple view of money. If I have money, it's because of me, and if I don't have money, that's because of me too.' No longer 'addicted' to money, as Jones puts it, Richard Cannon now earns about a third of what he did ten years or so ago, but is infinitely happier. He claims that: 'On the frugality side, it's just doing the same as our grandparents did. I'd love to meet them again!' And he can now see more of his family, and feels that he has the wherewithal to learn new skills and to achieve the things that matter to him in life.

With respect to facing his own mortality, he reflects: 'If I was sitting on the sofa, there was a bang at the door and it was the Reaper – and he said he was on his rounds and he'd be back in half an hour – what would I think about in that last half hour? If you like, the final goal is to die without a guilty conscience about yourself and others. It's not about having thousands of pounds saved. Every day becomes a bit more urgent – not in the negative sense, but in valuing it.'

Significantly, Richard Cannon does not see the world through rose-tinted spectacles. He has hard times too, and says he will need to earn a bit more money in the near future as he grows older; however, he is fortunate enough to have a pension to look forward to. Interestingly, he says that he would not advise younger people to downshift straight-away – and he should know, having done it. In his view, they should go to college, learn skills and make something of themselves first.

Nor does Richard think downshifting is for everyone; he explains that his nostalgia for the 1950s, and the sense of community and interconnectedness that he believes existed then, is part of his motivation. Others will not feel the same, and nor should they. But he does believe there is an element of sustainability in what he is doing: in his view, each human being is a custodian of the world for a certain number of years and should attempt to leave it a better place than it was before. But best of all, in Richard's eyes, is the way that downshifting has meant his life is under his own control: 'You deal the cards for yourself.'

Richard is by no means alone. Mark Boyle has lived entirely without money for over two years now, and talks of his surprise in 'how easy it's become'.[3] He wants to start a money-free movement, to which end he has set up the

Freeconomy website which enables members to share skills and tools for free. Nor is he is the first to attempt to live this way. Writing in the *Independent on Sunday*, Lena Corner describes the actions of others before him in the Noughties.[4] Artist Michael Landy, for example, spent a fortnight destroying all his belongings in an art piece called 'Breakdown'. His was perhaps the least dramatic case of those described: it was an art installation, after all, and his partner gave him cash with which to replace some of his stuff. The situation was quite different when self-confessed designer label addict Neil Boorman burned all his branded possessions in 2006. After the event, he became a virtual recluse for a while. He argues that it was an early reaction to rampant consumerism, and hopes that society will reach a 'nicer place where we can moderate our consumption'. The third example is artist Jasper Joffe, who put everything he owned up for sale after splitting with his girlfriend in 2009, calling it 'The Sale of a Lifetime'. He explained how the experience offered him a sense of transformation: getting rid of everything made him reassess his life and his relationships. Happily, he got back together with his girlfriend soon afterwards.

One last example as further food for thought: Patrick Barkham wanted to reduce his carbon footprint and, calculating that his clothes accounted for about half of the 10 per cent that he wanted to reduce it by, he decided to try to do without buying any more for a year.[5] A simple measure, perhaps – but potentially a life-changing one.

All of these forms of downshifting are motivated by different philosophies. There is the lifestyle of voluntary simplicity, the lifestyle of the Green movement and the increasingly popular do-it-yourself lifestyle choice in which you do not buy what you can make for yourself. There is spiritual frugality, frugality out of necessity and poverty;

and, finally, what seems to becoming increasingly common: accidental frugality. To my mind, this third kind of frugality is slightly reminiscent of Hilaire Belloc's playful warning about too much make-do-and-mend. In one of the 'cautionary tales' or humorous poems for which he was famous, the French-born British poet describes the fate of the fictional Lord Finchley, who attempted to 'mend the Electric Light / Himself'. The faulty light duly strikes the lord dead, and Belloc gleefully notes that it serves him right, as it is the business of the wealthy to 'give employment to the artisan', rather than to be penny-pinching and deprive them of work by attempting to do their jobs for them.

Moreover, while some of our current desire to rely on less stuff – to be frugal and self-reliant, to make do and mend – is utterly sensible, it is potentially fraught with dangers; of which mending the electrics, without skill or qualification, is only one!

Nevertheless, there are numerous websites devoted to downshifting, and plenty of life coaches who advise their clients to take the plunge. One such is Sally Lever, whose website page 'Voluntary Simplicity in a Nutshell' quotes Duane Elgin: 'To live more simply is to live more purposefully and with a minimum of needless distraction.'[6, 7] There is a list on how to go about it, which states: 'Reducing materialism. Voluntary simplicity is not the same as austerity. Rather, it is about living with less so as to free ourselves from the burdens of materialism … being authentic … finding a way of life that is more in keeping with what we authentically value, rather than what we believe will win the approval of others …'

Here we have the downshifter's paradigm: use less; have less; and think about what matters to you (which, indeed, is what this book is also trying to help you do!). But do we really need a life coach in order to downshift, or is this something we should be able to learn from the examples of people such as Richard Cannon, or simply by thinking for ourselves? And, moreover, is it mainly a lesson for the rich – for the overstuffed, the over-indulged, those too bound by their possessions – who do not seem to recognise that there are poor and deprived people out there for whom having 'too much' is not a problem and for whom 'enough' would be a huge relief?

It seems to me that there is little awareness of the benefits of redistribution in all this: a lot of the focus seems to be on the slash and burn of possessions, rather than on finding someone who might use them and want them. When downshifting becomes a case of burning possessions or selling them on, rather than giving them to those whose needs are greater, this begs a whole series of questions about how self-indulgent such a voluntary giving up of 'stuff' really is.

Despite being freshly fashionable and disseminated, the thinking behind downshifting is by no means new. Its philosophy owes much to the work of the American social philosopher Richard Bartlett Gregg, who was an influence on the thinking of Martin Luther King as well as an early convert to ecology and organic farming. His seminal essay 'The Value of Voluntary Simplicity' was written in the 1930s.

Even earlier is the thinking of the Religious Society of Friends, the Quakers, whose emphasis on simplicity predates Richard Bartlett Gregg and influential eco-educator Duane Elgin by a couple of hundred years. The Quakers' Testimony to Simplicity bears witness to their beliefs that people should live their lives simply in order to focus on what is most important. Quakers will try to focus on the Testimony to Simplicity in everyday life when using resources such as time, energy and money in order to make the world a better place. They consider it even when dressing themselves or speaking to others (Quakers do not use titles, using the 'simplicity' of first name and surname for everyone alike, irrespective of rank). The prison reformer Elizabeth Fry was known for her simple grey dresses. Quaker Oats packets still show a man plainly attired in a Quaker hat. Quakers traditionally focus on their inner state rather than outer appearance, and on the welfare of others rather than on themselves.

In the eighteenth and nineteenth centuries particularly, Friends often set a limit on the quantity of material possessions that they could own. This went hand-in-hand with business succes, notably in the chocolate trade and banking, enjoyed by many of the British Friends families such as the Frys, Rowntrees and Gurneys. Having gone into business because, as nonconformists, other avenues were closed to them, they used their wealth for practical purposes such as alleviating poverty, although some simply gave it away.

In more recent times, Friends have been leaders in the debate about using the earth's resources carefully, in some respects anticipating the thinking of Gregg and Duane Elgin by many years. Indeed, much of current thinking about ecology and simplicity owes a huge, and often unrecognised, debt to the thinking of the Religious Society of Friends.

But for Quakers poverty itself is not ennobling: they do not consider being poor a good thing, but prefer to use their own wealth to alleviate it. Much like the traditional Jewish view (e.g. as expressed by Maimonides), they believe that it is best to alleviate poverty in such a way that the recipient of charity does not ever need to ask for it again. [8] Hence there is a strong Quaker tradition of encouraging poor children into apprenticeships, and of working in prisons to give those who finally emerge from the system a chance to find employment and live a decent, self-sufficient life. The Quakers' emphasis on simplicity gives them the spiritual discipline to recognise hardship in others, even when it is not necessarily visible on the outside. Although their lifestyle may be satisfactory to them (and indeed to others), to my mind, it is not the satisfaction gained from living in this way that is important, but rather the sensibilities that it sharpens and the good acts it leads to.

Others adopt the simple life because they choose to earn less money, or, in the case of a couple, for example, decide that one partner should stay at home with the children. Sometimes the two factors combine, as in the case of the Jackson family in Whitstable, Kent. This family uses and reuses everything in true make-do-and-mend style to save money, but also because they see 'the economic and the environmental benefits of reducing waste, not buying new and making clothes and household objects last longer'. [9] They are 'part of a group of local families involved in the Transition Towns movement, which encourages the more efficient use of resources'. They go in for jam-making, winemaking and foraging; they darn and mend; they use hand-me-downs for the children and reuse towels and sheets until there is nothing left.

A couple of my friends in Ireland have chosen to live in a similar way. Not only do they grow their own food and bottle their own drinks, mend old clothes and forage, they use wind power and alternative heating sources, and recycle absolutely everything. They say that they long to see an end of waste and the rise of people living together in mutually supportive communities, where they look after each other, fix things for each other, grow things for each other and save the earth's resources. The mini-village in which they live is a cross between a commune and a kibbutz fuelled by a strong moral impetus to save the planet, but there is also a huge respect for privacy.

Roughly my own age, these friends have also learned from the example of the Second World War. My own parents saved every scrap of brown paper, every piece of string. And I know I am not alone in clearing out the home of elderly parents to find stacks of rubber bands, boxes, old birthday cards and bits of wool all neatly labelled and stored for possible re-use. This way of thinking was common during the War and afterwards until the 1950s, and not all of it was bad. Indeed, as I have mentioned, there is pleasure to be had from recreating things out of bits and bobs, and a sense of joy in avoiding waste.

Architectural salvage has been fashionable for some time, and salvage firms have made a great deal of money out of other people's waste. Now, however, smaller items are being salvaged and recreated – from old tiles and wooden surfaces to butler's sinks and electrical goods. Adam Hills, who founded the salvage and design firm Retrouvius in London, is on record as saying: 'Seeing the potential beauty in a battered old wooden cabinet, or giving something a new lease of life by mending it is hugely satisfying.' Indeed, Adam Hills' work is extraordinarily beautiful, although presumably you need to have a good eye, as he does, to achieve the results that he gets from other people's 'junk'. Part of this way of thinking and designing is being able to recognise that almost everything has possibilities, if we can only think what they might be. To make the point, one of

Adam Hills' most stylish inventions involves a new use for old glass funnels, which he turns into elegant lampshades for kitchen worktops: an idea that requires imagination, but also a particular determination to find a use for everything, whatever it might be.

With imagination, there is no end to invention: it's even proved possible to come up with an inventive way to recycle used chewing gum, a real pest and form of garbage which it costs local councils millions of pounds each year to remove and dispose of. One fantastic example of this is a young woman called Anna Bullus, who spent eight months working in a lab, trying to turn old gum into a new material. Everyone thought she was 'mad and a little bit disgusting' at the time, but:

> ... from getting it to make a foam, [she] was able to make a used-gum pellet; then ... she extracted a polymer that she calls BRGP (Bullus Recycled Gum Polymer). This is the substance she uses to make the pink bubble bins now dotted around Orpington College, where they're being trialled as gum-specific litter bins. When the bins are full, both bin and innards are recycled into new BRGP, which in turn become more bins and possibly other products, too.[10]

Although not usually taken to the same extremes as Anna Bullus did, recycling has become something of a trend, as has self-sufficiency. Keeping chickens is now commonplace in urban gardens, with the Eglu hen house turning into a runaway success for its inventors – and for good reason:

> It looks like a cross between an iMac screen and a giant Lego brick as it sits in a city backyard ...

until one chicken pokes its beak out of the Eglu's bright red door and another comes strutting out. A 21st-century plastic henhouse for urban gardens, complete with two organically reared hens, the Eglu is the invention of four Royal College of Art graduates. The company they founded – called Omlet in honour of the 10,000 fresh eggs a week laid by Eglu chickens – allows the coop's owners in British towns and cities to flirt with basic self-sufficiency. [11]

Omlet now provides Eglus for ducks and for multiple chickens. Its website offers courses on poultry, beekeeping and other kinds of self-sufficiency. Keeping chickens has also encouraged people to develop vegetable plots, as they can feed any waste to the chickens, whilst allotments in towns are in huge demand, with long waiting lists.

The recession of the late 2000s made people much more careful with money of course. The Green movement also exerted an influence, with many of us looking to be green and economical. The concept of 'Staycations' became common in 2009 and shows no sign of diminishing in popularity. Similarly, more people took up baking and knitting, with companies such as Lakeland and John Lewis reporting increased sales of bakeware and haberdashery. Meanwhile, the department store John Lewis republished what it calls a 'modern reworking' of the famous 1943 government booklet on making the most of minimal resources: *Make Do And Mend*. It includes such tips as freezing leftover cake until you have enough for a trifle, or setting central heating controls economically. There were no freezers for our grandparents in wartime, and not much central heating, but the idea is the same.

The original World War Two *Make Do And Mend* booklet has been republished by the Imperial War Museum and is described as: 'a delightful reminder of the techniques for household economies extolled by the wartime government'. There are old-fashioned remedies for everything from washing silks and mending clothes, to repelling the 'moth menace'![12] A modern equivalent might include dusting the element on the back of the fridge to save energy, shining shoes with the inside of a banana skin, and stopping ladders in tights with clear nail varnish (an old schoolgirl trick I remember from the 1960s). The museum's booklet sells well, which is no surprise: the interest today in saving and living more conscientiously is palpable.

And these things matter. We should not waste resources, whether water, energy or food. The knowledge that we throw away vast quantities of food when much of the world is starving or hungry offends me as much now as it did when I was a child and forced to eat everything on my plate because of 'the poor starving Russians'. Admittedly, I still do not quite get that particular connection: my growing even fatter would not help the Russians. But cooking less, serving smaller portions and not wasting food seems to me as sensible now as it did to my parents and grandparents; it's curious that it has taken us so long to realise that their values of 'waste not, want not' were the right ones.

We need a conscious moral response to scarcity and waste today; and we need to understand how to live differently from the way we live now – hence the significance of the messages of the Green movement, the increasingly green messages of mainstream politicians, and the growing awareness of the fragility of the earth's resources amongst the young.

Just as it is worth doing a spiritual spring-clean every few years, in my view it is well worth doing a physical audit of our possessions every decade or so, to see what can go and what needs to stay, and to force ourselves not to acquire more and more stuff accompanied by less and less joy.

To return to the old man whose flat was crowded with possessions that he planned to leave to his friends and family, I believe that we need to re-examine our attitudes to the inheritance we intend to leave behind us. My mother always said, 'Better to give with a warm hand than a cold one' – and I think she was right. Perhaps there is something in the Hindu concept of *sannyasa* – of getting rid of all our possessions, bar a few necessities, before we die – and we should be asking ourselves what the Western equivalent would be. Would it mean to get rid of our possessions? Would doing so be a mark of consideration to those who otherwise would be left to sort out our belongings once we are dead? As the situation stands, one in four of us may have to go into a care or nursing home, which means leaving most of our possessions behind.

Perhaps we should develop a new ritual whereby we shed physical possessions in older age (bar those which bring comfort or are necessary), if only in order to lighten the physical and mental load we bequeath to others when we are gone? Surely it is better to give lovingly while we are alive, than at our death. And maybe doing this in the guise of a ritual, as a normal thing to do at a particular stage of life, would make us feel less of a fundamental sense of loss (as my refugee grandparents felt when they left their lives in Germany), and would represent a way of coming to terms with older age; of finally accepting the fact that we cannot take our possessions with us when we die, and that everything around us is finite.

CHAPTER 9

SUFFERING AND LOSS

The deep pain that is felt at the death of every friendly soul arises from the feeling that there is in every individual something which is inexpressible, peculiar to him alone, and is, therefore, absolutely and irretrievably lost.

Arthur Schopenhauer (1788–1860)

Autumn 1999, West Cork, Ireland: a friend lost her husband to heart disease. He had been ill for a long time and survived many heart attacks. But that year he died and she found herself unable to cope. Her house was in turmoil, an outward expression of her inner pain. There was stuff everywhere and she began to press his old clothes, his tools, his belongings on to all comers. She could not talk rationally, and didn't even know the day of the week or the date. This was no early Alzheimer's. This was the effect of unbearable grief, of not knowing how she would manage, of fearing life alone and an even greater fear of living with relatives. This was a dread of having to deal with bills and managing all the everyday things she had always let him do, such as drive. Her life had been turned upside down. Although she learned to cope and to live again, she was never as easy in herself as she had been before her husband died. But the complete chaos caused by her grief during those first few weeks became an object lesson to me.

If we only ever look at the positive things in life, we will deny a very large part of what gives life its meaning, however much we would prefer to gloss over those aspects. Acknowledging the things we hate, rage about and fear is part and parcel of realising that life, albeit short, has much to offer that lies beyond our expectations. By virtue of simply being alive, we will need to face the truth that most of us will experience loss in one way or another – for the nature of life means that the story goes on, and us with it, although often in ways we would have hated to predict, and which we would rather not have to face. Nevertheless, when we do experience loss, we often find that we do not want to die imminently, however terrible our lives may now seem to us to be. Moreover, the process of learning how to cope with suffering and loss can help us grow as individuals. At best, it might inspire us to give something back to those in our families and social circle who have also experienced suffering.

For there will always be suffering in life. Suffering goes with the territory of being human and often involves loss of some kind, whether the loss of dreams and hopes, or the loss of loved ones. Loss can take many forms: the deaths of parents or older siblings, failing to get a longed-for job, loss of face, embarrassment, even loss of reputation. And there will be (unless we die young) loss of looks and life expecta- tions as we face the narrowing horizons of old age.

Despite increasing evidence that older people are happier than younger people, many of us reach a point – usually in our mid-forties to mid-fifties – when we reach a low in the form of a midlife crisis or the so-called male menopause, and we realise that many of our dreams and aspirations are simply never going to be realised. We are never going to be the chairman of the bank or run a four-minute mile. We are not even going to finish that PhD or travel to Africa as a volunteer. Somehow, the majority of us (but not everyone) will learn to deal with that loss of hope and aspiration, to turn the corner and become more content with our lot. We find that we are satisfied to be the assistant manager or the clerk, to travel only as far as Calais from London, Boston from New York, or from one Sydney suburb to another; we no longer dream of roaming the world or running a huge company. But, although we eventually turn that corner and become happier, this also has to do with loss – and the loss of dreams is often very hard to cope with.

Take, for instance, a friend of mine who was widowed many years ago: now in her early sixties, she has finally realised she is not going to meet another soul mate. Her hopes and aspirations for a second happy marriage are unattainable, and she must cope with the loss of her cherished ambition to set up home with someone new and beloved. She will be entering old age alone.

Or take the acute pain and yearning loss of infertile couples, desperate for children, who hope each month that this time, maybe this time, she will be pregnant. And then she is not. And there follows the long round of consultations and treatments, of cycle after cycle of IVF which fail despite all the drugs and the stimulation to the ovaries: just imagine the sense of loss and anguish that this couple, longing for children, must feel as they walk down the street and see parents out with children to whom they barely give a second glance, or may even mistreat.

And then there is the loss caused by illness, from the temporary and distressing hair loss experienced by some of those undergoing cancer treatment, to facial disfigurement, the loss of a body part or the loss of looks not through the normal process of ageing but through disease or treatment, and the loss of expectations and aspirations that ties in with this. Depending on the nature of their treatment, these individuals may fear that they will never work again, that they will never be able to have children or never even be sufficiently desirable again to form new partnerships.

Loss hurts us in many ways throughout our lives. While it may sometimes be expected, such as the death of an elderly parent, there is also what might be called 'abnormal' loss. This involves loss that is unexpected, particularly hard to face or unbearable – although most of us do somehow manage to bear the unbearable.

There is the loss of a child before the parent dies: an unnatural order of events, as these days we do not expect to lose our children, but expect to go to our graves in chronological order. Such a loss can come about through illness or accident and feels unnatural, hard, impossible to deal with – an experience from which we are unlikely to recover. However, our Victorian forebears had no choice but to deal with it, as infant mortality was so high during that period. Similarly, our ancestors who lived through the 1914–1918 Great War, and the worldwide flu pandemic that followed it, had to live with this sort of loss too. It changed our ancestors for two or three generations, making it impossible to speak of death thereafter, yet equally impossible to face the reality of traumatised young men returning from battle with shell shock, a condition that often went unrecognised or poorly treated. Here, loss often meant not the death of a loved one but the disappearance of the person he once was.

Today, unless we have been caught up in warfare or acts of terrorism, our losses are more likely to be of a domestic nature – but painful nevertheless. The loss of reputation, for instance, can be so great that it may lead to an unwillingness to face the world and even to suicidal thoughts. Or there is the pain that a loss of position can bring, as evidenced by the look of deep sorrow on the face of the outgoing UK Prime Minister Gordon Brown in May 2010, as I was working on this book.

Loss of appetite, hearing or sight can all impact on our lives. A loss of taste sounds relatively insignificant but it can be terrifying when it occurs, particularly when is accompanied, as it usually is, with a loss of smell, so a person can no longer tell if his food is rotten or his flat filled with gas.

And then there is the loss of memory, of mind, of the capacity to cope – a very topical subject given our ageing population in the West. A terrifying sense of panic and loss must accompany impending dementia as a person becomes aware that she is losing her memory and her mind – and is completely unable to do anything about it.

∞

So, whoever we are, we will inevitably need to face, endure, live with and accept suffering and loss in our lives. We cannot push loss away, nor pretend we live in a fairytale world where suffering does not happen. However, we can prepare for loss by being tough with ourselves and by training ourselves physically and mentally to meet it. And we can also prepare ourselves by being gentle, understanding and kind to ourselves, and by being generous-spirited and supportive towards others. Both approaches – clinical tough-mindedness and sympathetic gentleness – can be helpful, even in combination: the cold showers and warm fire approach!

We don't have to enjoy living with loss (although some people, masochistic souls, find in the strangest of ways that they do). But we do need to learn how to deal with it, from learning to cope with grief to learning how to deal with other forms of loss in which the normal grieving processes don't seem quite appropriate or effective. For while society sanctions our grief for someone who has died, grieving – and certainly ritualising the grief – for someone who is still alive with, say, severe dementia, is more difficult. In this instance, while we may experience the loss, we cannot put an end to it until the person actually dies.

Some religious traditions say that suffering is good for us: it ennobles the spirit; we can learn from the experience of suffering. And various Christian paths have argued that suffering brings us closer to the sufferings of Jesus on the cross, and therefore closer to God. There are those who argue that, through suffering, we learn how each of us depends upon the other: suffering teaches us that we fall to pieces by ourselves. As we suffer, we may also learn patience – the true meaning of suffering – and discover that material possessions are not much help when we are in this sort of crisis.

They also say – and I believe there is something in this – that suffering, like death, strips away the differences of class, status and degrees of importance that human beings have created for themselves. Suffering is a sort of elemental emotion. It may mean that those who are supportive and who know how to get through the pain in order to offer help are not our close friends, but people from different walks of life who somehow know what it is to suffer, and how the right comforting word might assuage the intensity of our pain. In some respects, then, suffering is an experience which offers insights into humanity.

All the same, I think we have to challenge the idea that suffering is ever good for us. It is just a part of life and we learn from it as we learn from other things. Mostly, what people might gain spiritually through suffering is not the product of the suffering itself – and I think the majority of liberal Christians would acknowledge that. Instead, we gain from our own efforts, from discovering how to deal with pain, changing our former perceptions in the process, and learning to depend on others for support and comfort.

Indeed, a more general argument that people can gain spiritually from indiscriminate suffering seems to me to be really cruel. How can anyone say to someone who lives with a major disability, or to person who has just lost a loved one, that there is any benefit to be gained for them through suffering? Patently, there is not. We have, I believe, to stick to the view that suffering is not 'good' for people, and is in fact positively bad for the majority of us, although there may nevertheless be a few people who can gain new spiritual insights and other perceptions from suffering. But that is by virtue of their hard work and the support they receive from others – and not a straightforward 'gain' that comes of the profoundly miserable experience of suffering and loss.

As we have seen, suffering is an integral part of the human condition; as Tennessee Williams famously said: 'Don't look forward to the day you stop suffering, because when it comes you'll know you're dead.'[1] But how we deal with suffering remains a genuine test of our strength of will and endurance, especially when we can't 'fix' the situation. It is also a test of self-discipline and character, of our determination to keep going and achieve not only our own ambitions but also those things that the person whom we have lost –

to death, dementia or permanent disability – would have wanted for us too.

As we will all face suffering and loss; thinking about how we will cope with the hard times, and learning how to do so, is an essential part of preparing to live a better life in general. And a simple way to begin to prepare is by making a list of the things which it would be really important to us to have accomplished in the face of prospective loss. We can use this as a means to measure ourselves, ticking off those things we have achieved or could still manage to achieve in however long is left either for ourselves or for a dying loved one. Such a list represents a way to ensure that at least the loss of aspiration is no greater than it has to be.

Suffering, however dreadful, can also be an experience that makes us feel fully alive – although anything but happy. Real suffering is extremely painful and the sensations very marked. We can't ignore them; it's not like being mildly depressed, when we may allow life to go by in a blur. Here, we really feel pain, often physically: sickness, nausea, pins and needles, headaches and stomach aches are amongst the most common physical symptoms of grief, along with extreme tiredness and a sense, when waking up in the morning, of having had no sleep. Alongside those physical symptoms there is an awful sense of longing – for the clock to be put back, for the person to reappear, for all the things we resented about them to be washed away.

Often, when I speak to people who have been recently bereaved, they tell me about the things that irritated them about the person who died. Women, for instance, may complain about their late husband's snoring. But I must have heard on a dozen occasions or more how much those same women, ready to throttle their men while their snoring kept them awake, now long for them to be lying in bed beside them, snoring – and still keeping them awake!

I've mentioned before how my mother used to say to me, as I rushed about trying to sort things out for her in her final years, 'Take it easy!' It used to drive me mad. As if, working full-time, looking after her and my family, I could take it easy … And yet now I find myself saying the same thing to my children. I can even hear her voice when I do – and how I wish she were still here to say those words to me again. For part of grieving is the wish for things to be different; grief is full of the 'might have beens' and 'should have dones', full of regrets about impatience and bad behaviour – full of all the things we wish we could now undo, too late.

People tend to experience grief in their minds, bodies and spirits – it is as if there is no part of us that is not transformed by grief. My colleague Jonathan Wittenberg has written of this experience most movingly and accurately, in my view, in *The Silence of Dark Water*:

> Everything in the outside world can be seen and touched; the shops, the street, the room, the mug of tea, the photographs, they are all right there, exactly as they were before. But a strange invisible layer clings to the heart and wraps itself around the mind. Though not impermeable, this curtain alters whatever passes through it; inside is a different atmospheric pressure. Sounds echo and clang. The most ordinary physical sensations feel strange. One stands up and tries to walk; it is as if gravity itself has become unreliable. Time doesn't function in the way it used to do. The semi-silent humming of the air is filled with the

> vibrations of tremendous shock; the ordinary
> daylight makes no sense, this simply cannot be.
> Inside the invisible membrane, the waves of sight
> and sound founder in slow motion. But the hours
> remain implacable and the calendar irreversible;
> the world refuses to be tugged back to where it
> ought to be.[2]

That longing – the wish for the clock to be put back, the sense that everything is out of kilter, everything topsy-turvy – is absolutely what people describe to me as they try to define the texture of their grief and loss.

But, however awful the experience (and it truly is awful), loss can make the good times feel very good in contrast. It can teach us that we need to celebrate the present moment, emphasising the philosophy of *carpe diem* – seize the day, because we have no idea what tomorrow will bring.

And there are many different ways to ritualise loss that can help us come to terms with it. Most faiths and cultures have set ways for dealing with grief when someone has died. Some traditions bury or cremate the body very soon after death, whilst others wait a few days or even weeks. Some cover mirrors, light candles or prepare special meals. There are even particular phrases to be used in greeting the bereaved: 'I'm sorry for your troubles,' as the Irish say, or 'I wish you long life,' as Jews in the UK say. Some put flowers on the grave, whilst for other traditions flowers are completely unwanted and wrong. Chrysanthemums are the flowers of funerals in Italy, whilst in the UK they simply mark the arrival of the autumn. Depending on our cultural and spiritual heritage, we may express our grief by wearing black, white or purple, by fasting, eating or even being fed because we do not have the wherewithal to cook for ourselves.

Grief is a natural human reaction. Even if we are the one who is actually dying, we will grieve: this well-recorded psychological phenomenon is not entirely dissimilar to the emotions experienced by the bereaved. It is a process of extreme pain, with all kinds of attendant emotions – and there is no way out of it. We must grieve after a death of a loved one if we are to emerge on the other side.

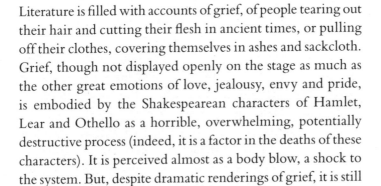

Literature is filled with accounts of grief, of people tearing out their hair and cutting their flesh in ancient times, or pulling off their clothes, covering themselves in ashes and sackcloth. Grief, though not displayed openly on the stage as much as the other great emotions of love, jealousy, envy and pride, is embodied by the Shakespearean characters of Hamlet, Lear and Othello as a horrible, overwhelming, potentially destructive process (indeed, it is a factor in the deaths of these characters). It is perceived almost as a body blow, a shock to the system. But, despite dramatic renderings of grief, it is still something that people in contemporary Western society are expected to keep hidden and private in ordinary life – even when it feels virtually impossible to do so.

And I think we should challenge this prevailing attitude. Personally, I come from a tradition in which mourning within the community is expected and encouraged – and brings comfort. The Muslim, Sikh, Hindu, Italian and Irish Catholic communities all do similar things, bringing people together, feeding them, allowing them to talk about their loss. There is a communal response: everyone is expected to turn out and give support. Having seen the benefits of this type of response, I feel there is a real imperative for us to change the Western secular idea that the bereaved should cope with their grief privately, behind closed doors, in silence. This is a sorry state of affairs that, collectively, we ought to be able to influence and change. And, if we are able to achieve this, we will truly have learned from loss: we will have invented a communal response, with a shared sense of responsibility for the welfare of those grieving. As a society, we will have discovered the ability to talk to bereaved people and thereby help them to learn from their own experiences, enabling them eventually to help others who are undergoing the same experience.

Today, there is an immense amount of literature concerned with the processes of grief and mourning, much of it written to help society learn how to deal with death again and talk openly about it, having failed to do so for much of the century following World War One. However, the cycle of grief was first explained fully by the Swiss psychiatrist Elisabeth Kübler-Ross in the 1960s.[3] She held a seminar at the University of Chicago where she considered the implications of terminal illness for patients and for those involved in their care. Her accounts of people's attitudes to grief are recorded in her book *On Death and Dying*, in which she suggested that there are various key stages through which someone is likely to pass when coming to terms with his or her own death. These are: Denial and Isolation, Anger, Bargaining, Depression, Acceptance and (some have added) Hope. Kübler-Ross originally listed Acceptance as a stage almost 'void of feeling' (rather than happiness or relief) near the end of the cycle.

In the fifty years since Kübler-Ross published her ground-breaking work, other scholars and observers have tested her theories. Among them, British psychiatrist Colin Murray Parkes has argued, 'Others might (and probably will) adopt a different terminology when describing the phases through which the dying person passes in the course of his illness.

Since individual variation is so great, it is unlikely that any one conceptual system could be applied to all.[4] As Murray Parkes suggests, many people's grief does not follow the whole of this clearly prescribed pattern.

Nevertheless, I think that the concept of stages of grief does help us understand what is going on. The idea of a cycle of grief also helps explain the need for the dying and bereaved to have the time and space in which to think, contemplate, explore loss and say their goodbyes. It is therefore very helpful to those who are dying and who want to think about how to do it well, as well as to those who are caring for them such as family or close friends.

Since anger is the first reaction that many of us have to the news of an impending death, we need to think about how best to deal with this emotion. Unfortunately, anger can lead to a degree of dishonesty within family relationships, as the spouse who experiences anger on first hearing about the impending death of his or her loved one may subvert that response into a form of denial: 'I don't want him to get any more upset, dear', or 'I cannot go through that ill-temper again, dear ...' It's a natural response: we are facing loss – our own life or someone else's very dear to us. But nevertheless dishonesty is surely to be avoided, for who wants the precious last few days, weeks or months of life to be a period of lies and false smiles, truths told behind hands in corridors or on draughty staircases? Surely learning to live with loss means learning to be honest about it too, particularly as, after the anger, acceptance comes to most of us; and, with acceptance, we might be able to talk honestly and openly about what things we can still do together or separately with whatever remains of our lives.

Those close to a person who is dying will do some of their own grieving whilst that person is still alive. If we are to be completely honest with each other, it is ideal if we can grieve together. For the experience of grief is universal. As we have seen, it is a completely normal response to the loss of a person, a period of life, a part of oneself, even an object. But if we are dying, all our losses come together at the same time, encapsulated in the impending loss of life itself, and the loss of everything that has ever meant anything to us.

Loss through bereavement is a crisis in which our whole previous equilibrium is upset, just as my colleague Jonathan Wittenberg's description suggests. Our normal responses are inadequate. Our behaviour may become very unpredictable and lead us, later on, to embarrassment at the upset we think we have caused. In this period of crisis, the various other phases or stages of grief are often evident: numbness, shock, and partial disregard of the reality of the loss; a phase of yearning, an urge to recover what has been lost; a phase of disorganisation, despair, and gradual coming to terms with the reality of the loss; a phase of reorganisation and resolution. All this can lead to a sense of shame as we find ourselves transgressing the rules of our 'normal' everyday behaviour and, although grief usually includes one or other of these phases, there is, of course, no universal way of providing help to those going through it, other than to show understanding and support.

Individuals also vary in how long the acute stage of their grief lasts. For some people, it will continue for a long time, or never really be completed; whilst for others it seems to progress gradually without the need for professional intervention, except for a sensitive listening ear on the part of family and friends. The phases of grief often overlap and are sometimes repeated in different ways and in different contexts. C. S. Lewis's collection of reflections, *A Grief*

Observed (1961), is a personal and painful description of his own bereavement which illustrates this:

> Tonight all the hells of young grief have
> opened again; the mad words, the bitter
> resentment, the fluttering in the stomach,
> the nightmare unreality, the wallowed-in
> tears. For in grief nothing 'stays put'. One
> keeps on emerging from a phase, but it always
> recurs. Round and round. Everything repeats.
> Am I going in circles, or dare I hope I am
> on a spiral? But if a spiral, am I going up
> or down it? [5]

The play and film *Shadowlands* is based on *A Grief Observed* and tells the story of Lewis's relationship with the American author Joy Gresham, who became his wife but was to die from a terminal illness. In the film, there is relatively little about their early love for each other, perhaps because Lewis had been such a confirmed bachelor until he became involved with Gresham. But when it came to depicting the loss forced on them by the cruel cancer which destroyed her, then the picture of grief was a real and terrible one. It encompassed the emotionally and physically agonising pain of loss and the impossibility that Lewis certainly felt in trying to comfort her sons from a previous relationship, whose grief was perhaps even greater than his own. Such representations are important, for they can sometimes be better than words at explaining the grieving process, as they have no qualms about showing the intensity of pain.

We all have to go through grief at our own pace, allowing time for anger, dealing with the pain, reminiscence and exploring some of the emotions that it is so necessary for us to go through. If we are grieving, then others around us may have to be helped to understand this process, and to give us the time and space we need. For grief can neither be rushed nor denied. And if we are helping those who have been bereaved, we may find that they need us to give them permission to weep, or simply acknowledge that a particular reaction – be it of anger, resentment, loneliness, relief – is entirely normal. For it usually is. People who are dying, who are about to be bereaved or who have lost someone, need reassurance: they need to understand that what they are going through, albeit horrible, is entirely normal.

However, we can never get our support for others, or the process of living with it ourselves, wholly right. We can only get it less wrong. Grief is painful. It is lonely, soul-destroying, difficult, depressing. What we can do is support people through the normal stages of their grief, encourage them with the thought that they are not alone, and nurse them into a more normal life, whereby they will be able to live with their loss perhaps a year or so after the bereavement.

And we can encourage them to mark the first anniversary of the death, as some faith groups do, using it to consecrate the tombstone or memorial as Jews do, or to say a particular memorial mass – whatever is appropriate. The anniversary does not need to be a formal religious event, but acknowledgement of the anniversary is very valuable, and makes people feel (at least in one way) that the first acute stage of grief is past. We do not forget; but we can carry on with normal life more easily after the first birthday, the first Christmas, the first set of significant dates, have been passed.

Nevertheless, some of us will find it hard to acknowledge death in the course of our daily lives. There are those of us who have a tendency to lose ourselves in activities, which means that we avoid facing the reality of the loss. Some people's denial takes the form of 'mummifying' the deceased person's room or belongings, which is why I think we should make sure we start dealing with the dead person's possessions as soon as possible. The normal weeping most of us do over a scruffy pair of shoes or a disliked jacket can be very therapeutic. Facing the loss of the person by immersing ourselves in their belongings also helps us come to terms with the loss of aspiration – both for them and for ourselves – which their loss has brought about.

The later phase in grieving, of acceptance and of gradually coming to terms with the loss, can be delayed or prevented altogether if the bereaved person withdraws completely from their friends and family. Many bereaved people, and particularly widowed older people who have problems in getting out of the house, can become reclusive. But that is no way to live with loss, and becoming reclusive may stop us finishing the normal journey through the stages of grief. However, the opposite can happen too: when a grieving person becomes over-dependent on others and develops a hopeless, irresponsible helplessness, so that he or she is apparently not fit to be left alone for even five minutes.

All these are reactions that we may experience ourselves or see in others. Living with loss means being clear that, sometimes, we cannot go through grief on our own. Sometimes, we will need professional help. And needing professional help to support us through bereavement is not something of which we should be in the least bit ashamed: we have taken a body blow. Going to the doctor about a broken bone does not seem abnormal. Why then when we have had a metaphorical body blow, with its physical and emotional symptoms, should we worry about seeking help – particularly given that specialist bereavement counsellors have a deservedly good reputation these days?

While it is absolutely normal to go through all sorts of emotional adjustments in the process of coming to terms with bereavement, there are some particular circumstances in which we may need to make adjustments that are not absolutely run of the mill. This applies especially after physical traumas and in certain sorts of illness, when people often experience difficulty in coming to terms with a change of body image such as a loss of leg, arm, vision or hearing. Similarly, those who have been involved in accidents, and find themselves left with only a few days or hours in which to live, may worry intensely about what will happen to the family left behind. They often want to try to plan for their family and friends from 'beyond the grave' as it were – to make sure everything goes according to plan when they are gone, as if somehow their unexpected death could possibly be slotted into any kind of plan and be normalised.

As I mentioned in the introduction to this chapter, dying out of turn – child before parent – brings with it particular problems, because it just all seems so unbearable. Here I am thinking of elderly parents sitting at the bedside of their terminally ill only daughter, who will leave behind motherless children and a father with whom the parents do not get on too well. Another scenario is the case of elderly parents who find themselves by the deathbed of a much loved son, who leaves a wife and children – and too little financial provision for them. Or there are the parents of the twenty-year-old who has been in a terrible accident; or the teenager who has untreatable myeloid leukaemia.

The list of tragedies goes on and on. But what is significant is the fact that these 'out of the correct order' deaths have a particularly powerful effect on our families. We can accept, albeit unwillingly, that a spouse will die as we get old. As middle-aged children, we know we will lose elderly parents. That is the way of the world. But the death of a child or a younger sibling, the death of a friend at a young age – somehow these are less acceptable, therefore less absorbable and less tolerable. They lead to a sense of cataclysmic loss. The reaction is even more agonised than that of other forms of bereavement, for the pain is not only of our loss, but of injustice as well. In these circumstances, the pain of not knowing how to cope can be overwhelming.

So how should we cope? In Judaism, one of the ways we deal with a death is by burying the person very quickly, giving those who are bereaved no time in which to stop and think. At the funeral, the sound of shovelled earth landing on the coffin lid brings home what has happened to the mourners. For, unlike common Anglican practice, with a few crumbs of earth being scattered into the hole, Jews and Muslims literally bury their dead communally. The chief mourner puts in the first spadeful of earth, with the other mourners following suit. The separation of the dead from the living is very clearly marked by what is a brutal, but useful, tradition. There is no hiding the finality as you hear the lumps of clay descend. At a cremation (now the form that more than half of funerals take around the Western world) the sight of the coffin sliding away through double doors, or a curtain coming round to hide it from view, can provide a similar effect.

So a funeral, if properly planned and carried out, can be an important part of the grieving process. It provides a formal and ritualised context in which the strong emotions of grief, which we all share, can be appropriately and publicly acknowledged; and in which those who have been bereaved can be helped by the whole community, who are there to provide support as well as share in their grief. For that is what we need in order to come to terms with loss.

When the well-known cartoonist Mel Calman, Deborah Moggach's partner of ten years standing, suddenly died at Moggach's side in a cinema, she wrote about her experiences in *The Times*.[6] She described the support of friends, who rang for a chat and to see that she was all right, who came round clutching a bottle of vodka and lunch, who filled her empty fridge. She said that she was asked all the time if she had hit the bottle yet and explained that she couldn't because every time she stretched out her hand towards it the phone rang. Meanwhile her sister stayed over at night, slipping away in the morning, and friends visited to talk about Mel.

That kind of love and friendship has to be right. Social networks, our friends, neighbours and families, have in the end to be our prime sources of support. We have to remember everything that has ever been said about the disadvantages of retired people moving away to live in places they do not know – and where the local people do not know them. This sort of relocation in old age is not a good idea for most of us: if one part of a couple dies, for example, the other will be left isolated. Far better to stay in the old home, in the old area, and to know that, when the time comes and we need help, it will be there.

For old friends, family and neighbours tend to come up trumps. In the first eleven weeks after my father died in 1996, there was not a single day when somebody did not ask my mother out or come to visit her – quite apart from the support that her family offered her. The role of our personal support networks is never as clearly defined as during bereavement, and often springs into action when someone is dying.

Whether a family has traditional bereavement rituals or not, the value of their wider social network and the fact that today people are increasingly willing to talk about the dead and offer words of comfort is to be greatly welcomed. It is now comparatively rare for people to cross the street when they see a bereaved person coming because they are embarrassed and do not know what to say to them. Much more often, they will say something along the lines of: 'I'm sorry for your grief.' They will send a sympathy card or a condolence letter, writing in it that they will be in touch – and then they truly will be in touch.

Our attitudes to bereavement have changed for the better in recent years. But, even so, I believe that we need to describe the mourning process more, support it more and perhaps even institutionalise it more than we do at present. For, if we can make sure that we both give and receive it when the time comes, the support that we can offer each other through a loved one's dying and after death is probably the best action we can take to cope with loss and help others face loss, too.

But the support we offer each other is not always perfect. There are often heightened tensions after a death, and families can be tense and unforgiving institutions. Some family members will just not know what to do, while others will want to talk about wills, money and possessions, with all the rows and arguments that can accompany this. The resulting tension may be unintentional, but it makes the grieving process even more challenging than it has to be. It can be very hard to deal with these sorts of situation; in my view, the best advice is to face them down, calmly and politely: 'I know you are very upset, but I don't think this is the time to talk about the will/the house/the silver, the things she did that you so disapproved of. Let's just sit down together, remember her with pleasure and tell funny stories about her.' For talking and remembering together can offer real comfort and allow the bereaved, or those facing the loss of their possibilities and aspirations, to feel less alone.

As we have seen, each person experiences the cycle of grief differently. Similarly, we process our loss in different ways. When my father died in 1996 and six other people who were close to me died in the space of ten weeks, I took to gardening. There was something about the texture of the earth, the fact that I was making things grow and, yes, stopping them from dying, which felt curiously therapeutic.

As a rabbi, I had done my training in bereavement support and I knew the stages of grief that I might go through. However, I had not read much about gardening as a mechanism for dealing with loss. I had not expected nor anticipated in any way this utterly primeval urge to get my hands in the earth. I have no idea – and psychiatrists and psychologists could probably spend hours debating this – whether there was a curious primeval link between gardening and the fact we had just buried my father in the earth, shovelling great lumps of clay on top of his coffin.

My father had been a keen gardener and I tried for the remaining five years of my mother's life to sustain his pride and joy – the brilliantly planted mini-garden on the balcony of their London flat, where my father had created a riot of colour and even produce in a space of about three foot by ten! I wanted to keep their balcony garden going for his sake, for my mother did not really care.

But digging my own garden was different. I do like gardening, but it is not the passion it became for my father in his later years. Yet dig and shovel, weed with a passion, hack and trim, tie back and split, is all I did. I spent hours in the garden, finding a curious kind of solace, a sense of inner peace amid the turbulence caused by my anger at my father having left me (he and I were very close) and my frustration that he had left my mother in my care.

I gardened my way out of the intensity of grief, and thought I was alone in the experience until I was having lunch with two friends who had lost parents at the same time. Both are even more unlikely gardeners than I am, yet they described how they too had spent every opportunity during the first few weeks, when not with the surviving parent, hacking and strimming, weeding and digging. We laughed at first, but then realised it was a phenomenon.

Much more recently, Catherine Horwood has written about how women have been doing this form of gardening for generations: 'gardening has always been a source of solace to women ... Mary, later Duchess of Beaufort, having been widowed ... at a young age, sank into a deep depression. She had ... "gone almost into a mopishness with melancholy".'[7] But then she started gardening, and built up a collection of exotic plants which became the envy of every horticulturist in the country! And Horwood describes how she herself took to gardening when her mother, a really keen gardener, developed Alzheimer's and started to neglect her previously cherished garden. But she adds that she would have been reaching for the antidepressants had she not tilled and pruned like a fiend, and that working in the garden somehow kept her in touch with her mother, whose mental absence caused her deep distress and led to a profound sense of loss.

It could be gardening, making bread or physical exercise that helps us cope with loss. It could be sorting through the dead person's clothes, or washing the dead person's body (which is done in faiths such as Islam and also in many secular hospices today). It could be painting, or rejoicing in the countryside: it could be any activity that helps us personally cope with our loss.

In her book *If The Spirit Moves You*, Justine Picardie writes movingly of working out on a treadmill on the Good Friday after her sister Ruth died aged just thirty-three in 2000, leaving two small children.[8] Justine describes how she feels heartbroken, but the treadmill is 'supposed to be good therapy, and sometimes it works'. Hard exercise. Thinking, working out – and a year later some kind of calm, some kind of accommodation.

Our communities and our faiths (if we have one) have their own rituals for coping with grief and loss, of course. But we often need more. Not only to talk, although that helps, but also to be active, to use our hands, our hearts and our heads in such a way as to connect with the world around us and assuage our burning grief. We should think too what we can do to lessen the grief of others when it is our turn to die: what kind of legacy we can leave behind that might help them to cope with the loss that we all have to face.

CHAPTER 10

LEAVING A LEGACY

*What we leave behind in this life is the memory of
who we were and what we did. An imprint, no more.*

Kate Mosse, *Labyrinth*

A friend in her hundredth year is writing her will. She
has already written one that divides up her possessions amongst her family and friends. She has even
written a letter of intent for her children to follow, which
lists small bequests – a favourite piece of jewellery here or a
treasured book there – for various friends and carers who do
not get a slice of the major bequests. And now she is typing
away at what she calls her 'moral last will and testament'.

She is concerned that her children should know how,
over the years, she has changed her mind on issues such as
homosexuality and gay marriage, the cap on immigration
(she thinks it should be removed), on women working and
looking after their children (she does not think it is possible
to do both well), and music (she has taken to liking jazz in
the evenings). What she wants her children to know is that
she does not believe it is a sign of weakness to change one's
mind. Indeed, it is a sign of strength. It is only the fear of
being thought weak that prevents intelligent people from

changing their minds more often, on the basis of evidence. And she wants her children to read this for themselves in black and white in her last moral will. She also wants them to use every moment of their lives to good purpose.

'Do Jews believe in an afterlife?' she asks me.

'Well,' I answer, 'Orthodox Jews say daily that they do, but all of Judaism is predicated on the belief that it is what you do in this life that matters: you leave a legacy, your memory lives on, you have "an afterlife" in how you are remembered for what you did.'

'I like that,' she says, as a deeply unobservant Jew. 'I'll tell them that.'

And she did.

When I was studying to become a rabbi, I became absolutely fascinated by another sort of 'moral will' – more precisely Jewish ethical wills. I came across a series of documents written by rabbis in the mediaeval period and later to their children and descendants. There were similar documents amongst the Muslim and Christian communities at that time.

These were not wills as we now know them – about money, possessions, property and dividing things up. These ethical wills made for fine, if sometimes eccentric, reading. They instructed their children on when to read particular religious books, and when to think about getting married. They told them to look after their mothers and their sisters. They warned them to beware of dishonest traders and always to give the benefit of the doubt to people who came begging. And they tried to sketch out what a good life might be. They represent a lovely custom, as parents try to sum up in them all that they have learned in life, expressing what they most want for and from their children. The letters were a precious legacy, because the parents believed that the wisdom they had acquired was just as much a part of what they wanted to leave their children as any material possessions they could pass on.

Studying the ethical wills, I puzzled from time to time about whether we could turn that kind of thinking into something more modern and applicable to people facing death today. I was talking to a friend who is a hospice nurse when I mentioned in passing that I'd been reading a particular ethical will by a seventeenth-century rabbi; she said that the idea reminded her of something that terminally ill young women, usually dying of breast cancer, sometimes put together for their children. They create boxes filled with objects of purely sentimental value which they want to pass on to their children, who they will never see grow up. Alongside the objects, they place letters in which they describe the things that have meant so much to them – beauty, art, helping others, books – and of course how much their children mean to them and how they were the apples of their eye ... In the letters they also often suggest how their children might want to live, given that they – their mothers – will not be there to guide them through life.

It's almost unbearably painful to hear young women talk about doing this, said my friend. But the value of preparing such a box, of leaving it for the children for when they are older, is enormous. It helps the mother cope with the loss of her children's future and it helps the children, when older, learn a little more about the mother they never really knew or can barely remember. Although it is heart-rending for both mother and child to realise what they did not know of each other, it brings some comfort. Although it can only offer a taste of the mother's personality, values, passions and love, it is nevertheless of immense value.

Before she died of breast cancer, Ruth Picardie also created memory boxes for her two-year-old twins. I mentioned Ruth's sister, Justine Picardie, in the last chapter on grief; Ruth was also a writer: she was a columnist for the *Observer* newspaper for five weeks before she died, recording what was happening to her. Her sister Justine and her husband, Matt Seaton, turned her writings into a book, *Before I Say Goodbye.*[1] It is almost unbearably moving, but it makes the point forcefully about the value of leaving some sort of ethical will for children to enjoy.

The letters in the memory boxes that she left to her two-year-old twins are published in the book; to Joe, she says, 'You are as musical as an angel,' and advises, 'Always enjoy your music – I played piano (grade 7 failed) and cello, string quartet and orchestras.' To Lola, she notes: 'You love clothes! Same here! Your godmother Big Lola will take you shopping at Harvey Nicks! So will Joe's godmother, Lizzie!' Finally, she says to both of them: 'You were the best thing that ever happened to me and Daddy and the hardest thing to let go.'

Memory boxes are also put together by young parents dying of AIDS-related illness in Southern Africa. The boxes are often simple: a discarded shoebox painted in bright colours with food dyes, with a bit of favourite material inside to remind the child of the parent who has died; a couple of trinkets; and, most importantly where possible, a note about the family. Indeed, the memory boxes are often used by the grandparents who take over the children's upbringing to tell them about their family history, and to place the lost parents in some sort of context.

There are elements of this desire – to understand who we are in relation to our families – in the current interest in tracing family trees and discovering distant ancestors. The fact that our forebears often did not leave us anything inspires us now – in the internet age – to go looking for them and find what their legacy was, to unearth the non-material legacy of people we may never have met or even known existed.

It is not only learned rabbis or young parents who are about to die who feel the need to leave a moral legacy. Some years ago, on the Jeremy Vine Show on BBC Radio 2, I took part in a discussion about children and young people who were facing untimely deaths. A young woman of fifteen phoned in and talked about how she was trying to prepare her mother and her sister for her own impending death. When she spoke, there was no anger, no bitterness, but a strong awareness that preparing them and leaving something for them in the form of a letter or box of cherished things was something she wanted to do for them, when they had expended so much love and care on her. And a few weeks later, after her death, her mother and sister came into the studio and talked about what her preparations had meant to them, and how she had helped them face her death. Her thoughtfulness before dying showed immense wisdom and courage for such a young woman.

After my own mother's death, I was very moved to find a short note that she had written and put amongst her emergency money, thanking both my husband and myself for being so good to her during her last long illness. The fact that, in extreme pain and sadness, she had bothered to write the note meant a great deal to me, as did her instruction that we should continue to add to her picture collection (which was actually too vast for us to manage). It was an ethical will of a sort, but also just a simple yet heartfelt thank-you letter, and very dear to us because of that. And maybe her little note is as good an example – so kind, so generous, brief and memorable – as any of the longer and somewhat bossy ethical wills to be found amongst the rabbinic literature.

And yet I remain very fond of the ethical wills of the mediaeval rabbis. Some make me laugh and others make me cry. I love, for instance, the very lengthy ethical will of Nathaniel Trabotti, an Italian rabbi who died in 1658, as recorded by his disciple, Samuel Belgradi.[2] Trabotti's will is a bit different from a simple letter written in private. He actually gathered the leaders of his community around his deathbed to dictate this testament, and his disciple Samuel Belgradi wrote it down later on. But the idea is the same:

> I am now eighty-six years of age, no more can I
> go and come in your midst as I have done from
> my early youth … I have wronged none, but
> have tried my best to maintain union among you
> all small and great, so as to prevent scandals in
> your midst. Be gracious to me, my friends, and
> let your prayers be made on behalf of my soul,
> and I on my part will never cease to pray for you.

There's a bit of self-justification there, to put it mildly, that perhaps a modern ethical will would not need. He carries on by giving them a bit of a bollocking, to put it not too politely, something some of us might be all too tempted to do in such a document! 'Many a time and oft,' he said to them:

> … as I went about I heard the idle talk of
> gossiping women, who stood in the crossroads
> doing their work. They would croak like the
> frogs in Egypt while uttering the name of
> God and these doings were like needles in my
> flesh. I desired to suppress the fashion, but for
> various reasons was unable to translate thought
> into act. I do now order that any instance be

reported forthwith to the Rabbi and the latter
shall prevent the continuance of the nuisance.
Similarly I impose the same rule against men
who waste their time in gaming houses, playing
at dice and amusing themselves with cards,
which they always carry in their pockets. Let
them desist from their habit of using the Name
of God in vain. Woe to them, woe to their souls,
woe to their latter end! I call heaven and earth
to witness that they must perish under the dire
wrath of God unless they mend their ways.

Gossip, cards and blasphemy – nothing new there then, not
to mention his slights against women! But nevertheless this
represented his final attempt to get his community to think
about behaving a bit differently.

Trabotti's represents one kind of ethical will, calling on
the whole community. But there's another kind altogether,
which appeals to me for other reasons, in which fathers try
to get their sons to do things in a certain order, such as read
particular books that fit their increasing maturity. If he is
not already on track to do what is said in the letter, the son
is likely to be racked by guilt and confusion.

A famous letter written by Judah Ibn Tibbon (1120–
c. 1190) to his son Samuel is an example of this type of will.[3]
In it, he berates his child over and over again, reminding
him how much he has done for him; and he ends with the
instruction that his child should consult this will regularly,
as if it would make welcome bedtime reading!

My son, list to my precepts, neglect none of my
injunctions. Set my admonition before your eyes;
thus shall you prosper and prolong your days in
pleasantness! … But you, my son! did deceive

my hopes. You did not choose to employ your
abilities, hiding yourself from all your books, not
caring to know them or even their titles. Had
you seen your own books in the hand of others,
you would not have recognised them; had you
needed one of them, you would not have known
whether it was with you or not, without asking
me; you did not even consult the catalogue of
your library...

Let your countenance shine upon the sons
of men; tend their sick and may your advice
cure them. Though you take fees from the rich,
heal the poor gratuitously; the Lord will requite
you. Thereby shall you find favour and good
understanding in the sight of God and man ...
My son! Examine regularly, once a week, your
drugs and medicinal herbs, and do not employ an
ingredient whose properties are unknown to you.
I have often impressed this on you in vain ...

There are many more different kinds of ethical will. The
tradition dates back to the Bible, when Jacob gathered his
children round his bedside and told them how to live after he
was gone; and when Moses instructed his people before his
death. David prepared Solomon before he died by warning
him whom to be wary of when he became king, and by
asking him to complete the task he had begun.

Later and into modern times we find these sorts of ethical
will become increasingly common. I have in my possession,
thanks to my friend Willie Kessler, a facsimile and translation of the book his grandfather Bernhard Kessler (who
got out of Vienna in time to escape the Nazi occupation)
gave him on his bar-mitzvah in April 1940.[4] It is in the

same tradition: 'If ever anyone does you an injustice, do not practise revenge! Show your mettle, however heavy your heart. For only love, truth and justice will prevail! Do not, therefore complain and do not sin ... Everything in life comes at the right time! ... I often feel my heart will break! But I wait patiently for God's judgment ...' At the end he writes: 'I wrote this booklet on the typewriter which your dear father gave me for my sixty-ninth birthday on the first of August 1939. I did not, however, write it in great happiness, but rather in anguish and heartache, in fear and agony of mind. For to me the present family circumstances of my beloved children are intolerable.' Yet he had already told Willie to make no enemies – and to visit his grandmother's grave in Vienna, despite the circumstances surrounding both Bernhard's refugee life and his family's uncertain future.

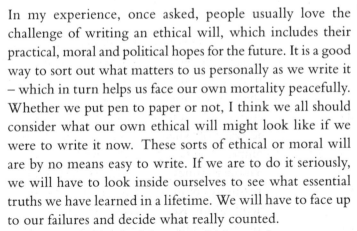

In my experience, once asked, people usually love the challenge of writing an ethical will, which includes their practical, moral and political hopes for the future. It is a good way to sort out what matters to us personally as we write it – which in turn helps us face our own mortality peacefully. Whether we put pen to paper or not, I think we all should consider what our own ethical will might look like if we were to write it now. These sorts of ethical or moral will are by no means easy to write. If we are to do it seriously, we will have to look inside ourselves to see what essential truths we have learned in a lifetime. We will have to face up to our failures and decide what really counted.

There is a school of thought which says that, no matter what we do, we are part of all we have met (and they of us). The message from this way of thinking is that we don't have to do great things for our contribution to matter, as in a way everything matters. Tennyson's poem 'Ulysses' makes this point very well and offers an inspirational call for us to make the most of life:

> I am part of all that I have met;
> Yet all experience is an arch where through
> Gleams that untravelled world, whose margin fades
> For ever and for ever when I move.
> … Life piled on life
> Were all too little, and of one to me
> Little remains: but every hour is saved
> From that eternal silence, something more,
> A bringer of new things; and vile it were
> For some three suns to store and hoard myself,
> And this grey spirit yearning in desire
> To follow knowledge like a sinking star,
> Beyond the utmost bound of human thought.[5]

We are all part of everything and leave our mark, however great or small we were, however memorable or otherwise our lives. No need, then, to leave greatness behind, but simply a good life in which we made a difference, even if that difference cannot be measured or recorded.

An ethical will offers a chance to reflect, to think about what we want to say as a last message to our most beloved people, and then to craft something special – with a little humour and perhaps a measure of self-awareness so that it is neither too smug, nor too fierce to be a bearable read. For these wills should give pleasure and joy, as well as instruction. They should be letters of kindness as well as of acquired wisdom. And they should make the recipient feel that they were written just for them.

While writing an ethical will can teach us a great deal about ourselves, it is likely to beg many questions too. Are we only going to be kind? Or should we follow the example of the mediaeval rabbis and be highly critical of our children? Is it going to be a last-ditch attempt at retaining control from beyond the grave, or a means of encouraging our children to be the best at whatever it is they want to be? Will we thank our children for all that they have been for us, or simply tell them what we want them to do next? If you write an ethical will, you will need to think about how it might be received, and whether your kindness will be more of a corrective to your children, should they go astray, than if you were to leave them a rebuke from beyond the grave.

It's important not to underestimate the value of leaving such a letter to our descendants about what mattered to us and what we think they could profit from in our experience. Not only is there value to us in the actual experience of writing it, but it may also be valuable to those who read it when the time comes. Whatever emotions they stir up, it is clear that ethical wills have an impact. Therefore, it must be right for us to recreate this tradition for our time – not just for Jews but for everyone. If we did, I truly think we would achieve something important – and that the next generation would gain considerably from our efforts.

In a short radio series for the BBC's World Service a few years ago, I asked several well-known people to put together an ethical will. I wanted to know what they would like to say to their children, if they had them, or to the next generation more generally. The politician Shirley Williams said that she would like to create a garden for her daughter and grandchildren as part of her ethical will, as she believes peace and a sense of meaning can be found in these spaces. Her thoughts will resonate with many of us; after all, although we plant gardens for ourselves they are also for the benefit of generations to come – for people whom we will never know, and who may have no relationship with us other than through enjoying the space we have created.

Planting slow-growing trees, for example, represents an act of faith in future generations, and is also a form of legacy. I am reminded of a wonderful story about New College, Oxford:

> After the giant oak beams in the New College's great hall rotted out, the Dons of the college were at a loss to source replacement oak timbers of sufficient size. The college forester came to the rescue – it turned out that when the New College was built, 500 years previously, the Dons of the college had planted oaks in Oxford's forest. Now, 500 years later, they were ready to be harvested and put into service in the great hall. The modern-day Dons thanked the forester, chopped down the trees and sold the forest.[6]

The discovery of lost gardens, such as at Heligan in Cornwall, is part of that same quest to unearth forgotten legacies.

In the same BBC World Service series, I spoke to the Reverend Calvin Butts, minister at the Abyssinian Baptist Church in New York and one of the people responsible for the regeneration of Harlem. He argued that the only section of an ethical will that really matters is the instruction to our children to put their hearts and souls into doing whatever they really believe in, and making the world a better place. That applied to his children, of course, but also to the next generation more widely: his was a general message for the future.

Our hopes for the future can be difficult to explore without sounding trite and clichéd. After all, it is hard for us to know what sort of world our children will be living in. Ethical dilemmas may arise for them that we cannot dream of. So Calvin Butts' request that children make a commitment to building a brighter future, without specifying exactly what that might entail, seems about right. Just how they achieve this must be for them.

These days there are issues of sustainability, of ensuring the whole world has enough to eat, and of protecting the environment, so it is challenging for us to imagine a future that does not include a notion of fairness and justice. But it cannot be for us to lay down the law about how to live in a world we will not inhabit. In leaving a legacy, we ought to be wary of imposing our own moral judgements on others (which is why I so like the idea of my centenarian friend telling her children that it's fine to change their minds!).

However, Ros Levenson, a friend who helped me with the research for this book, makes an interesting point. She reasons that if we are presently building towards a brighter future in the hope that our children will do the same, it follows that we cannot just give up as older people. We must vote for governments who will plan improvements that we may not be around to see; we must support developments now that may only yield fruit when our grandchildren or great-grandchildren are old – such as space exploration and other forms of scientific endeavour, which may yield results beyond our present dreams.

This sort of legacy requires us to become involved in decisions that may not necessarily affect us directly; it goes beyond an ethical will, although it has links with it. It is about making decisions now which will affect future generations. Indeed, some would argue that having more than two children – our physical legacy in human form – is in itself selfish, as over-population will inevitably do great harm to the planet: if we are concerned for the future of our earth, a decision about how many children we bring into the world should be of paramount importance.[7] So perhaps we have to make an ethical gesture in this respect too, as well as through writing an ethical will for those offspring we do have.

In a sermon he preached at a major ministers' conference in 2008, Pastor Jim Feeney made similar points to those made by my friend Ros. He argued that we can – and indeed should – have an impact upon others that outlasts our lifespan on this earth: 'Following certain biblical principles, you can leave a legacy, a spiritual inheritance, that will affect the lives of others for all eternity.' He opened his sermon by discussing the ways in which politicians approach leaving a legacy:

> Presidents speak of leaving a 'legacy' when
> their term is done. You hear expressions like:
> 'President Clinton's legacy is …' or 'What will
> President Bush's legacy be?' These expressions
> are referring to the impact that their presidency
> will have upon future generations. I wish to
> speak today about leaving a spiritual legacy, a
> spiritual inheritance, for those who come after
> us. Passing on to the next generations a legacy
> with eternal value is far more important than a
> temporal inheritance of money and property …
> Leave a legacy of good deeds, of acts of kindness,
> of loving service wherever you go.[8]

Such a legacy is a tribute to our hopes for the future.

And there are other forms of legacy which seek to hand on our present hopes and beliefs to our descendants. In a curious set of internet blogs called 'faithbooking', Donna Riner Weber asks: 'What will happen when you are no longer here on Planet Earth? Maybe you've taken care of a will so that your material possessions will be distributed according to your wishes but what about the spiritual part? Those experiences that happened to you – will they die when you pass on?'[9] She encourages her readers to share those experiences, which include acquired knowledge, wisdom and faith. She writes: 'It took me a long time to understand that God wants me to tell my son and grandchild the stories of how God has been present in our lives …'

Churches and individuals are latching onto the general concept behind 'Scrapbooking your Faith' or 'Faithbooking.' In some respects it is similar to composing an ethical will, in that it is about leaving a 'spiritual legacy – for the love of your family' (to quote Riner Weber) and is often created by grandparents for grandchildren. But, to my mind, it is as much about telling the story of our own lives in new ways as it is about leaving children guidance on how to live their own lives.

Indeed, the University of Southern Maine runs their Life Story Center website which encourages people to tell their own stories. The website instructs its readers: 'Leave Your Spiritual Legacy'. It continues: 'Our story is who we are. All that will remain of us after we are gone is our story. Stories connect us to our roots. Our stories contain our common spiritual heritage. They are also our legacy for future generations. All we are is the story we leave behind.'[10]

After all, a legacy is all too often thought of as something tangible, something material that we have worked hard to achieve. We leave it in a will to our family or friends, to our community, church or town. We may leave it as something that testifies that we were here – 'this is the bench he gave to the city', or 'she donated this picture to the gallery'. But our legacy can be more than this.

According to the Life Story Center website, a legacy is first and foremost: 'who we are at our core. What becomes more and more important as we age is the desire to be known …What might be one of the saddest things is to leave this earth without those you love the most ever really knowing who you were.' The site suggests that we tell our life stories as a feat of spiritual endeavour, which leads us to the heart of who we are and what matters to us most of all.

Of course, the authors of the website are right that story-telling holds a unique power. It is not for nothing that professors of ethics the world over now use story as a means of evoking the main messages that they want to convey in a particular situation. Today, the practice of using literature to teach medical ethics is commonplace, as it is in the way that situational ethics is taught in universities.

Stories matter – and, as we face the end of life, our own stories matter hugely. We should all consider how to use those stories to help others, as Randy Pausch did in his 'Last Lecture' (see Chapter 1). The experience of passing on our story can be immensely empowering and give others a deeper understanding of what matters to us. Put simply, it entails writing our own life story as a form of ethical will: it is about what matters, who we are, what we want for those who live after us. If we are not quite ready to tell our own stories yet, perhaps we can help others to do so.

I nevertheless think that we need to reflect deeply on our reasons for leaving a legacy of any kind. Is it simply that we wish to be remembered after we are gone – a sort of 'Dido's Lament' from Purcell's opera *Dido and Aeneas*, with that plangent aria singing over and over again, 'Remember me, remember me ...'? If so, presumably we will have to achieve something pretty amazing if we are to be remembered more widely than by our immediate friends and family. They will remember us for the texture of our personal relationships with them, but, beyond that, we will need to leave a mark of some kind on the world – and many of us experience the urge very strongly to make an impression that shows we were here.

The majority of us do want to leave something behind – to mark our lives when we go. I wonder whether the desire to leave a legacy stems from the fact that we cannot, in our bones, bear the idea of simply being no more – of being gone. If our remains are cremated, perhaps there won't even be a place that can be visited by those who wish to see where we lie? Is this desire to make an impact and leave a legacy about a search for immortality? Or is it an attempt to pass on that which has given our own lives meaning? For, as we prepare to leave, many of us will work out more clearly what really matters to us and cut out the dross.

The evidence throughout history suggests that our ancestors also felt strongly about leaving a legacy. Roman buildings often have the names of their builders carved into the stone; architects from all eras have left their mark on some aspect of the houses they've designed; traditionally, builders might sink a coin into the mortar; and sometimes even decorators today will inscribe a little something under the wallpaper.

This practice of making a mark reminds me a little of

the way that time capsules reach out towards the future. Filled with items designed to tell generations to come a bit about who we are now, time capsules can take many forms, from the homemade to the likes of the one buried at the BBC studios in the Blue Peter garden many years ago; or the time capsule containing a stash of Puffin Books which Kaye Webb, inspirational head of Puffin Books in the Sixties and Seventies, organised at Penguin's old headquarters in Harmondsworth, or those sent on space missions.[11] In a sense the form matters not: it is all about leaving a legacy of a kind, however strange it may seem to those who come after us.

I mentioned in Chapter 8 the citrus juicer that I inherited from my parents and which my father repaired time and again. Every time I look at it, I think of my early childhood when my most common words to my father when he returned from work were: 'Daddy, repair!' Even the sorts of everyday items that are unlikely to be listed in a last will and testament can carry memories. I still use my father's stapler (even if it's a bit rusty). I still wear my mother's scarf. This, like many other inherited items of clothing, retained the smell of its previous owner for a few years, bringing back vivid memories – a form of legacy in how I remember her.

We might also leave a legacy based on our work: the pictures we have painted; the books we have written or edited; the things we have made, and even – as one friend has done – the food we have loved. My friend with terminal breast cancer cooked up a storm in her last days before she finally took to her bed. She left a freezer and larder full of stews and casseroles, jams and chutneys for her family and friends. There are many different ways to leave a valuable legacy, of which an ethical will is just one.

I have mentioned earlier my own delight in creating things. Of course there is a limit to how many cushion covers or pots of jam anyone can make and give away, but there is nevertheless something especially gratifying in the act of passing on a creation made by your own hands – especially in this deskbound age. While jam does not last, something sown or knitted, or a personalised photograph frame or hand-decorated tray, could become a form of durable legacy, as are mementoes such as recipes, recordings and photos in a different way.

Those of us who work – or, like myself, play – at making practical things are creating a form of legacy. My friend Ros Levenson tells the story of her neighbour's funeral: 'He was a carpenter and the vicar said something like, "Most of us here have part of John in the work he did in our homes" – and everyone nodded as indeed, we had. That was nice; I still think of him when I use the bookshelves he built. They are part of him.'

There are other legacies in the act of remembering too. Ros Levenson continues: 'Just the other day, I went to a local fête which was a bit retro, and it reminded me strongly of going to the funfair with my dad, which we used to do every year when I was a child … the best way of leaving a legacy may be to live life fully and joyfully, as that leaves behind memories that cascade down the generations.' Absolutely. And every time I see the now rather sad-looking fair on Hampstead Heath at Bank Holidays – or come across a similar funfair – I think of my father too, who took me regularly to the fair, where he had the unenviable task of taking me down the helter-skelter, which I loved but he found terrifying. Of such stuff are memories made, and those memories are a kind of legacy from parents to children, and beyond, in how we are remembered.

As we have seen, there are many different ways to leave a legacy. Ethical, spiritual wills could form part of the answer, as could the act of telling our story in one form or another. Having witnessed the confusion of those who do not know their heritage – who may be adopted, foundlings or otherwise confused about their identity, and who struggle to find their roots, I believe that we ignore the need to know who we are and to pass that information on to future generations at our own peril.

And there are our physical possessions too. Although not all of us have children to whom we can leave our belongings and consign the future, most of us nevertheless feel a sense of obligation to the future generations who will inhabit the earth. Bearing this in mind, I am drawn once more to the writings of Maimonides, the great Jewish philosopher of the twelfth century whose eight-tiered theory of charity I mentioned in Chapter 4. I wonder if we could make use of his theories today, when considering how to create legacies? Here are some suggestions of my own, based on his principles:

- The lowest order of leaving a legacy would entail leaving things to our own children if we have them, or to our nearest and dearest if not. This would be for their future betterment, but perhaps also to control what they do.
- The second order would involve giving to those we love, such as friends and other family members, as an act of generosity – and also because there's a clear connection.
- The third order of legacy would mean leaving money to charity – with our name firmly on the bequest, and with some kind of control

over what the money is used for, such as not for administration purposes.

- The fourth is the same, but uncontrolled, for a cause in which we believed during life.
- The fifth is to give anonymously, but in the same way.
- The sixth would entail giving in such a way that it benefits generations long after we are dead and forgotten. It could take the form of planting trees, buying pictures for the nation, or another public-spirited gesture.
- The seventh would be to leave a legacy to someone unknown, in such a way that they will never need to ask for help again – just like the intention in Maimonides' highest orders of charity.
- And the eighth is similar, but would mean giving anonymously, with there being no idea who the recipient is and the recipient having no idea who the giver is: a legacy to be proud of.

In spite of the various forms that a legacy can take – such as an ethical will, generous bequest, or lovingly crafted bits and pieces – some of us will be remembered for none of these. We will leave unwritten legacies through our acts of kindness, through those small private gestures as well as public acts which can change the ways in which the people around us live, think and act. This sort of legacy may not be celebrated and may indeed pass unremarked, but it will nonetheless allow us to approach our graves in the certain knowledge, in our hearts, that we made a difference whilst we were here on earth.

If we are to leave this sort of legacy we will have to

prepare in advance. We may wish to include a charitable donation in our will, or, if necessary, even set up our own charity if there is a cause which we particularly want to support once we are gone – but it is the way in which we live our lives that will ultimately determine the nature of our legacy. We have to lead our lives well, here and now. In true Boy Scout and Girl Guide fashion, we have to 'be prepared' in order to face death peacefully.

CHAPTER 11

FACING DEATH

Today, you have sent a messenger of death to my door.
Carrying your invitation, he has crossed the ocean and
*   come to this shore.*
Today, the night is dark
and my heart is anxious with fear.
Yet, with a lamp in my hands,
I will open the door and greet him humbly.

From *Naibedya*, 'Dialogues with the Lord of the Heart',
by Rabindranath Tagore (1861–1941)[1]

A while ago, I visited an old friend who was in her early seventies and dying of breast cancer. She told me that she was determined to plan her own funeral down to the very last detail, including exactly who should be there. I remonstrated. 'It's up to them to decide whether to come, not you,' I argued.

But she was having none of it: 'I'll decide who comes and who stays away. I don't want my ex there, but I do want my children. I don't want the grandchildren to be there, but I do want my friends. I'm giving you a list and you can see to it!'

I really didn't want to accept the task; after all, funerals are not for the dead but for the living. And yet she was focusing on something that so many of us fail to do: she was looking her impending death in the eye, dealing with it, planning her funeral (and her memorial service, and her tombstone consecration), and she wanted her friends to help her make sure it would all be as she desired. And in the end it was.

In the late twentieth century and early twenty-first century, those of us living in Western countries are often reluctant to look death in the eye. Despite the fact that the countless images of dead bodies we see every day mean that many of us have become almost inured to depictions of death (on TV, in computer games, in magazines and films), most people have never seen a real dead body. Nor will they have given much thought to their own death or the prospective death of their family members or friends. Yet it is almost a truism to say that facing death needs to be done while we are still young enough and healthy enough to give it real thought, including what we want to achieve before we die, and give some context to our lives.

 ∞

Of course we all know we will have to die one day, however much we may try to avoid the subject. The proverb 'nothing is certain but death and taxes' has a particular fatalism about it. Despite tax avoidance schemes, and indeed advances in cryopreservation techniques, the truth is that we all end up paying taxes and we all die. Death is a certainty, which is why faiths frequently remind us of it in their liturgies and theology.

The Christian burial service, for example, makes the nature of death abundantly clear: 'Man that is born of a woman hath but a short time to live, and is full of misery. He cometh up and is cut down like a flower; he flieth as it were a shadow, and never continueth in one stay.'[2] We have only a short time to live, says the service and indeed other Biblical sources say much the same: 'In the midst of life we be in death ...' If that is not a reminder of mortality, it is hard to know what is. Similarly, in Judaism the funeral service includes the prayer 'What is Man?', which is a collection of verses from Psalms and which has much the same message:

> O Lord, what is man that You regard him, or the
> son of man that You take account of him? Man is
> like a breath, his days are like a passing shadow.
> You sweep men away. They are like a dream;
> like grass which is renewed in the morning. In
> the morning it flourishes and grows, but in the
> evening it fades and withers. The years of our
> life are threescore and ten, or even by reason of
> special strength fourscore; yet their pride is but
> toil and trouble. They are soon gone, and we fly
> away. So teach us to treasure our days that we
> may get a wise heart ...[3]

There follows an instruction in the prayer to value our days and look for forgiveness.

The message is not very different to that in Christianity or, for that matter, to Islam, which, like Judaism, regards this life as being a preparation for the world to come and for eternal life after death. Islam suggests that those who deny the truth of this simply become the slaves of their passions and desires, and realise their folly only at the time of their death. It is only then that they beg to be given a further chance in this world, to no avail: 'Until, when death comes unto one of them, he says, "My Lord send me back, that I may do right in that which I have left behind!" But nay!

It is but a word that he speaks; and behind them is a barrier until the day when they are raised …' (Qur'an, 23:99-104)

In Islam, Allah (God) is thought to be the creator of life and death as in Judaism and Christianity: 'Blessed be he in whose hand is the kingdom, he is powerful over all things, who created death and life that he might examine which of you is best in deeds, and he is the almighty, the forgiving.' (Qur'an 67:1-2) And in Islam, as in the other two Abrahamic faiths, the wise person is conscious of his mortality: 'A man from amongst the Ansaar (People of Medina) stood up and said, "O Nabi of Allah! Who is the wisest and the most resolute amongst people?" He replied, "He who remembers death the most, and prepares most diligently for death before it overtakes him. Undoubtedly, these are the wisest. They have acquired the nobility of this world and the dignity of the Hereafter."' [4]

Hinduism and Eastern faiths which believe in reincarnation take a different view, but the requirement to think about our mortality is no less pressing. Hinduism argues that we have four stages in our lives, of which the final one, that of the *Sannyasi* (the renounced one in full retirement), is about facing death. Traditionally, men used to undergo *sannyasa*, or renunciation, during which they would leave home with nothing but a begging bowl, and prepare for their inevitable death.

In Hinduism, there is the awareness that: 'In one sense, the whole of life, with its various stages and *samskaras*, is a preparation for death and beyond.' [5] During *sannyasa*, the preparations have physical implications; a person should even sit in a particular way: 'Having reached the last order of life, one should sit in a solitary place in a relaxed posture, with pure heart, with head, neck and body straight, controlling all the sense organs, having bowed with devotion to the

248

master.'[6] This advice could, arguably, be influenced by yoga positions such as the posture adopted in order to meditate properly. Those undergoing *sannyasa* are also advised: 'Having studied the Vedas in accordance with the rule, having begat sons according to the sacred law and having offered sacrifices according to his ability, he may direct his mind to final liberation' – the ultimate goal of death.[7]

Buddhism is equally directed towards thoughts of death as liberation and a journey. The present leader of Tibetan Buddhism, the Dalai Lama, has explained that his daily meditation involves preparation for death. Some Buddhists study death to the extent that they even rehearse how to behave at the moment of passing. In *The Tibetan Book of the Dead*, there are several scenarios presented for the dying process. The practitioners have to be mentally and emotionally prepared at the time of dying, so that they can reincarnate to the higher and better realms in the next rebirth.[8] The process of dying is in itself an opportunity for spiritual liberation if – and only if – the mind is calm. In fact, *The Tibetan Book of the Dead* can act as a guide to passing through the state of being that intervenes between death and the next rebirth. It is read aloud to the recently deceased, so that the departed's soul can recognise the nature of the mind and attain liberation from the cycle of rebirth.[9] It is yet another ritual to link the experience of reading aloud, and of creating sound, to a form of meditation, although this time it is for the benefit of the dead rather than the living.

Sikhs also believe that immortality (*amarapad*) is the ultimate objective (*paramartha*) of life. But Sikhs are always aware of the biological reality that everyone is going to die. Even the prophets have no immunity from death, and mortality reigns over the realm of the gods as well:

Death will inevitably strike

Even in the land of Lord Indra

Nor is Brahma's domain free from it.

Likewise is Lord Shiva's world decreed to
   come to naught.[10]

All these different faiths share the view that life is short, that death needs to be prepared for, that this life is some form of preparation or anteroom to the next life or After World – and that the living need to reflect carefully on their mortality.

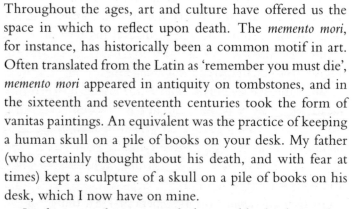

Throughout the ages, art and culture have offered us the space in which to reflect upon death. The *memento mori*, for instance, has historically been a common motif in art. Often translated from the Latin as 'remember you must die', *memento mori* appeared in antiquity on tombstones, and in the sixteenth and seventeenth centuries took the form of vanitas paintings. An equivalent was the practice of keeping a human skull on a pile of books on your desk. My father (who certainly thought about his death, and with fear at times) kept a sculpture of a skull on a pile of books on his desk, which I now have on mine.

In drama and art around the world, death is often paired with fear as well as reflection. The Danse Macabre, or Totentanz, is another part of the Western tradition. It probably originated as a late mediaeval allegory on the universality of death: the Dance of Death tells us that we must all die and thereby unites us. Some argue that its roots lie in the endless horrors of the fourteenth century with that period's recurring famines, the Hundred Years' War in France, and, most of all, the presence of the Black Death. These factors were culturally assimilated throughout Europe into a realisation that death was everywhere. It represented a religious response to mortality, expressed as a desire for penitence.

But the Danse Macabre is also partly satirical, as illustrations of it often show the dead or the personified figure of Death summoning representatives from all walks of life to dance to the grave, typically including a pope, emperor, king, youngster and labourer, sometimes in a chain of alternating dead and live dancers. From the highest ranks of the mediaeval hierarchy descending to its lowest, each mortal's hand is taken by a skeleton or an extremely decayed body. In the Middle Ages, there was also an almost hysterical desire for amusement while still possible, so this last dance became a form of cold comfort. Darkly humorous, unsettling, and in many ways similar to the mediaeval mystery plays, the Danse Macabre reminds us of the inevitability of death and advises us to be prepared for it at all times.

Similarly, the legend of 'The Three Living and the Three Dead' was widely painted in church frescoes. This is the story of three young gentlemen who are out enjoying a ride or hunt when they meet three cadavers who warn them: '*Quod fuimus, estis; quod sumus, vos eritis.*' What we were, you are; what we are, you will be.

In *Don Giovanni*, Mozart's opera of 1787, there is also a moral undercurrent when the statue of the commandant whom Giovanni has murdered becomes the harbinger of death. The stone guest refuses to eat with Giovanni: 'He who has sat at a heavenly banquet does not break the bread of mortals ...' But his huge stone hand closes upon Giovanni and he asks him to repent. Don Giovanni refuses and is consequently dragged down by demons to a nasty end. Here death is represented by a dead man who returns to take his murderer back with him. Similarly, in Noël Coward's comedy *Blithe Spirit*, the dead return to take the living away.

The idea that death is the ultimate equaliser can be found in contemporary culture too, although film and TV's standard depiction of a still body, sprawled on its front after a violent end, does not usually make us afraid. Indeed, it could be argued that the portrayal of death in modern culture is anything but designed to make us afraid: it is about computer games, about 'extinguishing' lives on screen and about a single hit in a round of bullets in a movie. Or it is about the frankly unbelievable deaths meted out in horror movies, when strange outlandish creatures come to get us.

Today, the only realistic pictures most of us will see of death are those shown on the news or in charitable appeals, when strangers die from starvation, in wars and genocides, or in terrorist incidents. However, the imperative of the phrase *memento mori* – 'remember you must die' – remains as present in what we witness through the media and in our religious teachings as it does when captured through the imaginative world of art.

In December 2008, Sky filmed the death of Craig Ewert, a retired university professor from Harrogate, Yorkshire.[11] Ewert had travelled to Dignitas, an organisation in Zurich that helps people to die, because he did not want to spend the rest of his days in a 'living tomb'. When the programme about his death was broadcast, it met with considerable criticism from anti-euthanasia campaigners and television watchdogs, although it had been made with his consent.

Perhaps the outcry was because, today, we believe that death should be kept private, not part of everyday experience. Although we seem drawn to the ghoulishness of horror movies, to rubber-necking at road fatalities, to the fantasy as well as the real world of gun culture, many of us believe that the normal processes of death and dying should be kept out of sight, behind closed doors at home, in a hospice or hospital. And yet death is a part of all that we are.

∞

There are many different notions about what death is, where – if anywhere – we go afterwards: from a firm belief in an afterlife, through a hazy sense that this life may not be all there is, to the view that it almost certainly is.

Many years ago, my father, a Reform Jew, spent a few days in intensive care in hospital. When he emerged and was placed on another ward, he was looked after by a lovely young Irish Catholic nurse. They got talking and it transpired she had been a patient in intensive care a few weeks before my father, having suffered an allergic reaction to an injection. She was quite convinced that she had glimpsed heaven during that period: it was shining and white, she could see a cross on the wall and, to cap it all, her grandmother was there – so she knew that's where she was. My father, meanwhile, said the ward hadn't been like that at all: it had been grey and shadowy, with shady figures flitting about, dull and soundless, a bit like the Jewish idea of Sheol, the destination after death.

Laughing, the nurse pushed my father in a wheelchair over to the intensive care ward to look. They peered in. Neither was right! The walls were greenish in colour – with staff in green gowns flitting about. While it was anything but shady and silent, it certainly wasn't white or shining either. Each of them had in their deepest psyche a view of what the afterlife was – and which they had seen in intensive care – only it wasn't this place!

I tell this story because I think it is important to realise how conditioned we are by our expectations. Jews and Muslims, alike in their view of the value of human life, have traditionally been astonishingly affirming of this life. They share a belief in a somewhat hazy afterlife (perhaps better developed in Islam than in Judaism), which is why some of their adherents might find it hard to be enthusiastic about modern ideas on what constitutes a good death, with adequate pain relief which may, by the so-called double effect, shorten life slightly.

Yet these days all of us need to be enthusiastic about dying well. We need to know what to expect and what to be wary of. Besides preparing ourselves for the undeniable fact that we are not immortal and will die, we need to consider how we want to die. For otherwise we risk dying in degrees, suffering to no purpose. It is this that has led to strong calls for assisted death, from forms of euthanasia in which health professionals give a fatal injection to their patients, to physician-assisted suicide when terminally ill people in some jurisdictions are given the wherewithal to take their own lives.

My colleague and friend Rabbi Tony Bayfield wrote an extremely moving article six years after the death of his wife Linda from cancer. Called 'Why Preserve Life with No Meaning?', in it he made the point that, had Linda not died when she did, he would have helped her to go. She had said the first line of the *Shema* prayer, the line Jews say before they die, and told him she had had enough.[12] He had no doubt that there was no point in Linda's suffering any longer – and she thought it too.

In the article, Tony also made a point that few campaigners for euthanasia make properly in my view, which is that: the 'ability to prolong life has brought with it many benefits, but it has also brought with it largely unforeseen consequences – the many ways in which we can keep people alive beyond the point where that life has any meaning either to

the person dying or to those around them'. Precisely. There
has to be a moment when medical interventions should stop.

There is a point at which the number of days left can no
longer be a valid goal in itself. The time comes when dying
well and going peacefully into that 'good night' is the goal
to be desired. And, although this is not the place to discuss
euthanasia or assisted suicide in depth, the call for such intervention occurs when people feel that they are being kept
alive when life itself no longer holds any meaning for them.

In her superb analysis of our attitudes to youth and quality
of life in her book *The Denial of Aging*, Muriel Gillick asks
why the idea of dying by degrees or 'dying in bits' has come
about. She suggests that today, given most people's increased
life expectancy, there is a reluctance to accept that being in
our eighties and nineties means that we are really old:

> Centenarians have something important to
> teach. Often they have wisdom arising from
> their accumulated experiences which they enjoy
> sharing, and which they are able to share because
> they aren't burdened by multiple maladies.
> … Their world is the antithesis of the elderly
> community in Florida, which has developed a
> culture that revolves around their health. The
> average elderly Floridian sees multiple specialists,
> often making more than one physician visit each
> week … In parts of Florida … Medicare spends
> more than twice as much per capita for health
> care as it does anywhere else. What its citizens
> get in exchange for this largesse is more hospital
> days, more tests, more ICU admissions, and more
> subspecialty consultations in the last six months
> of life, with no evidence that the additional
> attention improves the quality of care.[13]

In many cases, it seems that the wrong things are being done for the wrong people – albeit at their request, because of their fears of dying or their belief that they are immortal. Gillick continues:

> Centenarians have another lesson for us as well. The usual claim is that centenarians remain robust until a catastrophic event occurs, at which time ... they collapse completely. Centenarians are different from other people in that the aging process has been postponed ... But there is no reason to believe that their organs are programmed to fail simultaneously. The reason the centenarian dies from his pneumonia or his heart attack is that doctors do not aggressively treat their 100-plus-year-old patients – they do not routinely admit them to the intensive care unit, place them on a breathing machine, start dialysis, or initiate any of the other interventions that are commonplace in octogenarians. Centenarians die quickly because we let them, and the 85-year-olds die slowly because we don't.

In light of this, I believe that we need to discuss more frequently and openly with our families, our doctors and nurses, and in the public domain, just what kind of death we want, and, more particularly, what treatment we do not want if it is offered to us.

There are many wonderful examples of people who have died exactly where they've wanted to. Most of us would like to die at home, but there are a few of us who want to die in our gardens or on a beloved boat, for example. In my days as a congregational rabbi, I was involved in helping a family enable their beloved father to fulfil his wish and die amongst the irises he had grown and adored – and, when it came, his death felt so right. Then there was the Chinese gentleman who wanted to make sure that his family made all the right preparations for his funeral, and who insisted on having the coffin in the room with him. We found his wish disturbing at first, but we soon realised that it gave him immense comfort. And it made me realise that people of all backgrounds like planning their own funerals – and telling their families what to do!

Although my own father was desperately ill, he didn't manage to die until he had returned from hospital to his own bed, in his own home. He had been in an acute coronary care ward, with end-stage heart failure. Having had heart disease for thirty years or more, he knew his days were numbered.

Four days before he died, we took him out to Regent's Park, returning him to the hospital at teatime on the instructions of the wonderful staff nurse, Ann Hamlet, who was caring for him. Ann warned us that he could 'go at any moment'. But he didn't: he stayed alive – just – until an ambulance could be organised to take him home after the Bank Holiday.

He had a wonderful last day at home, where his bed was made up by the family doctor, and where a Marie Curie nurse and the district nurse were on hand to help us, his family, look after him. He got to see his beloved plants on the balcony outside his bedroom and, with a book – as ever – on his knee, he knew he was back home. Like a dying animal, he had wanted to crawl back into his hole. As a dying human being, he wanted us around him and he wanted to be as free from pain and fear as it was humanly possible to be.

My father had a wonderful death. Five years later, my mother died in the same flat, having been seriously ill and disabled for far longer than my father was. She died in a bed supplied by the NHS, since by then she was too thin to sleep in her own without becoming sore. Her pain was controlled by the district nurses and the palliative care team called regularly. Her carer, Juliet Mwaniki, had visited her in the afternoons for years, but finally moved in to live with her. There was a great deal of hilarity and much red wine drunk around her kitchen table. My mother was determined to see her eighty-sixth birthday. She hadn't eaten anything for days, but on her birthday she ate a plate of asparagus (her favourite food), half a pizza, some chocolate with a cup of tea, and went to sleep. She never woke up properly again, and died four days later.

In both cases, I was convinced that this was the way to go: at home, surrounded by loved ones, cared for, pampered, pain-free, and in no doubt about what was happening. But my parents were lucky. All too often we don't get the chance to die well. There is no palliative care team available for most of us if we are not dying of cancer, motor neurone disease or AIDS. If we have Alzheimer's disease, we are all too often simply left to get on with it: it is as though our pain somehow goes unrecognised because we can't communicate properly, and in the end our deaths matter as little as our tragically demented lives.

∾

Christianity has lessons for us all in facing death. Broadly speaking, Christians are genuinely interested in the afterlife and some Christians find planning their funerals a very good way of thinking about what comes next. Others need to focus on the actual journey to the hereafter: for the founder of the modern hospice movement, Dame Cicely Saunders (1918–2005), it was very clear that the journey to the afterlife should be a good one. If suffering and pain made that impossible, something should be done about it. Part of Cicely Saunders' revulsion towards people dying in pain, without dignity, was related to her Christian faith. For her, and by extension for the rest of us, a good death is a goal much to be desired.

Some might argue that the fact that the modern hospice movement originated in Britain is related to the proverbial British 'stiff upper lip' – the sense that, whatever the pain, whatever the tragedy, we shouldn't scream or shout about it but resign ourselves to it with a measure of calm. There may be a grain of truth in this; however, I believe the fact that the movement's roots lie in the Christian tradition is a more compelling explanation. To journey with equanimity into the afterlife, we should have a good death. And a good death should give us the opportunity to think about this life, to come to terms with what we have and haven't done, sort out any complications or rows with family and friends – and then die at peace. This means determining the environment in which we die. Ideally, people's dying moments should not be clinical, in hospital, away from those they love. Rather, we should die at home, under our own control – experiencing human moments, not mechanical ones.

To my mind, a bad death would mean dying slowly, with lots of interventions, in hospital. But I am aware that this will not ring true for everyone and that many of us will want to give the doctors every chance we can. All the same, I believe there comes a point at which we ought to recognise that we have reached the end, that further treatment is futile and that we should cease fighting to cling to life.

Can we avoid unnecessary long hospital stays at the end of our lives? Yes, we can on the whole in the West. We can write advance directives, saying what we want, which we give to our nearest and dearest and to our family doctor. We can tell our friends and family what we want and ask them to make sure it happens – or, perhaps more importantly, what we do not want to happen. And we can be very clear with our health professionals that, if the time should come when the treatments seem endless and are of little benefit, we don't want them. Or, if we wish to accept every treatment that is available, we should be allowed to choose that option too. One part of preparing for death today involves telling others how we wish to die or be kept alive – and what those choices really mean to us.

Death must be the last great taboo subject in the UK. Nevertheless, we have wonderful palliative care services and our hospices are the envy of the world. We ought to learn the lessons they provide and make their style of care available to everyone. But that means being prepared to talk about dying, to think about it and study it, in the realisation that death can touch our lives at any moment through accident or illness. All of us should think now, while we can, about how we want to be treated when the time comes for us.

That is, in part, why I think we should listen when the world's faiths ask us to consider our own mortality. Whether we are believers or not, we must come to terms with the emotional reality of death, as well as its practical side. In this respect, the Open University has played an important role in the UK in encouraging us to examine our attitudes to dying. In a documentary co-produced by the Open University and the BBC in 2009, for example, actor Richard Wilson undertook a poignant journey in which he explored why we're so afraid of death and if there's a better way to approach the end of life in twenty-first century Britain than by simply ignoring it. Wilson himself said that, 'Death is the only certainty in life – so why do so few people want to talk about it?'

Although there are those of us who are ready to embrace death when the time comes, by no means all of us will meet death with equanimity. We do not all share the view that sometimes it is simply no longer right to hang on to life. Here, my thoughts are drawn to Susan Sontag, the writer and intellectual who died in 2004. To the very last, she refused to admit she was dying and gave her son, David Rieff, a terrible time, insisting on having a transplant that brought her no quality of life, but which prevented her death for a short period, and which afforded him no opportunity in which to say goodbye to her:

> It was impossible even to tell her – in a deep
> way, I mean – that I loved her, because to have
> done so would have been to say: 'You're dying.'
> And if that wasn't on, then there was no chance
> whatsoever of real conversations about the past
> since all she really wanted to focus on was the
> future, on 'all the things I need to do when I
> finally get out of this hospital bed', as she often
> put it while lying on that bed out of which she
> would never rise.[14]

Complete denial, anger, desolation, and an inability to say goodbye: not perhaps what we might have expected of one of the twentieth-century's great thinkers, and certainly not an attitude that showed much consideration for her son. However, perhaps more than most, her story makes the case for franker discussion and greater public acceptance of death. We need to acknowledge death, even if this means our being more exposed than we currently are, from childhood on, to the sight of dead bodies and funerals.

An old family friend tried to deny he was dying and insisted on carrying on with normal life for years, even though everyone around him knew he was terminally ill. His backache and a 'severe cold' were used as explanations for his being unable to stand or speak at public events. The stress that his denial caused to family and friends was enormous and, ultimately, unfair. Not only do we need to prepare for our deaths individually, but we also need to be able to prepare for the loss of someone dear to us – which we cannot very well do if that person insists that she is not dying, when it is clear that, in fact, she is.

We need to face up to death on our own behalf and on the behalf of those we love. Ned Stutman shows the importance of this. A lawyer for the US Department of Justice who prosecuted Nazi war criminals, Stutman died from a peculiarly aggressive form of lymphoma. However, first he wrote a book called *Facing Up* about his experiences, which was finished by his widow, Suzanne, and his children. It makes for astonishingly moving reading.[15]

Ned Stutman knew he had little chance of surviving his illness. However, a stem cell transplant gave him a little more time, and his letter (reprinted in the book) to the anonymous donor tears at the heartstrings, as his gratitude shines out and his belief in the value of doing good anonymously comes to the fore. He was an observant but not orthodox Jew. The attitude he takes to his illness and impending death contains a strong Jewish element of reflection, but a fair amount of alternative approaches are thrown in – not least in the section about his aura, which makes for hilarious reading. His book is honest, unflinching in its descriptions, tender, and yet, surprisingly and importantly, funny. Stutman often said that he felt the best medicine was humour, and he obviously laughed and laughed with family and friends as the illness took its grip and killed him. But he and they faced up to what was going on.

He died young, shortly after his sixtieth birthday, the age I am now. Many of us will go on for much longer, to our eighties and nineties, when reflecting on our death may become a part of our everyday life.

How can we approach extreme old age and our impending deaths in ways that are of benefit to us now? What do we want from the life that remains to us? In her eightieth year the psychologist and writer Dorothy Rowe wrote: 'All the knowledge that I have acquired makes my old age the pleasantest time in all my life. I know what matters and what doesn't. Old age isn't to be feared but to be enjoyed and cherished.'[16] Despite the awful publicity it often gets, extreme old age need not be dreaded and is in fact not awful for most people. In the approach to death as older people, we may have, quite literally, the opportunity to count our blessings. As we saw in Chapter 3, the evidence suggests that people become happier as they get older, with recent research suggesting that middle age is comparatively the time of greatest stress and disappointment. Older age allows for fewer mood swings, enabling us to make the best of things.

Perhaps not surprisingly, the Quakers have some lovely advice on approaching old age and death:

> Approach old age with courage and hope. As
> far as possible, make arrangements for your care

in good time, so that an undue burden does not fall on others. Although old age may bring increasing disability and loneliness, it can also bring serenity, detachment and wisdom. Pray that in your final years you may be enabled to find new ways of receiving and reflecting God's love ...

Are you able to contemplate your death and the death of those closest to you?

Accepting the fact of death, we are freed to live more fully. In bereavement, give yourself time to grieve. When others mourn, let your love embrace them.[17]

Good advice indeed, with a strong steer on how to prepare for our own death and also help others come to terms with bereavement! And this advice is predicated on actively thinking about old age and death, not denying it.

Julian Barnes picks up on this idea in his thought-provoking book, *Nothing to be Frightened Of*, in which he cites his doctor who is, like him, writing about death: 'She argues for a reconsideration of pain, which is not necessarily a pure enemy, but something the patient can turn to use. She wants more room for "secular shriving", a time for a drawing-up of accounts, for expressions of forgiveness, and – yes – remorse.'[18] Barnes continues by saying that, like Sherwin Nuland, whose attack on US-style healthcare with intubated dying in intensive care makes such good reading, his doctor regards life as a narrative with death as the final act. Barnes disagrees – although it is hard to see how he can do so logically. It is as if he is simply saying that some of our lives may not be much of a story. While that may be true, it's nonetheless the best story we've got, and death is the final chapter that we need to get to grips with and use for good in some way, if we can.

And whether we believe in an afterlife peopled with angels, a shady realm populated with dancing girls, or in reincarnation, the real test of our quality and of whether we have found meaning in life lies in whether we can accept the fact that we are dying and prepare ourselves for our final act; then leave the world, having made peace with our enemies and having said all we need to say to our family and friends.

Yet, for all our good intentions, the majority of us will find it difficult to come terms with the concept of our own deaths. Jane Miller, author of *Crazy Age*, was not at all sure she would die – ever! 'I should come clean,' she writes: 'I'm not sure that I really believe that I will be dead one day, any more than I entirely believe that I'm as old as I am. I would like to think that everyone has moments when they think of themselves as the exception to the rule. Writing about my own old age is a way of convincing myself that I really am old and that I really will die.'[19] She cites the hero of Philip Roth's brilliant novel, *Everyman*, in which the hero becomes more and more interested in 'the manner of his friend's dying'. And she also reflects on the experience of getting out of bed, and how she might not be doing that so easily in years to come:

> If I find it painful getting out of bed in the
> morning, I am likely to find it harder still in five
> years' time. Then you have to add that, though
> that is undoubtedly so, it is also quite possible that
> you won't be there in five years. And given that
> it's pain you're thinking about, you're faced with a
> dilemma. Do you really want to be there having a

much worse version of the pain that's bothering you now? Might it possibly be a relief not to be there?

To some extent, facing mortality is about taking control. It is about asking and answering ordinary questions about dying, about the place of death and manner of going, about what pain control we may need and who will be present. In the year 2000, the charity Age Concern published *The Millennium Debate of the Age*. In the volume on health and social care (the working group I chaired), we came up with a charter for what the charity believed everybody should know about preparing for death. It is in fact a charter of rights for the dying:

- To know when death is coming and to understand what can be expected.
- To be able to retain control of what happens.
- To be afforded dignity and privacy.
- To have control over pain relief and other symptoms.
- To have choice and control over where death occurs.
- To have access to any spiritual and emotional support required.
- To have access to hospice care in any location, not only in hospital.
- To have control over who's present and who shares the end.
- To be able to issue advance directives which ensure wishes are respected.
- To have time to say goodbye and control over other aspects of timing.
- To be able to leave when it's time to go and not have life prolonged pointlessly.[20]

In the years I have spent in Ireland on and off, I have been struck by how Irish families treat a family member who is dying. Normally (although by no means always), the dying person stays at home, where he may be brought downstairs to the kitchen during the day so that he is in the middle of everything that goes on. Preparing to die should not inevitably mean being left alone to get on with it, because those around us do not know what to say. As we have seen, dying can teach us all important lessons.

The inevitability of death can help us find meaning in life. Mitch Albom's book *Tuesdays with Morrie* became a worldwide bestseller – and rightly so in my opinion.[21] It is the account of a remarkable dying man who agrees to give one-to-one tutorials to a former student. Morrie Schwartz was Mitch Albom's favourite professor at Brandeis University in greater Boston, and he gave his final message to the nation in his last interview with Ted Koppel: 'Be compassionate and take responsibility for each other ... love each other or die.'

Although he was dying, Schwartz's spirit shone through and his words have become a light to many people through Albom's book. He wanted only to die when the time was right: 'Don't let go too soon, but don't hang on too long.' He got his wish and in the end he had a wonderful funeral conducted by another force of nature and influence for good: Rabbi Al Axelrad. Today, Schwartz is almost immortal in the respect that his ideas have travelled around the world and helped others.

Grief at the loss of our loved ones is a barren place, but it is gentled if we feel that all that could have been done has been done, and that the people we loved had the kind of death they wanted. Morrie Schwartz's family felt he had the right kind of death and the right kind of funeral. We know how to provide a good death when we try. But, all too often, we fail.

Whether we profess ourselves to be religious or not, we all need access to spiritual support when we consider our mortality; for the majority of us will begin to question the meaning of our lives as we approach our deaths. However, that support may not always come in an official religious capacity, as I found to be the case in the early days of the North London Hospice. My colleagues and I went to considerable effort to draw up a roster of willing clergy to provide spiritual support to the hospice's patients; and we were somewhat surprised when virtually none of them was ever called out.

Only one person, the Unitarian minister in Golders Green, was ever summoned. Partly, this was because those who wanted spiritual support clearly had their own resources. For those who had no particular faith but who still wanted to talk, the minister came closest to providing the sort of support they were looking for. And also it seemed that many people received their spiritual support from friends and relatives who had the language in which to talk about such issues.

For facing death involves many different sorts of support. Sometimes what is needed is quite practical, such as checking whether there is an up-to-date will, or whether the dying person has had the final conversations they want with those they want to have them with. Are they ready to go in peace; are they sure they have tidied up where they live, which may mean throwing away embarrassing personal papers? These are relatively practical matters, but have a huge impact on how people prepare themselves for death and how they envisage a future in which they will not be present.

If we are confident we have thought about the things that are within our power to change, strengthen and deepen, we will have the confidence to face the unknown with equanimity, including death. We do all have to die – but facing death well is not always easy in a culture of denial. Making sense of our lives in the here and now represents an important way of making sense of our deaths – and starting to do so in our thirties is not too early. How we die will affect the lives of those we leave behind. We all want to be remembered for good. What we most want to avoid is leaving people with a sense of agony in their loss – of issues that have not been resolved; with no good memories, particularly of the last few weeks, months, years before our passing. In order to die well, we must live well. We must embrace our lives, work on giving them meaning, finding a sense of purpose and arriving at our own satisfying answers to the question: 'Is that all there is?'

LIVING WELL

So we have worked, played and volunteered, faced suffering, loss and our own mortality. Where does that leave us? Many of us today will live to a ripe old age, facing our share of joy and grief, love and losses, success and failure, loneliness and parties, joy and sadness and even depression in the process. It is all part of life.

In view of this, what do I hope can be learned from this little volume?

1. How reflecting on finding meaning and purpose in life matters, and can profoundly affect the way we live.

2. Why our friends are important and need cherishing – just as we do ourselves. We should spend time and energy on keeping up with them, appreciating them and simply enjoying them. We should try to be on hand whenever they need us to look after them, so that they will be there for us in turn.

3. The significance of being needed, as this can give us a sense of purpose in life. Whether we are needed by family, friends, through informal volunteering or paid hard graft – it does not really matter. We owe it to ourselves to find environments in which we feel valued, appreciated and part of a bigger whole.

4. Why we need to be honest about how we tackle our own issues in relation to happiness, sadness, joy and depression. We should look after our mental wellbeing as well as our physical wellbeing. And we should try harder to help others suffering from depression or other sorts of mental disorders. Actively working on being happy may help us function better as human beings – to the benefit of all around us as well as ourselves.

5. How to face loss, grief and suffering, and learn from these experiences, discovering how to cope with them and ultimately helping others deal with them too. If we learn how to cope with grief, we will be happier, more fulfilled people and less dragged down by unresolved guilt and confusion.

6. Why taking risks may be an inevitable part of life, but we should be clear about what we are doing and why. We should visit our reasons for doing risky things from various perspectives: our own and that of our loved ones. If we believe that only the experience of risk and its attendant thrills are what make us fully human, we may need to examine our sense of self.

7. The impact of our pace in life. Some of us rush about too much; others of us are slow to the point of sloth. Let's look at how to pace our lives by asking whether we might sometimes speed up or sometimes slow down, and whether we can find a rewarding pace, or a range of paces.

8. How to exercise self-discipline, and how to order and organise our lives. Every few years, we would do well to sort out our possessions and examine our lives more closely. What have we achieved? What do we hope to achieve? What needs to be done to fulfil our goals?

9. The role that our possessions play in our lives. Could we do with less? Do we need more? Could we recycle and reuse? Is there value in making things ourselves? Can we think about our stuff differently, not only for ourselves but for generations to come?

10. The many different forms that a legacy can take, such as goods and chattels, or simply a letter such as an ethical will, which lists the values we want to pass on. But can we make thinking about our legacy a part of the discipline we impose on ourselves as we work out how to live our lives?

11. The inevitability of death. To meet it, let us sort out our lives as best we can, look deliberately for whatever will give them purpose and meaning, and thereby create legacies of which we can be proud.

12. How there are many different ways to find meaning
and a sense of purpose in life. We need to find
those that resonate with us personally and have the
courage to follow our hearts.

If we can achieve these things, we will have discovered a few
answers to the question, 'Is that all there is?' This, in turn,
should enable us to go to our deaths secure in the knowledge
that we have loved and learned, helped others and ourselves,
and realised that our own happiness and wellbeing are not
the most important things in the world: being needed and
finding a sense of purpose through our interactions with
others are what make us humans tick. Herein lies a lesson by
which to live our lives and face our deaths, having achieved
all that we hoped to achieve, and at peace with ourselves
and those around us.

REFERENCES

Introduction
1   François, Lelord, *Hector and the Search for Happiness* (London: Gallic Books, 2010)
2   Mitch Albom, *Tuesdays with Morrie* (London: Little, Brown, 1998)

1: Is That All There Is?
1   Richard Dawkins, *The Selfish Gene* (Oxford: Oxford University Press, 1976), p.x
2   H. Von Foerster, 'On Constructing a Reality', from an adaptation of an address given on April 17, 1973, to the Fourth International Environmental Design Research Association Conference at the College of Architecture, Virginia Polytechnic Institute, Blacksburg, Virginia. Originally published in *Environmental Design Research*, Vol. 2, F.E. Preiser (ed.), (Stroudberg: Dowden, Hutchinson & Ross, 1973) pp. 35–46
3   John Milton, 'Samson Agonistes', 1671
4   Primo Levi, *If This Is a Man* (London: Abacus, 1988)
5   Rachel Sylvester, 'There's a God-shaped hole in Westminster' in *The Times*, 21 October 2008
6   Mark Vernon, 'School of life: Ideas for Modern Living 10, Carpe Diem' in *Observer Magazine*, 25 April 2010, p. 21
7   Dalai Lama, 'Voices from the Heart' in *The Art of Happiness: A Handbook for Living*, edited by Ed and Debbie Shapiro (Tarcher, 1998)
8   http://www.qog.pol.gu.se/working_papers/2010_1_Samanni_ Holmberg.pdf Quality of Government Makes People Happy
9   John Rawls, *A Theory of Justice* (Harvard University Press, 1991)
10   Oliver James, *Affluenza* (London: Vermilion books, 2007)
11   Eugene Watson Burlinghame, *Buddhist Parables* (Delhi: Motilal Banarsidas Publishers Pvt. Ltd. 1999, first published 1922)
12   Randy Pausch, *The Last Lecture* (Hyperion, New York, 2008)

2: Being a Good Friend

1 Mark Vernon, 'What is friendship? "You've got a friend". But what have you got?' in *The Philosopher's Magazine*, 29 September 2005 http://www.markvernon.com/friendshiponline/dotclear/index.php?post/2005/09/29/109-youve-got-a-friend-but-what-have-you-got

2 Bill McBride, 'Teaching to Gender Differences: Boys Will Be Boys and Girls Will Be Girls: A Quick-Reference Resource to Help Educators Modify Instruction for Gender', 2009

3 Carol Gilligan, *In a Different Voice* (Cambridge Massachusetts and London: Harvard University Press, 1982)

4 Claire Prentice, 'Is a rented friend a real friend?' BBC, 5 October 2010

5 David Loxterkamp, 'A friend in need: why friendship matters in medicine' in BMJ 2008

6 Raymond Tallis, 'Warning: Don't Let Auld Acquaintance be Forgot' in *The Times*, 21 December 2009

7 Elizabeth Day, 'Nobody cared when they were alive or mourned when they died alone' in *Observer*, 17 August 2008

8 'The Lonely Society?' Mental Health Foundation, 2010

9 Emily White, *Lonely: A Memoir* (London: HarperCollins, 2010)

10 Julia Neuberger, 'Face to faith' in *Guardian*, 2 January 2010

11 Carole Stone, *Networking: The Art of Making More Friends* (London: Vermilion, 2001)

12 Bruce Feiler, *The Council of Dads: My daughters, my illness, and the men who could be me* (London: Little, Brown, 2010)

13 Aristotle, quoted in Diogenes Laertius, *Lives of Eminent Philosophers* (Forgotten Books, 2010)

14 John 15:13-15

15 Bihar-ul-Anwar, vol. 74, p. 192

16 Proverbs 12:26

3: Learning to Be Happy

1 Ian Sample, 'Why do some people enjoy life and others don't?' in *Guardian*, 19 November 2003

2 Marilyn Elias, 'Psychologists now know what makes people happy' in *New York Times*, 10 September 2009

3 M.E.P. Seligman, *Authentic Happiness: Using the New Positive*

Psychology to Realize Your Potential for Lasting Fulfillment (New York: Free Press, 2002)

4 Richard Layard, *Happiness: Lessons from a new science* (Oxford: Oxford University Press, 2005)

5 BBC News: Why hard work makes people happy, http://news.bbc.co.uk/go/pr/fr/-/2/hi/health/4577392.stm

6 Jon Henley, 'Is John Lewis the best company in Britain to work for' in *Guardian*, 16 March 2010

7 J.M. Keynes, *Economic Possibilities for Our Grandchildren*, eds Lorenzo Pecchi and Gustavo Piga (MIT Press, 2008, first published 1931)

8 Rowan Williams, *Crisis and Recovery: Ethics, Economics and Justice* (London: Palgrave Macmillan, 2010)

9 'Being happy starts with a £42,000 job' in *Daily Mail*, 26 April 2010 (http://www.thisismoney.co.uk/news/article.html?in_article_id=503403&in_page_id=2)

10 BBC: 'Money 'can buy you happiness'', 9 January 2002 http://news.bbc.co.uk/1/hi/health/1750337.stm)

11 Vani K. Borooah, 'What Makes People Happy? Some Evidence from Ireland' in *Journal of Happiness Studies* (2006), vol 7, pp. 427–65

12 http://news.bbc.co.uk/1/hi/programmes/happiness_formula/4771908.stm

13 http://news.bbc.co.uk/1/hi/programmes/happiness_formula/4809828.stm

14 Roger Scruton, *The Uses of Pessimism and the Danger of False Hope* (London: Atlantic Books, 2010)

15 from Ruut Veenhoven's World Database of Happiness, http://worlddatabaseofhappiness.eur.nl/ updated to include the results from the 2005–2007 World Values Survey

16 http://biopsychiatry.com/happiness/happycountry.html

17 Harry Wallop, 'Happiness begins at 55' in *Telegraph*, 2 September 2010 http://www.telegraph.co.uk/finance/personalfinance/7976262/Happiness-begins-at-55.html

18 Michael A Kisley, Stacey Wood and Christina L Burrows, 'Looking at the Sunny Side of Life. Age-Related Change in an Event-Related Potential Measure of the Negativity Bias' in *Psychological Science* (2007) 18: 838-843

19 http://www.dallasnews.com/sharedcontent/dws/fea/
    healthyliving/health/stories/DN-nh_bestyears_0506liv.ART.
    State.Edition1.465122e.html

20 'Promoting mental health and wellbeing in later life: A first report
    from the UK inquiry into Mental Health and Well-being' in *Later
    Life* (Age Concern and Mental Health Foundation, 2006)

21 Elaine Feinstein, 'Getting Older' in *Collected Poems and Translations*
    (Carcanet Press, 2002)

22 Marcus Buckingham, 'What's Happening To Women's
    Happiness?' in *Huffington Post*, September 17, 2009 http://www.
    huffingtonpost.com/marcus-buckingham/whats-happening-to-
    womens_b_289511.html

23 Anke C. Plagnol and Richard A. Easterlin, 'Aspirations,
    Attainments, and Satisfaction: Life Cycle Differences Between
    American Women and Men' in *Journal of Happiness Studies*; DOI:
    10.1007/s10902-008-9106-5. Referred to in http://www.
    sciencedaily.com/releases/2008/07/080729133605.htm

24 Geraldine Bedell, 'What makes women happy?' in *Observer*, 11
    June 2006

25 http://www.statistics.gov.uk/cci/nugget.asp?id=322

26 http://www.statistics.gov.uk/cci/nugget.asp?id=1685

27 Kate Devlin, 'Having children "can raise a woman's self-esteem"'
    in *Telegraph*, 23 March 2010 http://www.telegraph.co.uk/health/
    healthnews/7498063/Having-children-can-raise-a-womans-self-
    esteem.html

28 The Joy Of Economics: http://www.newsweek.com/2007/
    04/04/the-joy-of-economics.html

29 'One born every minute', Channel 4, 2010, plus accompanying
    website Life begins, http://lifebegins.channel4.com/

30 http://www.visitpeakdistrict.com/trailtribe/thedms.aspx?dms=13
    &feature=1015&GroupId=1&venue=6090821&easi=true

31 http://www.enjoythebook.com/ChaptersEnjoy/23_ch15.pdf
    Gini Graham Scott Ph.D.:Enjoy! 101 Ways to Add Fun to Your
    Work Every Day, Amacom – American Management Association,
    2008) (see http://www.enjoythebook.com)

32 Jon Henley, 'The rise and rise of the tattoo' in *Guardian*, 20 July
    2010

33 Gaby Hinsliff, 'Government seeks secret of keeping us all happy'
    in *Observer*, 4 March 2007

34 K. M. Sheldon & S. Lyubomirsky, 'Achieving sustainable gains
    in happiness: Change your actions, not your circumstances'
    in *Journal of Happiness Studies*, (2006) 7, 55-86., referenced in
    http://www.spring.org.uk/2007/11/being-happy-activities-
    beat.php

4: Belonging and Feeling Needed
 1 K. M. Sheldon & S. Lyubomirsky, ibid.
 2 Jan Oyebode, *Advances in Psychiatric Treatment* (2003), vol. 9,
    45–53
 3 R. A. Pruchno & N. L Resch, 'Husbands and wives as caregivers:
    antecedents of depression and burden' in *Gerontologist*, 29,
    159–165, 1989
 4 http://www.healthtalkonline.org/carers/mentalhealthcarers/
    Topic/3476/topicList
 5 Mary Larkin, 'Life after Caring: The Post-Caring Experiences
    of Former Carers' in *British Journal of Social Work* (2009) 39,
    1026–1042, doi:10.1093/bjsw/bcn030
 6 M Nolan, G Grant and J Keady, *Understanding Family Care*
    (Milton Keynes: Open University Press, 1996)
 7 Anna Pierce, www.ipsos-mori.com/newsevents/blogs/
    thebigsociety/598/Big-Society-and-the-Bigger-Picture, 29
    November 2010
 8 Melanie Oppenheimer, *Volunteering: Why We Can't Survive
    Without It* (Sydney, University of New South Wales, 2008)
 9 England Volunteering Development Council, *Report of the
    Commission on the Future of Volunteering and Manifesto for Change*
    (London: Volunteering England, 2008)
10 Janet Christie, 'An HIV diagnosis is no longer a death sentence,
    and buddy schemes are an important factor in removing the old
    stigma' in *Northumberland Gazette*, 27 September 2009
11 Gaby Hinsliff, 'Government Seeks Secret of Keeping Us All
    Happy' in *Observer*, 4 March 2007
12 http://www.csv.org.uk/resources-library?page=1&tid=
    329&term_node_tid_depth=All)
13 Mary Greene, 'The £50 Million Giveaway' in *Saga Magazine*,
    July 2007
14 Denis Campbell, 'Gift of life: the UK's living organ donors' in
    Guardian, 22 June 2010

15 Caitlin Moran, 'Giving to Charity is one of my Favourite Things' in *The Times*, 13 March 2010
16 Adam Phillips and Barbara Taylor, *On Kindness*, (New York: Picador, 2009)
17 Maimonides, *Hilchot Mat'not Ani'im* 10:1, 7-14

5: Taking Risks and Feeling Alive

1 Lynn Ponton, *The Romance of Risk: why teenagers do the things they do* (New York: Basic Books, 1997)
2 (http://search.barnesandnoble.com/The-Romance-of-Risk/Lynn-Ponton/e/9780465070763#TABS
3 Laura Clark, 'The Children who are too Frightened to Play Outside' in *Daily Mail,* 24 May 2004; Amelia Hill, '"Stranger danger" Harms Kids' in *Observer*, 23 May 2004
4 Gillian Thomas quoted in Julie Wheelwright, 'Streets of Fear' in *Guardian,* 26 May 2004
5 Edmund Burke, *A Philosophical Enquiry into the Origin of Our Ideas of the Sublime and Beautiful,* 1757, quoted by Robert Macfarlane in *Mountains of the Mind – History of a Fascination* (London: Granta Books, 2003)
6 'In Gone By Ages' quoted by Francis Spufford in *I May be Some Time: Ice and the English Imagination* (London: Faber, 1996)
7 Joe Simpson, *Touching the Void* (London: Jonathan Cape, 1988)
8 Mike Belitz quoted in Mark Henricks, 'There's Risk Involved: Can risking your life on a mountainside make you a better entrepreneur?' in *Entrepreneur Magazine*, February 2003
9 Robert Macfarlane, *Mountains of the Mind – History of a Fascination* (London: Granta Books, 2003)
10 Samuel Smiles quoted in *Service of the Heart* (London: Union of Liberal and Progressive Synagogues, 1968)
11 Jim Ring, *How the English Made the Alps* (London: John Murray, 2000)
12 http://www.rockclimbing.com/Articles/Training_and_Technique/Why_Are_You_Taking_a_Risk__215.html
13 Carl Hiebert is referred to in Mark Henricks, 'There's Risk Involved: can risking your life on a mountainside make you a better entrepreneur?' *See* http://findarticles.com/p/articles/mi_m0DTI/is_2_31/ai_n12937327/ from BNetUK

14 David Rose, 'Why it is life enhancing to risk death on a mountain', http://www.independent.co.uk/opinion/why-it-is-lifeenhancing-to-risk-death-on-a-mountain-1044830.html

15 Reverend Neil Elliot quoted in Mike Higgins, 'The Sky's the Limit' in *Independent on Sunday*, 24 January 2010

16 Maria Coffey, *Where the Mountain Casts its Shadow* (New York: St Martin's Press, 2005)

17 Quoted by Francis Spufford, above

18 Adam Phillips and Barbara Taylor, *On Kindness* (New York: Picador, 2009)

19 http://www.thebmc.co.uk/Feature.aspx?id=1493

20 Tim McGirk, 'Climber's family keep K2 pledge' in *Independent*, 16 October 1995

21 Stuart MacDonald, 'Tom Ballard: "It killed my mother, Alison Hargreaves, but I'll climb K2"' in *Sunday Times*, 7 March 2010

6: When to Go Slow

1 Satish Kumar quoted in Giulio Sica, 'What part does spirituality play in the green movement?' in *Guardian*, 16 January 2008

2 Charlotte Mathivet, 'Enjoying Slow Life: Let's Slow Down Cities!' in *Cities for All: Experiences and Proposals for the Right to the City*, edited by A Sugranyes and C Mathivet (Santiago: Habitat International Coalition, 2010)

3 E.F. Schumacher, *Small Is Beautiful: Economics As If People Mattered* (London, Abacus, 1991, org. 1973)

4 www.cittaslow.org.uk/images/Download/cittaslow_charter.pdf

5 Tom Leonard, 'US cities may have to be bulldozed in order to survive' in *Telegraph*, 12 June 2009

6 'If you think one person can't really make a difference, just watch the nun who won't take "no" for an answer: Nun a champion for the homeless' on NBC News, Ron Allen, Correspondent, 16 November 2005

7 Charlotte Mathivet, 'Enjoying Slow Life: Let's Slow Down Cities!', 2009, http://base.d-p-h.info/es/fiches/dph/fiche-dph-8541.html

8 Jeannette Winterson, 'Once upon a Life' in *Observer*, 13 June 2010

9 Kate Connolly, 'How Going Green May Make You Mean' in *Guardian*, 16 March 2010

10 Matthew Crawford, *The Case for Working with Your Hands* (London: Penguin, 2010)

11 Darina Allen, *Forgotten Skills of Cooking* (London: Kyle Cathie, 2009)

12 Christopher Richards: www.slowdownnow.org

13 Fiona Macdonald Smith, 'The switched-on generation: have you got *Freizeitstress?*' in *The Times*, 8 May 2010

14 Qayyum Johnson, *Slow Shopping Saves Lives: Stories of a Farmers Marketeer, Including Gentle Recommendations for How To Shop During Times of Ecological, Social and Financial Collapse* (San Francisco Zen Centre, 2009)

15 Zindel V. Segal; Peter Bieling; Trevor Young; Glenda MacQueen; Robert Cooke; Lawrence Martin; Richard Bloch; Robert D. Levitan 'Antidepressant Monotherapy vs Sequential Pharmacotherapy and Mindfulness-Based Cognitive Therapy, or Placebo, for Relapse Prophylaxis in Recurrent Depression' in *Archives of General Psychiatry*, Dec 2010; 67: 1256–1264.

16 William Skidelsky: '"Slow down and inhabit the now": Britain enjoys a Meditation Boom' in *Observer*, 2 January 2011

17 Carl Honoré, *In Praise of Slow: How a Worldwide Movement is Challenging the Cult of Speed* (London: Orion Books, 2004)

7: The Benefits of Being Tough (on Yourself)

1 http://www.buddhanet.net/e-learning/snapshot01.htm)

2 http://www.age-of-the-sage.org/buddhism/buddhist_philosophy.html

3 http://jcsu.jesus.cam.ac.uk/~mma29/essays/speakingself/

4 Advices and Queries, http://qfp.quakerweb.org.uk/qfp1-02.html

5 http://www.dlshq.org/teachings/sadhana.htm

6 http://www.retreats.org.uk/

7 Joan Smith, 'Help Me, Rhonda, Help, Help Me' in *The Times*, 21 August 2010

8 Ibid.

9 http://www.cluttergoneco.uk/?gclid=CM-T5-mN0qACFQ Isl Aodu1VX0g

10 http://zenhabits.net/2008/07/life-laundry-day-get-your-affairs-in-order-each-week-to-clear-your-mind/

11 Babylonian Talmud, Moed Katan 27a–27b
12 Hershey H. Friedman, 'The Simple Life: The Case Against Ostentation in Jewish Law', http://www.jlaw.com/Articles/againstosten.html

8: Having It All?

1 Matthew Barnett, 'I can't live without …' in *The Times*, 19 May 2010
2 'Priest turns pauper: new BBC series to show clergyman living without money for eight months in return to "the simple life"' in *Daily Mail*, 22 January 2010
3 Holly Williams, '"I live entirely without money", Mark Boyle, 30' in *Independent*, 30 January 2010
4 Lena Corner, 'That was the moment I decided to destroy all my worldly goods' in *Independent on Sunday*, 10 January 2010
5 'Can I give up buying clothes for a year' in *Guardian*, 31 December 2009
6 Sally Lever, 'Voluntary Simplicity in a Nutshell', www.sallylever.co.uk, 8 June 2009
7 Duane Elgin, *Voluntary Simplicity: Toward a Way of Life that is Outwardly Simple, Inwardly Rich* (New York: HarperCollins, 2010)
8 Maimonides, Mishneh Torah, Hilchot Mat'not Ani'im 10:1, 7–14
9 Sarah Lonsdale, 'A new generation is on the mend' in *Daily Telegraph*, 22 January 2010
10 Lucy Siegle, 'Anna Bullus's innovation: chewing gum recycling' in *Observer*, 25 April 2010
11 Lucy Siegle, 'Fresh way of life sweeps suburbia' in *Observer*, 7 November 2004
12 Ministry of Information (Author), *Make Do and Mend*, first published in 1943, now published by the Imperial War Museum, London, 2007

9: Suffering and Loss

1 Quoted in *Observer*, 26 January 1958
2 Jonathan Wittenberg, *The Silence of Dark Water* (London: Joseph's Bookstore, 2008)
3 E Kübler-Ross, *On Death and Dying* (London: Tavistock, 1970)
4 C. M. Parkes, *Bereavement* (Harmondsworth: Penguin, 1972)
5 C. S. Lewis, *A Grief Observed* (London: Faber, 1961)
6 Deborah Moggach, 'And Now I Miss the Rest of Me' in *The Times*, 19 February 1994
7 Catherine Horwood, 'Sowing the seeds of a happier life' in *The Times*, 4 May 2010
8 Justine Picardie, *If the Spirit Moves You* (London: Picador, 2002)

10: Leaving a Legacy

1 Ruth Picardie, *Before I Say Goodbye* (London: Penguin, 1998)
2 Samuel Belgradi quoted in Israel Abrahams, *Hebrew Ethical Wills* (Philadelphia: Jewish Publication Society, 1976) from a 1926 original
3 Ibid. 1976
4 Bernhard Kessler, *To My Dear Grandchild on his Thirteenth Birthday!* (London 1940), facsimile and translation privately printed by Willie Kessler, London, December 1997, courtesy of Willie Kessler
5 Lord Alfred Tennyson, 'Ulysses' in *Selected Poems* (London: Everyman, 1997)
6 http://dropsafe.crypticide.com/article/2078
7 Margaret Ryan, 'Is it selfish to have more than two children?' on BBC News, 18 February 2009
8 Pastor Jim Feeney, PhD, 'Leaving a Spiritual Legacy' preached at Heritage Ministers Fellowship conference, Phoenix, Oregon, 19 September 2008, http://www.jimfeeney.org/leaving-legacy-inheritance.html
9 Donna Riner Weber, '5 Reasons to Leave a Spiritual Legacy For Your Child-Grandchild' and 'Scrap booking your Christian Faith', Ezine articles on Faithbooking http://ScrapbookYourChristianFaith.com
10 http://www.usm.maine.edu/olli/national/lifestorycenter/legacy.jsp
11 Valerie Grove, *So Much To Tell* (London: Viking, 2010)

11: Facing Death

1 Rabindranath Tagore, *Naibedya*, 'Dialogues with the Lord of the Heart', http://discovervedanta.wordpress.com/2009/06/27/facing-death-two-poems-from-naibedya-rabindranath-tagore/ This collection has been translated in English from Bengali by Shailesh Parekh and published by A Writers Workshop (Ahmedabad: Saffronbird Book, 2002)

2 The Burial Service, the Book of Common Prayer, 1662 Version: Includes Appendices from the 1549 Version and Other Commemorations (London: Everyman's Library, 1999)

3 Tzidduk Ha-Din, Funeral Service, Liberal Judaism (London, 1996; reprinted 2005) and all other Jewish funeral services

4 From 'Sayings of The Holy Prophet (S.A.W) on Death', guest author: Sadiyya Patel http://www.bellaonline.com/articles/art54607.asp Ibne-Majah, Tabrani, Majma-'uz Zawaid)

5 http://hinduism.iskcon.com/practice/604.htm

6 Atharva Veda, *Kaivalya Upanishad*, 5.VE, 442

7 *Manu Dharma Shastras*, 6.36. LM, 205

8 *The Tibetan Book of the Dead* quoted on http://www.buddhistdoor.com/OldWeb/bdoor/0606/sources/teach104.htm

9 http://www.near-death.com/experiences/buddhism01.html

10 Guru Granth Sahib, 237, http://www.sikhiwiki.org/index.php?title=Death

11 Sky Real Lives channel: 'Right to Die?', made by Oscar-winner John Zaritsky, December 2008, http://www.nowpublic.com/culture/assisted-suicide-televised-british-documentary-film#ixzz1ARfn0mkj

12 Tony Bayfield, 'Why preserve life with no meaning' in *The Times*, 5 August, 2009

13 Muriel Gillick, *The Denial of Aging: Perpetual Youth, Eternal Life, and Other Dangerous Fantasies* (Cambridge: Harvard University Press, 2006), pp. 213–14

14 David Rieff, 'Why I had to lie to my dying mother' in *Observer*, 18 May 2008

15 Ned Stutman, *Facing Up* (Indiana: Bloomington, 2009)

16 Dorothy Rowe, 'Why on earth would I want to be young?' in *Sunday Telegraph*, 6 June 2010

17 Advices and Queries, http://qfp.quakerweb.org.uk/qfp1-02.html

18 Julian Barnes, *Nothing to be Frightened Of* (London: Vintage, 2009)
19 Jane Miller: 'I'm not sure I really will die' in *Guardian*, 26 August 2010
20 Millennium Debate of the Age, Health and Social Care, 2000
21 Mitch Albom, *Tuesdays with Morrie* (London: Little, Brown, 1998)

SELECT BIBLIOGRAPHY

Abrahams, Israel, *Hebrew Ethical Wills* (Philadelphia: Jewish Publication Society, 1976) from a 1926 original

Age Concern and the Mental Health Foundation, 'Promoting mental health and well-being in later life: A first report from the UK inquiry into Mental Health and Well-being in Later Life', 2006

Ainsworth-Smith, I. and Speck, P., *Letting Go* (London: SPCK, 1982)

Albom, Mitch, *Tuesdays with Morrie* (London: Little, Brown, 1998)

Allen, Darina, *Forgotten Skills of Cooking* (London: Kyle Cathie, 2009)

Aristotle, *Nicomachaean Ethics* (London: Penguin, 2004)

Barnes, Julian, *Nothing to be Frightened Of* (London: Vintage, 2009)

Bettelheim, Bruno, *The Informed Heart: Autonomy in a Mass Age* (London: Penguin, 1991)

Bok, Derek, *The Politics of Happiness* (Oxford: Princeton University Press, 2010)

Book of Common Prayer, 1662 Version (London: Everyman's Library, 1999)

Borooah, Vani K, 'What Makes People Happy? Some Evidence from Ireland', in *Journal of Happiness Studies* (2006), vol 7, pp. 427–65

Burke, Edmund, *A Philosophical Enquiry into the Origin of Our Ideas of the Sublime and Beautiful* (Oxford: Oxford University Press, 2008)

Burlinghame, Eugene Watson, *Buddhist Parables* (Delhi: Motilal Banarsidas, 1999)

Carroll, Lewis, *Alice Through the Looking Glass* (London: Penguin, 2003)

Coffey, Maria, *Where the Mountain Casts Its Shadow* (New York: St Martin's Press, 2005)

− *Explorers of the Infinite* (New York: Tarcher, 2008)

Crawford, Matthew, *The Case for Working with Your Hands* (London: Penguin, 2010)

Dawkins, Richard, *The Selfish Gene* (Oxford: Oxford University Press, 1976)

Elgin, Duane, *Voluntary Simplicity* (New York: HarperCollins, 2010)

Epicurus, *Essential Epicurus*, ed. Eugene Michael O'Connor (Amherst: Prometheus Books, 1993)

Feiler, Bruce, The Council of Dads (London: Little Brown, 2010)

Feinstein, Elaine, *Collected Poems and Translations* (London: Carcanet Press, 2002)

Gillick, Muriel, *The Denial of Aging* (Cambridge, Mass: Harvard University Press, 2006)

Gilligan, Carol, *In a Different Voice* (Cambridge Mass: Harvard University Press, 1982)

Gregg, Richard Bartlett, *The Value of Voluntary Simplicity* (Wallingford, PA: Pendle Hill, 1936)

Grove, Valerie, *So Much To Tell* (Viking, London, 2010)

Horace, *Odes*, trans. C E Bennett (Cambridge, Mass: Harvard University Press, 1989)

Horwood, Catherine, *Gardening Women* (London: Virago, 2010)

James, Oliver, *Affluenza* (London: Vermilion, 2007)

Kessler, Bernhard, *To My Dear Grandchild on His Thirteenth Birthday!*, facsimile and translation privately printed by Willie Kessler (London, December 1997)

Keynes, J.M., *Essays in Persuasion* (London: Palgrave Macmillan, 2010)

Kübler-Ross, E., *On Death and Dying* (Tavistock, London, 1970)

Larkin, Mary, 'Life after Caring: The Post-Caring Experiences of Former Carers' in *British Journal of Social Work* (2009) 39, 1026–1042, doi:10.1093/bjsw/bcn030

Layard, R, *Happiness* (London: Penguin, 2006)

Lelord, François, *Hector and the Search for Happiness* (London: Gallic Books, 2010)

Levi, Primo, *If This is a Man* (London: Abacus, 1988)

Lewis, C. S., *A Grief Observed* (London: Faber, 1961)

Macfarlane, Robert, *Mountains of the Mind* (London, Granta Books, 2003)

Maimonides, *The Guide for the Perplexed* (Indianapolis: Hackett Publishing, 1995)

Mental Health Foundation, *The Lonely Society?* (London, 2010)

Neuberger, Julia (Chair), 'The Future of Health and Care of Older People' in *Age Concern Millennium Papers* (London: Age Concern, 1999)

Nolan, M., Grant, G., and Keady, J., *Understanding Family Care* (Buckingham: Open University Press, 1996)

Parkes, C. M., *Bereavement* (Harmondsworth: Penguin, 1972)

Pausch, Randy, *The Last Lecture* (New York: Hyperion, 2008)

Phillips, Adam and Taylor, Barbara, *On Kindness* (New York: Picador, 2009)

Picardie, Justine, *If the Spirit Moves You* (London: Picador, 2002)

Picardie, Ruth, *Before I Say Goodbye* (London: Penguin, 1998)

Putnam, Robert, *Bowling Alone* (New York: Simon and Schuster, 2001)

Qayyum Johnson, *Slow Shopping Saves Lives* (San Francisco: San Francisco Zen Centre, 2009)

Rawls, John, *A Theory of Justice* (Cambridge, Mass: Belknap, 1991)

Ring, Jim, *How the English Made the Alps* (London: John Murray, 2000)

Schumacher, E.F., *Small Is Beautiful: Economics As If People Mattered, 25 Years Later … With Commentaries* (Vancouver: Hartley & Marks Publishers, 1999)

Scott, Gini Graham Ph.D., *Enjoy! 101 Ways to Add Fun to Your Work Every Day* (New York: American Management Association, 2008)

Scruton, Roger, *The Uses of Pessimism and the Danger of False Hope* (London: Atlantic, 2010)

Simpson, Joe, *Touching the Void* (London: Jonathan Cape, 1988)

Smiles, Samuel, *Self-Help* (Oxford: Oxford University Press, 2008)

Spufford, Francis, *I May Be Some Time: Ice and the English Imagination* (London: Faber, 1996)

Stone, Carole, *Networking* (London: Random House, 1997)

– *The Ultimate Guide to Successful Networking* (London: Vermilion, 2004)

Stutman, Ned, *Facing Up* (Bloomington: iUniverse, 2009)

Titmuss, Richard M, *The Gift Relationship: From Human Blood to Social Policy*, eds Oakley, Ann and Ashton, John (New York: New Press, 1997)

Tzidduk Ha-Din: Funeral Service (London: Liberal Judaism, 1996), reprinted 2005

White, Emily, *Lonely: A Memoir* (London: HarperCollins, 2010)

Williams, Rowan and Elliott, Larry, *Crisis and Recovery* (London: Palgrave Macmillan, 2010)

Wittenberg, Jonathan, *The Silence of Dark Water* (London: Joseph's Bookstore, 2008)

WEBSITES

Cittaslow: www.cittaslow.org.uk/images/Download/cittaslow_charter.p

The Downshifter: http://www.thedownshifter.co.uk/index.html

Down The Lane Forum: http://www.downthelane.net/index.php

International Institute of Not Doing Much: www.SlowDownNow.org

Life Story Center: http://www.usm.maine.edu/olli/national/lifestorycenter/legacy.jsp

Religious Society of Friends: http://qfp.quakerweb.org.uk/qfp1-02.html

The Retreat Association: http://www.retreats.org.uk/

INDEX